Healing Outcomes

Raymond Hawkins • Scott Meier

Healing Outcomes

An Integrative Approach for Measuring Psychotherapy Effectiveness

Springer

Raymond Hawkins
Psychology
The University of Texas at Austin
Austin, TX, USA

Scott Meier
Counseling School and Educational Psychology
University at Buffalo
Buffalo, NY, USA

ISBN 978-3-032-33610-1 ISBN 978-3-032-33611-8 (eBook)
https://doi.org/10.1007/978-3-032-33611-8

This Springer imprint is published by the registered company Springer Nature Switzerland AG
The registered company address is: Gewerbestrasse 11, 6330 Cham, Switzerland

Preface

In 2015 we published a paper in Jeffrey Magnavita's and Jack Anchin's innovative *Journal of Unified Psychotherapy and Clinical Science* (JUPCS) (Hawkins & Meier, 2015). This paper was entitled "Psychotherapeutic change and measurement—An integrative theory." We believe that this paper was important and should be expanded into a book because it included an integrative multi-level theory called the systems-contextual integrative model (SCIM) that unites personality and contextual influences in an elaboration of Andras Angyal's (1965) theory of health (healing) and neurosis (trauma) systems principles. Methodologically, our book links this meta-theory of change with the latest innovations in idiographic, process-oriented measurement that will guide practice research network applications.

More recent work on the Early Therapeutic Environment (ETE; Meier, 2023) offers a potentially important reconceptualization of how and when core therapeutic processes unfold in psychotherapy. Traditionally, the working alliance has been understood as something that emerges gradually through face-to-face interaction, typically assessed no earlier than the fourth session, with therapeutic mechanisms assumed to be dormant before that contact begins. Recent research challenges that assumption on multiple fronts. Zilcha-Mano (2025) conducted a randomized controlled trial that demonstrated that measurable changes in patients' alliance perceptions can occur *before* they ever meet their therapist. These pre-treatment shifts significantly predict both subsequent alliance development and symptom reduction across the full course of treatment.

Our research on ceiling effects on working alliance measures suggest that, for a substantial proportion of patients, the alliance is not gradually built but rather rapidly established (Meier & Feeley, 2021). Thus, for a group of clients the alliance functions more like a threshold than a linear developmental process. Together, these observations point toward a broader reconceptualization in which the transition into psychotherapy itself—encompassing referral experiences, intake procedures, administrative contacts, and early expectancy formation—constitutes a distinct and clinically significant therapeutic phase. The ETE model formalizes this insight, situating pre-session and early-session processes as foundational rather than incidental, with direct implications for understanding early dropout, refining alliance measurement, and redesigning clinical practice to attend carefully to the relational environment patients encounter from their very first contact with a treatment setting.

We believe that our book will be useful for psychotherapy theorists who aim to develop unified models that will facilitate further research on core processes that will promote outcome effectiveness. Our book will be interesting to practitioners who wish not only to measure outcomes but also to understand and integrate holistic person-centered personality processes with environmental contexts to promote these healing outcomes. Students studying clinical and counseling psychology will learn a comprehensive, unified overview of current psychotherapy outcomes research and measurement.

We want to acknowledge Jack Anchin and Jeffrey Magnavita, former JUPCS editors, for graciously permitting us to use portions of our 2015 paper. Ray wants to thank Dr. Tom Borkovec for his guidance on creating practice research networks, Dr. Mary McCaulley of the Center for Applications of Psychological Type, and Dr. James Grice for his instruction on using Observation Oriented Modeling. Scott would like to thank his graduate school mentors—Dr. Patricia McCarthy, Dr. Ronald Schmeck, Dr. Barbara Yanico, and Dr. Howard Tinsley—for exemplifying what it means to be psychological research scientists.

Austin, TX, USA Raymond Hawkins
Buffalo, NY, USA Scott Meier

References

Angyal, A. (1965). *Neurosis & treatment: A holistic theory*. Wiley.

Hawkins, R. C. II, & Meier, S. (2015). Psychotherapeutic theories of change and measurement: An integrative model. *Journal of Unified Psychotherapy and Clinical Science, 3*, 80–119. http://unifiedpsychotherapyproject.org/journal/

Meier, S. T. (2023). A model of the early therapeutic environment: Predicting client attrition. *Journal of Psychotherapy Integration*, *33*, 235-247. https://doi.org/10.1037/int0000293

Meier, S. T., & Feeley, T. H. (2021). Ceiling effects indicate a possible threshold structure for working alliance. *Journal of Counseling Psychology, 69*(2), 235-245. https://doi.org/10.1037/cou0000564

Zilcha-Mano, S. (2025). Therapeutic change may begin before the therapist and patient ever meet: Pretreatment alliance changes predict clinical outcomes. *Psychotherapy and Psychosomatics*, 1–7. https://doi.org/10.1159/000548510

Contents

About the Authors

Scott T. Meier, PhD is Professor Emeritus, the Department of Counseling, School, and Educational Psychology, Graduate School of Education, and Affiliate Faculty Member with the Institute for Artificial Intelligence and Data Science, University at Buffalo. He is a licensed psychologist who received his PhD in Counseling Psychology from Southern Illinois University, Carbondale, in 1984. Meier's major research and teaching areas focus on psychological measurement (particularly progress monitoring and outcome assessment), research methods, and counseling and psychotherapy. Meier is the author or co-author of multiple books (including *Incorporating Progress Monitoring and Outcome Assessment into Counseling and Psychotherapy*, *Measuring Change in Counseling and Psychotherapy*, *Elements of Counseling,* and *Narratives and Language in Counseling and Psychotherapy*) and has published in the *American Psychologist, Professional Psychology: Research and Practice, Journal of Counseling Psychology*, *Measurement and Evaluation in Counseling and Development*, *The Clinical Supervisor*, and the *American Journal of Evaluation.*

Raymond C. Hawkins II, PhD, ABPP (Clinical Psychology) is a licensed psychologist who has been engaged in clinical health psychology research and practice for over 50 years, beginning with his doctoral studies at the University of Pennsylvania. Since 1975 Dr. Hawkins has conducted clinical psychology research as a faculty member of the Psychology Dept. at The University of Texas at Austin (former Director of the UT Clinical Psychology Training Clinic). From 2004 to 2024 he was a Core Faculty member (now Professor Emeritus) in the Clinical Psychology PhD Program at Fielding Graduate University. Dr. Hawkins has co-edited three books (*Exceptional Infant 4: Psychosocial Risks in Infant-Environment Transactions,* Brunner/Mazel; 1980; *The Binge—Purge Syndrome*, Springer, 1984; *Clinical Health Psychology: Cultural Considerations*, Fielding University Press, 2020) and has many peer-reviewed research publications and conference presentations. Dr. Hawkins co-founded the Austin Stress Clinic in 1980. He was a clinical psychologist at Austin Regional Clinic for 22 years, where he developed and led the Family Recovery Program, an outpatient treatment program for substance abuse patients. His research projects have included studying evidence-based assessment and interventions in two practice research networks (the UT Austin Clinical Psychology Training Clinic and the Fielding Training Clinic at New Life Institute, which he directed until December 2023). In November 2024 he received the "Outstanding Contribution to Education" award from the Texas Psychological Association.

List of Figures

List of Tables

Part I
Foundations

Chapter 1
Introduction: Healing Outcomes and a Broader Definition of Psychotherapeutic Change

Definitions of Healing and Psychotherapeutic Change

Advancing psychotherapy research and training requires a heuristic integrative theory capable of informing measurement of key change processes and outcomes. Two foundational questions must be addressed: (1) how broadly psychotherapy effectiveness should be defined, and (2) how theory and measurement can be more closely aligned.

The concept of *healing* provides a useful organizing framework. Derived from the proto-Germanic *hailijana*, meaning "to make whole," healing encompasses restoration of functioning as well as integration, meaning, and coherence. Jungian and contemporary perspectives emphasize healing as a holistic process that may occur even in the presence of enduring limitations. Hitchcock (1991, p. 21) states that Jung's approach is "from the first to the last…the development of a work of healing…Psychologically, healing embraces opposites, and therefore must remain as much non-rational as rational." Larson's (2017) book on psychological healing endorses this definition of healing as a holistic process, increasing one's sense of meaning and integration despite the possibility of there being enduring disability or limitation.

A seminal text describing the non-specific factors common to all psychotherapies is *Persuasion and Healing* (Frank & Frank, 2025). These ingredients for persuasion and healing include client demoralization, which provides the motivation for seeking psychotherapy; an emotionally charged, confiding relationship with a helping person; a healing setting where the healer is believed to be helpful and is trusted to do the healing; the healer's rationale, conceptual scheme, or myth that explains the patient's symptoms and proscribes a ritual or treatment to remedy them; the agreement of this rationale with the client's worldview and the client's acceptance of it; the therapist's and client's participation together in the healing process that is believed to be helpful; and the client's sense of match or alliance with

R. Hawkins, S. Meier, *Healing Outcomes*,
https://doi.org/10.1007/978-3-032-33611-8_1

the healer. Remoralization and hope result from this healing process. These factors were later adapted and elaborated by Wampold in his contextual model of psychotherapy process (e.g., Wampold, 2001; Wampold & Imel, 2015) and have, in turn, informed our own model.

The Centrality of Measurement

From the perspective of the history of science, innovations in measurement theory and techniques are tightly linked with progress in theory and application (Cone, 1988; Meier, 2008). This relationship is not merely correlational but fundamentally constitutive of scientific advancement itself. When researchers develop new ways to measure phenomena, they simultaneously open new conceptual spaces for theoretical development and create opportunities for practical applications that were previously unimaginable. Measurement breakthroughs do not merely serve as tools; they actively drive theoretical innovation by extending the reach of human perception and compensating for its limits (Tryon, 1991). By making the invisible visible, the intangible tangible, and the unmeasurable quantifiable, new measurement capabilities force scientists to reconceptualize existing theories and often reveal entirely new domains of inquiry. The instruments we create to measure the world shape not only what we can observe but also what we can conceive of as empirically meaningful questions.

Throughout scientific history, this pattern is evident across diverse fields and epochs: Galileo's telescope reshaped cosmology by providing empirical evidence that challenged geocentric models and revealed celestial phenomena that demanded new theoretical explanations; spectroscopy enabled chemical analysis of distant stars, transforming astronomy from a purely descriptive science of celestial positions into a discipline capable of determining the elemental composition of objects billions of miles away; and X-ray crystallography and nucleotide assays underpinned the discovery of DNA structure, providing Watson and Crick with the empirical foundation necessary to propose their double helix model (Meehl, 1991). Each of these measurement innovations fundamentally altered the trajectory of its respective field, demonstrating that advances in how we measure often precede and enable advances in what we understand.

In the contemporary era, advances in measurement continue to transform healthcare and psychotherapy in profound and multifaceted ways. The digital revolution has fundamentally altered not only the scale and speed at which clinical data can be collected but also the granularity and ecological validity of the information obtained. What was once confined to pre-treatment and post-treatment assessments conducted in controlled settings has evolved into continuous monitoring that captures the dynamic, fluctuating nature of psychological phenomena as they unfold in patients' daily lives. Technological developments now permit real-time, session-by-session outcome monitoring, modeling of nonlinear change trajectories, and data-driven clinical decision support (Barkham et al., 2023; Lutz et al., 2022). These capabilities enable clinicians to detect deterioration patterns before they become entrenched, identify which patients are not responding to treatment as expected, and adjust therapeutic approaches with a level of precision and timeliness that was previously impossible. Machine learning algorithms can now analyze patterns across thousands of treatment cases to generate personalized predictions about treatment outcomes and provide empirically grounded recommendations for clinical decision-making, effectively creating a feedback loop between aggregate clinical science and individual patient care.

These developments underscore the central role of measurement-based care (MBC) as both a scientific and clinical enterprise. On the scientific side, MBC generates rich datasets that allow researchers to test theories of therapeutic change with unprecedented temporal resolution and statistical power, moving beyond simple pre-post comparisons to examine the microprocesses through which change occurs. Clinically, MBC transforms psychotherapy from a practice guided primarily by intuition and retrospective recall into one informed by systematic, ongoing evaluation of patient progress. This dual nature of MBC—simultaneously advancing scientific knowledge and improving clinical outcomes—represents a powerful synthesis of the scientist-practitioner model, where the boundary between research and practice becomes increasingly permeable and mutually enriching.

The Systems-Contextual Integrative Model

To reduce the gap between psychotherapy theory and measurement of changes requires multi-method assessment and outcome measures that can capture the full complexity and multidimensionality of therapeutic change. Traditional approaches to outcome assessment have often been criticized for their narrow focus on symptom reduction, failing to account for the rich theoretical frameworks that guide different therapeutic modalities and the diverse ways in which clients experience and express psychological transformation. Single-method approaches, particularly those relying exclusively on self-report questionnaires, are vulnerable to method variance, response biases, and an inability to capture implicit or pre-reflective aspects of change that may be therapeutically significant. Different theoretical orientations emphasize different change mechanisms and outcomes: Psychodynamic approaches focus on insight and relational patterns, cognitive-behavioral therapies target thought patterns and behaviors, and humanistic approaches emphasize self-actualization and authenticity. Despite this, measurement systems have often imposed a one-size-fits-all approach that fails to honor these theoretical distinctions.

We have proposed a transtheoretical systems-contextual integrative model (SCIM; Hawkins & Meier, 2015) that guides selection and interpretation of progress and outcome measures while respecting the theoretical diversity of the field. This framework is explicitly designed to bridge competing paradigms by identifying common principles of therapeutic change without reducing them to a lowest common denominator. The SCIM recognizes that therapeutic change is inherently multilevel, occurring simultaneously across biological, psychological, interpersonal, and sociocultural domains, and that these levels are dynamically interrelated rather than independent. This model emphasizes multimethod assessment, including self-report questionnaires that capture subjective experience, clinician ratings that provide expert observational perspectives, performance-based tasks that assess implicit processes and behavioral capabilities, and narrative or text-based indicators that reveal meaning-making processes and identity transformations. By triangulating across these diverse data sources, clinicians and researchers can develop a more comprehensive and nuanced understanding of therapeutic change that is less susceptible to the limitations of any single assessment approach.

The model is organized across three nested levels that reflect both systems theory principles and the empirical literature on therapeutic change processes:

Macro level. This encompasses broad values, worldviews, and personality dimensions (e.g., agency and communion) that shape goals and meanings of change. At this level, we are concerned with the overarching narrative frameworks through which individuals interpret their experiences, their fundamental assumptions about self and world, and the deep personality structures that organize behavior and experience across contexts and time. Measures at this level extend beyond symptom relief to include interpersonal awareness, emotional depth, and personal meaning, recognizing that for many clients, the most significant therapeutic outcomes involve shifts in identity, purpose, or philosophical orientation rather than merely the reduction of distress. Assessment at the macro level might include measures of life meaning, values clarification, personality trait changes, narrative coherence, and existential concerns. These constructs often change more slowly than symptoms but may be more predictive of long-term well-being and resilience.

Meso level. This addresses social and ecological contexts (e.g., family, work, community) that support or constrain change. Therapeutic change does not occur in a vacuum but is embedded within and sustained by the social systems in which clients live their daily lives. Rituals, routines, and relational patterns at this level influence resilience and maintenance of gains, determining whether therapeutic insights and new behaviors can be integrated into everyday functioning or whether environmental contingencies will pull clients back toward old patterns. The meso level recognizes that even highly effective therapy can fail to produce lasting change if the client returns to toxic relationships, unsupportive work environments, or communities that lack resources for mental health and wellbeing. Assessment at this level includes measures of social support, family functioning, work satisfaction, community engagement, and the quality of important relationships. The meso level also encompasses environmental stressors and resources and the degree to which the client's social network reinforces or undermines therapeutic gains.

Micro level. This focuses on attachment relationships and the therapeutic alliance, where emotional processing and meaning making occur most intensely. The therapeutic relationship itself is understood not merely as a vehicle for delivering interventions but also as a primary mechanism of change, providing a safe relational context for exploring painful emotions, revising internal working models, and practicing new ways of relating. Narrative processes, emotional activation, and reflection are central mechanisms of change at this level (Mergenthaler, 1996), with therapeutic progress often marked by the ability to tell more coherent, complex, and emotionally flexible stories about one's experience. The micro level captures the moment-to-moment processes within therapy sessions, including the quality of the therapeutic bond, the depth of emotional engagement, the capacity for mentalizing and reflective functioning, and the integration of affective and cognitive processing. Assessment at this level might include alliance measures, in-session process ratings, AI-based linguistic analysis of therapy transcripts to identify emotional tone and narrative complexity, and moment-by-moment tracking of emotional arousal and regulation patterns.

Summary and Implications for Practice and Research

Theoretically aligned measurement based care is increasingly recognized as a core clinical competency. Integrative frameworks—such as the systems contextual model—provide a coherent structure for organizing existing measures, developing new theory-driven tools, and training clinicians to use data meaningfully. When aligned with psychotherapy theory, progress monitoring and outcome assessment can reduce treatment failure, support therapist responsiveness, and enhance clinical decision-making.

In subsequent chapters, we outline practical strategies for implementing theory-informed progress monitoring, assessment, and feedback systems. Strengthening the integration of psychotherapy theory and measurement holds promise for improving both empirical understanding and everyday clinical practice.

References

Barkham, M., et al. (2023). Trajectory-based approaches to psychotherapy outcomes. *Psychotherapy Research, 33*, 1–14. https://doi.org/10.1080/10503307.2022.XXXXX

Cone, J. D. (1988). *Psychometrics and measurement theory*. Brooks/Cole.

Frank, J. D., Frank, J. B., & Wampold, B. E. (2025). *Persuasion and healing: A comparative study of psychotherapy*. Baltimore, MD: Johns Hopkins University Press.

Hawkins, R. C. II., & Meier, S. (2015). Psychotherapeutic theories of change and measurement: An integrative model. *Journal of Unified Psychotherapy and Clinical Science, 3*(1), 80–119.

Hitchcock, D. (1991). *Jungian perspectives on healing*. Routledge.

Larson, D. B. (2017). *The healing process*. American Psychological Association.

Lutz, W., Schwartz, B., & Delgadillo, J. (2022). Measurement-based care in psychotherapy. *Annual Review of Clinical Psychology, 18*, 71–102. https://doi.org/10.1146/annurev-clinpsy-072220-014821

Meehl, P. E. (1991). Why summaries of research on psychological theories are often uninterpretable. *Psychological Reports, 68*, 195–244. https://doi.org/10.2466/pr0.1991.68.1.195

Meier, S. T. (2008). *Measuring change in counseling and psychotherapy*. Guilford.

Mergenthaler, E. (1996). Emotion–abstraction patterns in psychotherapy. *Psychotherapy Research, 6*, 237–251. https://doi.org/10.1080/10503309612331331660

Tryon, W. W. (1991). *Activity measurement in psychology and medicine*. Plenum. https://doi.org/10.1007/978-1-4757-9003-0

Wampold, B. (2001). *The great psychotherapy debate: Models, methods, and findings*. Lawrence Erlbaum Associates.

Wampold, B. E., & Imel, Z. E. (2015). *The great psychotherapy debate* (2nd ed.). Routledge. https://doi.org/10.4324/9780203582015

Chapter 2
The Theory–Measurement Gap and Why It Matters

Introduction

We propose that a substantial gap exists between psychotherapy theories and psychological measurement and assessment (Hawkins & Meier, 2015). Surveys of clinical practice indicate that only about 20% to 30% of mental health professionals report that they employ progress monitoring and outcome assessment (PMOA) (Clement, 1999; Hatfield & Ogles, 2004). We suggest that one of the major reasons for this neglect of PMOA is the gap that exists between psychotherapy theories and psychological measurement and assessment. That is, while the theories describe general change processes, they typically do not provide sufficient detail about the sequences of change events, how individuals may differ in change events, or how to track change events over time. Cognitive-behavioral therapy (CBT) interventions (e.g., Barlow, 2024) may be an exception to this generalization. In fact, however, many theories (including CBT) focus on one cluster of change events (e.g., changes in cognitions linked with changes in behavior) and assume those are sufficient to describe the psychotherapeutic events for most individual clients (at least within broad diagnostic categories).

This theory–measurement gap can be narrowed through a better integration of measurement and psychotherapy theories. One source of this gap lies in the construction and interpretation of existing measures. Clinicians report that the most useful assessment information concerns progress since intake and the need to alter treatment (Hatfield & Ogles, 2004). Interpretation of such data depends heavily on the theoretical assumptions embedded—explicitly or implicitly—within measures.

Working alliance measures (WAMs) illustrate this challenge. Alliance is consistently associated with outcome (average $r = 0.30$; Del Re et al., 2012; Flückiger et al., 2020), yet many alliance measures show pronounced ceiling effects early in treatment. Analyses across dozens of studies indicate that alliance development is often rapid and nonlinear rather than gradual (Meier & Feeley, 2021). Whether these ceiling effects reflect measurement artifacts or meaningful psychological

R. Hawkins, S. Meier, *Healing Outcomes*,
https://doi.org/10.1007/978-3-032-33611-8_2

processes remains debated (Paap et al., 2020). Emerging evidence suggests that psychological factors—such as distress-driven motivation or social anxiety—may account for early high scores, emphasizing the need for theory-driven interpretation. Interpretation of test score data about such progress depends substantially upon the theory on which the test is explicitly or implicitly based. For example, clinicians commonly observe significant variation in symptoms and functioning in their clients over the course of treatment, including evidence of improvement, worsening, stability, and cycling (Mergenthaler, 1996). Interpretation of these patterns depends upon the clinician's theoretical expectations about their meaning and implications for future events.

In the contemporary era, advances in measurement continue to transform healthcare and psychotherapy. Technological developments now permit real-time, session-by-session outcome monitoring, modeling of nonlinear change trajectories, and data-driven clinical decision support (Barkham et al., 2023; Lutz et al., 2022). These developments underscore the central role of measurement-based care (MBC) as both a scientific and clinical enterprise. (Barkham et al., 2023; Lutz et al., 2022).

Measurement-Based Care and Feedback in Psychotherapy

Evidence supporting feedback-based therapies (FBTs) and routine outcome monitoring (ROM) has accumulated over several decades (Beutler & Harwood, 2000; Meier, 2008; Persons, 1989). Measurement feedback systems, such as the Outcome Questionnaire–45 (OQ-45) and the Partners for Change Outcome Management System (PCOMS), provide clinicians with systematic information about client improvement, stability, or deterioration. Meta-analyses indicate modest but reliable benefits (Cohen's $d = 0.15–0.40$), particularly when feedback is shared collaboratively with clients (Delgadillo et al., 2022; Rognstad et al., 2023).

A key function of progress monitoring is the alert mechanism—identifying clients who deviate from expected recovery trajectories (Lambert et al., 2001, 2005). However, alerts alone do not specify how treatment should change. Effective use of feedback requires integration with psychotherapy theory, case conceptualization, and clinical judgment. Despite strong empirical support, systematic progress monitoring remains underutilized (Clement, 1999; Hatfield & Ogles, 2004). Barriers include perceived burden, limited theoretical fit, clinician anxiety, and skepticism regarding clinical utility (Ionita et al., 2015).

Why Measurement Matters: Treatment Failure and Dropout

Treatment failure rates in psychotherapy range from approximately 10% to 50% of clients (Kraus et al., 2011; Lambert, 2007; Lilienfield, 2007; Persons & Mikami, 2002). Failure includes premature dropout as well as deterioration or harm. In the

United States, average dropout rates approach 35–40%, with many clients discontinuing after only one or two sessions (Owen et al., 2012). Clients who experience unsuccessful therapy often report worsened symptoms, unmet goals, ruptured alliances, and long-term reluctance to seek future help (Knox et al., 2023).

Research suggests that therapist-related factors contribute substantially to treatment failure. Clients frequently cite poor assessment and understanding, inflexibility, inadequate knowledge, and problematic therapist behaviors as reasons for discontinuation (Alfonsson et al., 2024). These findings underscore the need for timely, theoretically meaningful feedback to guide intervention adjustments.

Progress Monitoring and its Limits

Progress monitoring (PM) data provide clinicians with information about current client status and likely future trends. Lambert and colleagues demonstrated that PM feedback can reduce deterioration and improve outcomes for clients who are not responding early in treatment (Lambert et al., 2001, 2005, 2018). Meta-analytic findings indicate that, among early non-responders, feedback reduces deterioration rates and increases improvement rates (de Jong et al., 2025). PM data alone, however, rarely explain *why* clients fail to improve. Identifying mechanisms underlying stagnation or deterioration requires theoretically informed measures that capture processes such as emotional avoidance, interpersonal functioning, and meaning-making. Short-term indicators—such as avoidance of negative affect—may offer additional predictive value for future symptom trajectories and inform more precise clinical decisions.

Summary and Implications for Research and Practice

Measurement-based care is increasingly recognized as a core clinical competency rather than a research luxury. When aligned with psychotherapy theory, progress monitoring and outcome assessment can reduce treatment failure, support therapist responsiveness, and enhance clinical decision-making. Integrative frameworks—such as our systems-contextual model (SCIM)—provide a coherent structure for organizing existing measures, developing new theory-driven tools, and training clinicians to use data meaningfully. In subsequent chapters, we outline practical strategies for implementing theory-informed progress monitoring, assessment, and feedback systems. Strengthening the integration of psychotherapy theory and measurement holds promise for improving both empirical understanding and everyday clinical practice.

References

Alfonsson, S., Fagernäs, S., Beckman, M., & Lundgren, T. (2024). Psychotherapist factors that patients perceive are associated with treatment failure. *Psychotherapy (Chicago, Ill.), 61*(3), 241–249. https://doi.org/10.1037/pst0000527

Barkham, M., De Jong, K., Delgadillo, J., & Lutz, W. (2023). Routine outcome monitoring (ROM) and feedback: Research review and recommendations. *Psychotherapy Research, 33*(7), 841–855. https://doi.org/10.1080/10503307.2023.2181114

Barlow, D. (2024). *Clinical handbook of psychological disorders: A step-by-step treatment manual* (6th ed.). Guilford.

Beutler, L. E., & Harwood, T. M. (2000). *Prescriptive psychotherapy: A practical guide to systematic treatment selection*. Oxford University Press. https://doi.org/10.1093/med:psych/9780195136692.001.0001

Clement, P. W. (1999). *Outcomes and incomes*. Guilford.

de Jong, K., Douglas, S., Wolpert, M., Delgadillo, J., Aas, B., Bovendeerd, B., Carlier, I., Compare, A., Edbrooke-Childs, J., Janse, P., Lutz, W., Moltu, C., Nordberg, S., Poulsen, S., Rubel, J. A., Schiepek, G., Schilling, V. N. L. S., van Sonsbeek, M., & Barkham, M. (2025). Using progress feedback to enhance treatment outcomes: A narrative review. *Administration and Policy in Mental Health, 52*(1), 210–222. https://doi.org/10.1007/s10488-024-01381-3

Del Re, A. C., Flückiger, C., Horvath, A. O., Symonds, D., & Wampold, B. E. (2012). Therapist effects in the therapeutic alliance-outcome relationship: A restricted-maximum likelihood meta-analysis. *Clinical Psychology Review, 232*(7), 642–649. https://doi.org/10.1016/j.cpr.2012.07.002

Delgadillo, J., Deisenhofer, A. K., Probst, T., Shimokawa, K., Lambert, M. J., & Kleinstäuber, M. (2022). Progress feedback narrows the gap between more and less effective therapists: A therapist effects meta-analysis of clinical trials. *Journal of Consulting & Clinical Psychology, 90*(7), 559–567. https://doi.org/10.1037/ccp0000747

Flückiger, C., Del Re, A. C., Wlodasch, D., Horvath, A. O., Solomonov, N., & Wampold, B. E. (2020). Assessing the alliance-outcome association adjusted for patient characteristics and treatment processes: A meta analytic summary of direct comparisons. *Journal of Counseling Psychology, 67*(6), 706–711. https://doi.org/10.1037/cou0000424

Hatfield, D. R., & Ogles, B. M. (2004). The use of outcome measures by psychologists in clinical practice. *Professional Psychology: Research and Practice, 35*, 485–491. https://doi.org/10.1037/0735-7028.35.5.485

Hawkins, R. C., II, & Meier, S. T. (2015). Psychotherapeutic theories of change and measurement: An integrative model. *Journal of Unified Psychotherapy and Clinical Science, 3*(1), 80–119.

Ionita, G., Fitzpatrick, M., Tomaro, J., Chen, V. V., & Overington, L. (2015). Challenges of using progress monitoring measures: Insights from practicing clinicians. *Journal of Counseling Psychology.*. Advance online publication. https://doi.org/10.1037/cou0000122

Knox, S., Miller, C., Twidwell, R. E., & Knowlton, G. (2023). Client perspectives on psychotherapy failure. *Psychotherapy Research, 33*(3), 298–315. https://doi.org/10.1080/10503307.2022.2110020

Kraus, D. R., Castonguay, L., Boswell, J. F., Nordberg, S. S., & Hayes, J. A. (2011). Therapist effectiveness: Implications for accountability and patient care. *Psychotherapy Research, 21*(3), 267–276. https://doi.org/10.1080/10503307.2011.563249

Lambert, M. J. (2007). What we have learned from a decade of research aimed at improving psychotherapy outcome in routine care. *Psychotherapy Research, 17*, 1–14. https://doi.org/10.1080/10503300601032506

Lambert, M. J., Hansen, N. B., & Finch, A. E. (2001). Patient-focused research: Using patient outcome data to enhance treatment effects. *Journal of Consulting and Clinical Psychology, 69*(2), 159–172. https://doi.org/10.1037/0022-006X.69.2.159

Lambert, M. J., Harmon, C., Slade, K., Whipple, J. L., & Hawkins, E. J. (2005). Providing feedback to psychotherapists on their patients' progress: Clinical results and practice suggestions. *Journal of Clinical Psychology, 61*, 165–174. https://doi.org/10.1002/jclp.20113

Lambert, M. J., Whipple, J. L., & Kleinstäuber, M. (2018). Collecting and delivering progress feedback: A meta-analysis of routine outcome monitoring. *Psychotherapy, 55*(4), 520–537. https://doi.org/10.1037/pst0000167

Lilienfield, S. O. (2007). Psychological treatments that cause harm. *Perspectives on Psychological Science, 2*, 53–70.

Lutz, W., Schwartz, B., & Delgadillo, J. (2022). Measurement-based and data-informed psychological therapy. *Annual Review of Clinical Psychology, 18*, 71–98. https://doi.org/10.1146/annurev-clinpsy-071720-014821

Meier, S. T. (2008). *Measuring change in counseling and psychotherapy*. Guilford.

Meier, S. T., & Feeley, T. H. (2021). Ceiling effects indicate a possible threshold structure for working alliance. *Journal of Counseling Psychology, 69*(2), 235–245. https://doi.org/10.1037/cou0000564

Mergenthaler, E. (1996). Emotion-abstraction patterns in verbatim protocols: A new way of describing psychotherapeutic processes. *Journal of Consulting and Clinical Psychology, 64*, 1306–1315. https://doi.org/10.1037/0022-006X.64.6.1306

Owen, J., Imel, Z., & Adelson, J. (2012). "No-show": Therapist racial/ethnic disparities in client unilateral termination. *Journal of Counseling Psychology, 59*, 314–320. https://doi.org/10.1037/a0027091

Paap, D., Schepers, M., & Dijkstra, P. U. (2020). Reducing ceiling effects in the working Alliance inventory-rehabilitation Dutch version. *Disability and Rehabilitation, 42*(20), 2944–2950. https://doi.org/10.1080/09638288.2018.1563833

Persons, J. B. (1989). *Cognitive therapy in practice: A case formulation approach*. Norton.

Persons, J. B., & Mikami, A. Y. (2002). Strategies for handling treatment failure successfully. *Psychotherapy: Theory/Research/Practice/Training, 39*, 139–151. https://doi.org/10.1037/0033-3204.39.2.139

Rognstad, K., Wentzel-Larsen, T., Neumer, S. P., & Kjøbli, J. (2023). A systematic review and meta-analysis of measurement feedback systems in treatment for common mental health disorders. *Administrative Policy in Mental Health, 50*(2), 269–282. https://doi.org/10.1007/s10488-022-01236-9

Lambert, M. J., Harmon, C., Slade, K., Whipple, J. L., & Hawkins, E. J. (2005). Providing feedback to psychotherapists on their patients' progress: Clinical results and practice suggestions. *Journal of Clinical Psychology, 61*, 165–174. https://doi.org/10.1002/jclp.20113

Lambert, M. J., Whipple, J. L., & Kleinstäuber, M. (2018). Collecting and delivering progress feedback: A meta-analysis of routine outcome monitoring. *Psychotherapy, 55*(4), 520–537. https://doi.org/10.1037/pst0000167

[illegible]

Lutz, W., Schwartz, B., & Delgadillo, J. (2022). Measurement-based and data-informed psychological therapy. *Annual Review of Clinical Psychology, 18*, 71–98. https://doi.org/10.1146/annurev-clinpsy-[illegible]

[illegible] Guilford.

[illegible]

[illegible]

[illegible]

[illegible]

[illegible]

[illegible]

[illegible]

Chapter 3
A Systems-Contextual Integrative Heuristic Model, Part 1: Healing and Levels of Change

Chapter 2 highlighted the need for bridging the gap between therapeutic theory and measurement methods. In this chapter, we outline a systems-contextual integrative model (SCIM) for organizing multimethod assessment and outcome measures. For each level of this model, we offer sample measures (self-report, clinician ratings, performance based, and narrative text based) to provide a helpful guide for clinical practice and research.

First, as described in Chap. 1, healing means not only restoration of optimal functioning but also indicates an integrative holistic mode of being. Our systems-contextual integrative model (SCIM; Hawkins & Meier, 2015), as we discuss in this chapter and particularly in Chap. 4, posits a core dynamic oscillation between opposites, the Trauma Cycle and the Healing Cycle.

In 1961, Jerome Frank wrote a book titled *Persuasion and Healing* (most recently updated in 2025), which presented a general model for psychotherapy that essentially described healing as a restoration of hope that would then lead to specific improvements as measured by particular outcome measures. This book was an early attempt at integration or unification at a more global and general level reminiscent of Freud's classic concept in psychoanalysis, for example, of psychic maturity as the capability "to love and to work." This same outcome was expressed in Andras Angyal's (1965) model of personality function according to the healthy system principle (i.e., autonomy and homonomy). Cognitive behavioral therapy conceptualizes healing in terms of reducing symptom distress in specific areas that correspond to DSM-5 diagnostic mental disorders. So, for example, there are domain specific measures for improvements in depression and anxiety (e.g., Beck Depression Inventory, Beck Anxiety Inventory). The humanistic existential paradigm expanded beyond the CBT emphasis upon functionality as measured in specific areas of symptom distress to include a more general capacity for making meaning of one's life and for developing purposefulness.

In our systems-contextual integrative model (SCIM) we provide a heuristic framework for organizing and listing not only mono-method evidence-based

R. Hawkins, S. Meier, *Healing Outcomes*,
https://doi.org/10.1007/978-3-032-33611-8_3

assessment measures (such as the BDI and BAI) (Youngstrom et al., 2017) but also multi-method clinical assessment at different levels of change, specifically exploring *macro* (societal, cultural), *meso* (interpersonal-relational), and *micro* (intra-individual) levels. An important assumption of the SCIM is that outcome should be described as "healing" using the connotation of healing as holistic and integrated functioning with purposefulness and a balance between one's ability to be functional and contented in both work (agency) and communion (love). Healing is a noun that has the same root as health or mental health. The SCIM also moves beyond general personality trait measures (e.g., Five-Factor Model) and domain-specific measures, such as those from CBT just mentioned, to consider more complex situation-behavior relationships that reflect the influence across the levels of change in this model. Thus, the behavior of individuals in therapy at the micro level is moderated by relationships at the meso level, including the therapeutic relationship, but also interactions within families, groups, etc., and at the macro level, involving not only larger systems such as communities or affiliations but also cultural factors including value orientations. The SCIM is a dynamic systems perspective in which there is a fusion or interconnection across these levels of change.

To introduce the evolution of the SCIM, consider an older model based upon research by Hawkins et al. (1984) to provide a framework for the development and maintenance of binge eating disorder in overweight individuals. Certain predisposing macro-level societal and meso-level family relational influences, which can be designated as "negative psychosocial processes," lead to expectations (particularly in young women) for compliance with thinness and dieting as socially desirable sex-role behaviors. At the micro intra-individual level, these cultural-familial pressures are hypothesized to become developmentally internalized as a personality and behavioral vulnerability which Hilde Bruch (1973) called the "thin fat person." This personality vulnerability involves sensitivity to external cues for overeating, fear of loss of control of eating leading to fatness (weight gain), and an absence of interoceptive awareness to regulate food intake, and then this vulnerability generalizes to lower self-esteem and lack of self-efficacy. Developmentally, an individual with this kind of vulnerability in an environment, which would pose high demands on self-regulation that would conflict with a developmental curiosity about relationships and new more adult like activities (e.g., college lifestyle environment), would differentially impact individuals with the "thin fat" personality structure, leading them to experiences that would involve affect dysregulation and resulting loss of control of eating (i.e., binge eating with compensatory behaviors including self-induced purging). Individuals who experience this loss of control of binge eating with resultant weight gain and internalized weight phobia or stigma would also attempt to compensate and develop what Hawkins et al. (1984) called the "purification promise" (i.e., to engage in dietary restriction) which would unfortunately set the stage for a subsequent loss of control and more binge episodes.

The limitation of this multifactorial "pathways to bulimia" model (Hawkins et al., 1984) is that it did not specify treatment outcome or change measures except for weight loss and decreased bingeing and purging, the latter measured by the Binge Scale developed by Hawkins and Clement (1980). This choice of mono-method assessment and outcome measures (body weight, Binge Scale) is not overall healing of these individuals' capacity for meaningful and satisfying relationships with others and/or an increased sense of increased hope and purposefulness in their subsequent development.

A related model for substance use disorder recovery, called the "stress-coping theory—life contextual view" (SCT-LCV), likewise situated micro individual-level choice responses for re-using drugs within the larger contexts of personal coping and social resources (Hawkins, 1992). This SCT-LCV did propose measures not only for substance use problem behaviors but also for purposefulness and spiritual well-being associated with participation in recovery programs and sustaining abstinence.

The purpose of the present systems-contextual integrative model is to correct this rather limited view by expanding upon the levels of change, operationalizing measures to include both self-report, other clinician reports, and observation and performance measures to describe how individuals would change and have overall improved overall healing outcomes. The SCIM is a transdiagnostic, complex dynamical systems network model (Roefs et al., 2022) in which the constitutive elements interact at multiple contextual levels, maintaining healthy states or disorders, and/or rapid shifts between them.

Psychotherapeutic Theories of Change and Measurement: A Systems-Contextual Integrative Model

As noted earlier, although conceptual models for psychotherapy have operationalized their key constructs in some instances, generally there has not been either a sufficient specification of the change process for monitoring progress, or a sufficient integration to cover diverse change mechanisms (e.g., the controversy between specific treatment techniques and the treatment alliance, see Zilcha-Mano et al., 2014) and well-agreed upon personality dimensions for mapping client and therapist characteristics (such as the Five Factor Model, McCrae & Costa, 1987; Widiger & Costa, 2013, or the Myers-Briggs Type Indicator, Jinkerson et al., 2014, 2015) to guide comprehensive outcome assessments. In contrast, theorists such as Hansen and Freimuth (1997) have provided a framework for assisting the clinical supervisor and psychotherapy trainee to formulate components of psychotherapy across theories and intervention approaches. Their seven-fold model comprising assumptive world views, schools of psychotherapy, theories, particular theorists (within a particular theoretical orientation), working hypotheses, strategies, and techniques represent concentric levels of analysis that become increasingly concrete and focused to enable the clinician to systematically formulate a given case. Mayer (2004, 2005) also provided a unified systems view for psychology in general and for mapping change techniques from psychotherapy onto personality. Mayer's modular view formulates system dynamics from which methods of measurement can be developed for these components of personality that relate to psychotherapy process and outcome. Epstein's (2014) cognitive-experiential theory of personality likewise provides an integrative framework for measurement with applications to psychotherapy. McAdams and Pals (2006) include narrative methods in their integrative model of personality. Finally, Castonguay (2011; Castonguay & Beutler, 2005) has argued cogently for continued study of the principles of psychotherapeutic change and measurement, and for building bridges of collaboration and integration across theoretical orientations and science-practitioner divides (e.g., through fostering practice research networks).

While such integrative frameworks exist, most notably recent proposals for unifying psychotherapy through metatheoretical biopsychosocial systems theories (Magnavita & Anchin, 2013; Melchert, 2013), current clinical assessment methods and measures of psychotherapy process and outcome variables do not fully align with these newer unifying metatheoretical frameworks nor do they span the major theoretical orientations of psychotherapy (e.g., see Hopwood & Bornstein, 2014, pp. 437–438, for discussion of a similar claim). In this section, we map psychotherapy outcomes (that we call *healing outcomes*) using an integrative model intended to be trans-theoretical and linked to specific measurement strategies that can facilitate effectiveness studies of psychotherapeutic change (Hawkins & Meier, 2015). This model is illustrated through application to a specific case, presented in the Appendix to Chap. 4.

Medical model versus *psychosocial and contextual models*. Traditionally, the contrast regarding models of psychotherapy has been between the so-called medical model and the psychosocial model (Albee, 1998; Szasz, 1974). Bruce Wampold in his provocative book *The Great Psychotherapy Debate* (Wampold, 2001; Wampold & Imel, 2015) contrasted the medical model with his own model for psychotherapy, which he termed a contextual model. Wampold's contextual model has elements that resemble broader-based healing principles that are found culturally in common within anthropology, medicine, and spirituality (Wampold & Budge, 2012). The contextual model for healing emphasizes the importance of psychosocial contextual factors in interaction with change processes within the psychotherapy client. This model is not based on DSM-IV or DSM-5 descriptive nomenclature, as are core batteries used for psychotherapy research (e.g., Horowitz et al., 1997); however, we contend that it can be adapted to the DSM disorder specific treatments with the provision of additional domain specific measures. Moreover, we believe that our own systems-contextual integrative model (SCIM) provides a coherent conceptual framework for integrating the person within the social environment (e.g., Horowitz, 2004) that will facilitate case formulation for clinical research and practice (e.g., Horowitz, 2005).

Three contextual levels (macro, meso, and micro). This type of contextual model (which we call the SCIM, shown in Fig. 3.1) should be integrated and systematically specified in terms of the major theories of personality and psychotherapy at

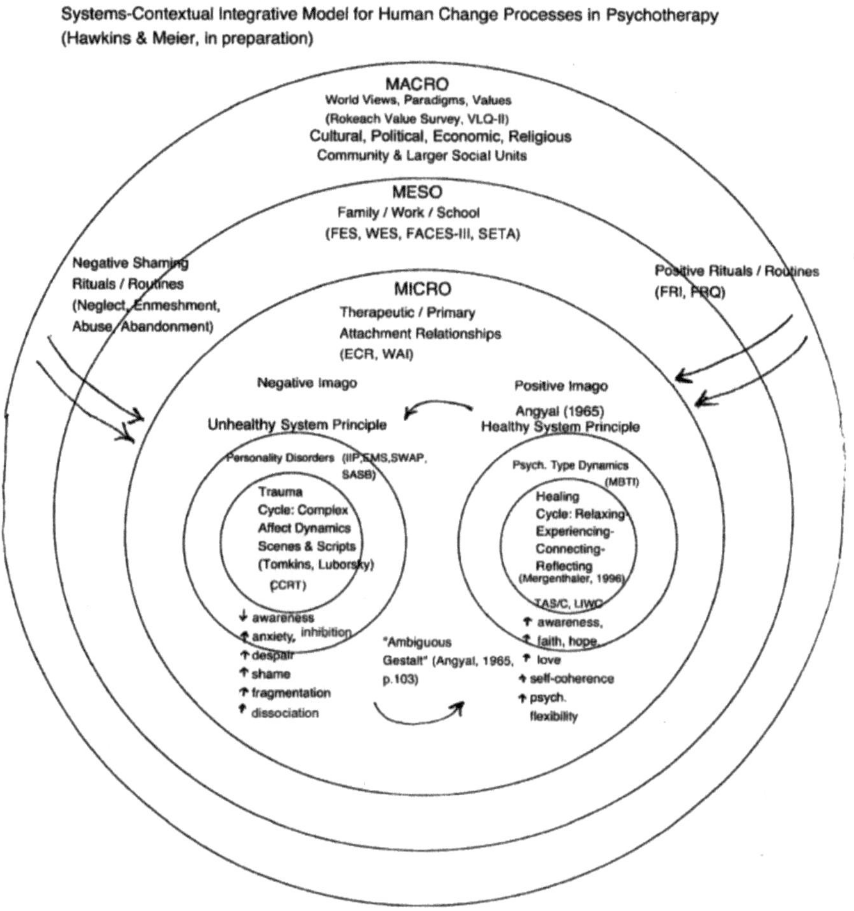

Fig. 3.1 Systems-contextual integrative model for human change processes in psychotherapy (Hawkins & Meier, 2015)

three levels of analysis.[1] At each level of analysis, examples of measurement tools should also be specified (Fig. 3.1 & Table 3.1). These are described below. The present model bears some resemblance to Wachtel's (1977, 1997, 2014) cyclical psychodynamics model in its integrative framework. But Wachtel's integration of psychodynamics, cognitive behavior therapy, and family systems approaches in the

[1] The levels of these social ecological contexts (i.e., micro, meso, and macro) should be viewed not as linear statistical mediators or moderators, but instead as fused, permeable coupled systems (as in Ford & Lerner, 1992). This model's operation can best be conveyed as the interplay of individual dispositional attributes and characteristic adaptations to perturbations from social ecological contexts at these three levels (as shown in Figure 3.1 and operationalized with suggested measures in Table 3.1) as this interplay is manifested in the unfolding of each person's unique life narrative as postulated by McAdams and Pals (2006).

Table 3.1 Examples of measures for the three levels of the systems-contextual integrative model

Measure	Level	Source
Rokeach value survey	Macro	Rokeach (1973)
World hypotheses	Macro	Pepper (1942)
Valued living Questionnaire-2	Macro	Wilson and DeFrene (2009)
Family environment scale	Meso	Moos and Moos (1994)
Work environment scale	Meso	Moos (1994)
Family adaptability and cohesion evaluation scale (FACES-IV)	Meso	Olson (2011)
Salter environmental type (SETA)	Meso	Salter (2000)
Family routines inventory	Meso	Jensen et al. (1983)
Family rituals questionnaire	Meso	Fiese (2006)
Attachment—Self-report [ECR], interview [AAI], projective [AAPS]	Micro	Fraley et al. (2000), Steel et al. (2009); George and West (2012)
Myers-Briggs type indicator	Micro	Myers (1980); Myers et al. (1998)
NEO-PI-3	Micro	McCrae and Costa (2010)
Five facet mindfulness questionnaire	Micro	Baer (2006)
Acceptance & Action Questionnaire II	Micro	Bond et al. (2011)
Thematic apperception test(TAT)	Micro	Westen (1991)
Inventory of interpersonal problems	Micro, meso	Horowitz et al. (2000)
Schema questionnaire	Micro	Young et al. (2003)
Structured clinical interviews	Micro	DSM-IV related (e.g., SCID-I & II, Hamilton scales)
SWAP-200	Micro	Shedler and Westen (2007)
Core conflictual relationship theme (CCRT)	Micro	Luborsky and Crits-Christoph (1997)
Structural analysis of social behavior (SASB)	Micro	Benjamin (2006)
Working Alliance inventory	Micro	Horvath and Greenberg (1989)
Therapy expectations (C/EQ, MPEQ)	Micro	Devilly and Borkovec (2000); Norberg et al. (2011)
The experiencing scales	Micro	Klein et al. (1986)
Sessions rating scale	Micro	Duncan et al. (2003)
Outcome rating scale	Micro	Miller et al. (2003)
Outcome questionnaire: 45	Micro	Lambert et al. (1996)
Treatment outcome package	Micro	Kraus et al. (2005)
CORE-OM	Micro	Barkham et al. (2001); Evans et al. (2002)
DANA	Micro	Meier (2012b)
Objective measures—computer text software (LIWC, TAS/C); audio-video sampling of behavior	Micro	Tausczik and Pennebaker (2010); Mergenthaler (1996)
Objective measures—Behavioral health (psychophysiology, physical health, biological markers)	Micro	Bornas et al. (2012); Doehrmann et al. (2012); McKay (2008); Moss (2005); Olff et al. (2007); Wheat and Larkin (2010)

(Continued)

Table 3.1 (Continued)

Measure	Level	Source
Domain specific CBT outcome measures (e.g., BDI-II, BAI, and PSWQ)	Micro	See Nezu (2000); Antony (2001)
Self-monitoring daily records—Target behaviors, emotions, thoughts, social interactions (hardcopy, or electronically mediated)	Micro	See Barlow (2021); Bolger et al. (2003); Conner et al. (2009); Fahrenberg et al. (2007); Mehl and Conner (2011)
Domain specific self-efficacy	Micro	Bandura (2006)

contextual framework of vicious circles that maintain dysfunctional relationships and conflictual behavioral patterns established in childhood does not provide guidelines for measuring key constructs and thereby building empirical support for his model. Magnavita and Anchin (2013) have also recently proposed a multi-level personality biopsychosocial theory for unifying psychotherapy that bears interesting similarities with the levels of our integrative model. Kiesler's (1996) seminal volume on interpersonal theory and research provided an important conceptualization of adaptive and maladaptive interpersonal transaction cycles with clinical guidelines for measuring and assessing them. Lorna Benjamin's (2003) object relations Interpersonal Reconstructive Therapy (IRT) for the treatment of personality disorders may be the closest analogue to our model in terms of its dual process core algorithm (i.e., the "Regressive Loyalist," and the "Growth Collaborator," Benjamin, 2003, p. 72), objectively measured with the Structural Analysis of Social Behavior (SASB) method, in which each IRT intervention promotes improved behavior through enhancing the growth collaborator and diminishing the client's need for deploying regressive loyalist defensive maneuvers.

Macro level. At this level, personality conceptions are at the most general abstraction of philosophies (e.g., the "assumptive world" views of Pepper, 1942, as framed by Hansen & Freimuth, 1997), values (including those of particular schools of psychotherapy), and ideals of the community, region, and nation. We subscribe to a pluralistic stance wherein therapists' (and clients') macro-level assumptions are identified through dialogue, differences are respected, and assessment and treatment strategies specified according to the specific context of a given case (see Safran & Messer, 1997). However, our pluralist, constructivist philosophy emphasizes behavior change, affective experience, and meaning making in an interpersonal context. These macro-level value dimensions such as agency and communion (Bakan, 1966) differ across individuals, groups, and situations, and need to be mapped as part of personality assessment and treatment planning.

Personality and psychotherapy thus involve interpersonal processes (Sullivan, 1953), measurable both within persons and in their interactions with others (Benjamin, 1996, 2003) at various levels from the nuclear family to the community and to broader cultural units. Timothy Leary (1957) conceptually pioneered this perspective and described the Interpersonal Checklist (ICL), a circumplex model with two dimensions: dominance / submission and affiliation / disaffiliation. Within this circumplex model, he identified two levels of interpersonal functioning, one adaptive and the other maladaptive. He also specified measures for these interpersonal facets, measures that would tap processes known to the individual consciously (and therefore self-reportable) and those that would be unknown (and therefore observable only by other persons); for example, the MMPI clinical scale elevations can be used to estimate individual psychopathology, whereas the MMPI content scales would reflect symptoms known to the test taker. More recent circumplex models include Wiggins' (1995, 1996) Interpersonal Adjective Scales (IAS), Benjamin's Structural Analysis of Social Behavior (SASB) (Benjamin, 2006), and the Inventory of Interpersonal Problems (IIP) (L. Horowitz et al., 2000). It is important to be clear that what we are designating as macro level are these personality dimensions as assumptive beliefs and values per se and not just their mapping in the interpersonal interactions of individuals and/or for describing intrapersonal object relations. The ICL, IAS, SASB, and IIP can also be used at the meso level for comparing individuals within dyads, families, and groups, and at the micro level for describing the development of the individual personality within these contexts, particularly in primary attachment dyads and in the therapeutic relationship.

Macro-level psychotherapy goals. Classifying the goals of psychotherapy for the purpose of selecting and comparing them in outcome studies is also a macro-level project that taps into assumptive worldviews and value dimensions. To illustrate the importance and implications of this aspect of the contextual model, we shall consider another contemporary measure of personality and personality disorders that has attracted considerable attention: the Shedler-Westen Assessment Procedure (SWAP-200; Shedler, 2010; Shedler & Westen, 2007). With the SWAP-200 (Shedler, 2010; Shedler & Westen, 2007; Westen et al., 2012), trained clinicians rate samples of interviews along 200 dimensions reflecting both optimal mental health functioning and degrees of psychopathology / personality disorder characteristics. Using the SWAP-200, clinician judges are able reliably to rate multiple dimensions of client functioning. Shedler (2010) provided a table entitled Definition of Mental Health listing 23 attributes of individuals' functioning, most in the context of interpersonal behaviors that are rated by observers, which can yield highly reliable judgments that are valid indicators of personality disorder diagnosis and psychotherapy process / outcome. Shedler (2010, Table 2, p. 106) described sample items such as "is able to use his/her talents, abilities, and energy effectively and productively," "enjoys challenges; takes pleasure in accomplishing things," "is empathic, is sensitive and responsive to other people's needs and feelings," "is able to find meaning and fulfillment in guiding, mentoring, or nurturing others," "appears comfortable and at ease in social situations," "generally finds contentment and happiness in life's activities," "is creative; is able to see things or approach problems in novel ways," "tends to be conscientious and responsible," and "is psychologically insightful; is able to understand self and others in subtle and sophisticated ways." The sample SWAP-200 items map the assumptive macro therapeutic goals of interest transtheoretically.

Indeed, Shedler (2010, pp. 99–100) claims that psychodynamic psychotherapy has identified distinctive features that apply to other forms of psychotherapy and are assumptive goals for psychotherapeutic change, which we believe are important for our holistic model of healing assessment and treatment. He contends that these assumptive goals embrace but transcend the focus of CBT upon symptom change to include emotional and interpersonal awareness. These seven characteristics comprise the following:

1. Focus on affect and expression of emotions.
2. Exploration of attempts to avoid experiencing distressing thoughts and feelings.
3. Identification of recurrent themes and patterns.
4. A developmental focus.
5. A focus on interpersonal relations.
6. A focus on the therapeutic relationship.
7. Exploration of fantasy life.

These distinctive features are particularly interesting for their emphasis on levels of functioning that supersede symptom distress, particularly the relational context and the valuing of emotional experience. This broader macro context for defining the goals of psychotherapy (and human flourishing) is also seen in the three questions that Westen et al. (2006, p. 348) have posed in their clinical model of personality structure. These questions appear to relate to the same underlying assumptive philosophies for goals for potential psychotherapeutic change measures:

1. What does the person wish for, fear, and value, and to what extent are these motives conscious or conflicting?
2. What psychological resources (affective, cognitive, and self-regulatory) does the person have to deal with reality and attain his/her goals?
3. How does the person experience the self, others, and relationships, and to what extent is s/he capable of mature, intimate relationships? (p. 348).

Macro-level goals and stages of psychotherapy change. The stages of psychotherapy change model and the related dose response model have been studied extensively by Kenneth Howard and colleagues (e.g., Howard et al., 1986; Howard et al., 1993; Lueger et al., 2001; Maling et al., 1995), using the COMPASS tracking system for outcome assessment. These models can be simply expressed as a set of sequential stages that may be seen as an unfolding contextual model of progressive change, comprising restoration of hope or remoralization (Frank & Frank, 1991), followed by decreased symptom distress and symptom improvement, improved interpersonal relations, and improved social role functioning. To this list, we would add systems/structural changes, such as cognitive and personality reorganization, and more subtle but important changes such as the ability to be creative, insightful, and integrated with a coherent sense of self and one's values, with the skillful use of all the psychological functions (Jung's concept of individuation). Howard et al. (1996) originated patient-focused research.[2] Lambert and colleagues (Lambert et al., 1996, 2001) developed the Outcome Questionnaire (OQ 45.2) and have shown that with the progression of psychotherapy beyond the initial eight sessions, where

[2] "Patient-focused research" (in contrast to variable-based research) is the term used to denote the emphasis placed upon the individual client as the unit of analysis for the evaluation of the effectiveness of psychotherapy in outcome research (e.g., Lambert et al., 2001).

much symptom improvement occurs, there is subsequent gradual improvement in interpersonal relations and social role performance (Lambert, 2007).

Meso-level social ecological contexts for psychotherapy change. At the meso level (Fig. 3.1, Table 3.1), as originally theorized by Brofenbrenner (1979) in his ecological systems model, we theorize that positive, promotive rituals and routines from the reciprocal influences of family, school, community, and work settings shape beliefs and values that develop and stabilize human strivings (Dahlke, 1999; Fiese, 2006). Unfortunately, these positive rituals and routines can be undermined and invaded by shame-based family systems arising from predominant negative rituals and routines (abuse, enmeshment, neglect, and abandonment, as described by Grant Jr et al., 1992) that often involve addictive behaviors (Hawkins & Hawkins, 2012). However, recent conceptual and empirical studies in prevention science (e.g., Biglan et al., 2012; Chen, 2012; Johnson, 2012; Yoshikawa et al., 2012) have emphasized the overarching importance of promotive social support factors in nurturing positive human development in the face of adversity, even possibly ameliorating the chronic stress-related neuroendocrine and neurocognitive damage (i.e., allostatic load, McEwen & Stellar, 1993) associated with adverse childhood experiences related to poverty through improving caregiving and social support (Blair & Raver, 2012). Promotive communal routines and rituals (e.g., parenting and classroom interventions, community-based violence prevention) support primary attachment in the parent-child relationship.

Two psychotherapeutic approaches that fit the meso level are family therapy and group counseling. Family systems theorists view individuals' social systems as a major source of individuals' problems. Families are most people's most important social systems, and these groups can act to preserve their status quo, including family members' acting to keep individuals dysfunctional (Meier & Davis, 2011). In group counseling, the group becomes a therapeutic social system. In contrast to clients' previous social interactions, therapeutic groups provide social and emotional support, models of how to cope and interact with others appropriately, and normalizing of client problems (Schneider-Corey & Corey, 2005; Yalom & Leszcz, 2005). In both families and groups, the therapist's tasks include pointing out maladaptive interactions and helping to initiate new behaviors, particularly around interpersonal communication (deShazer, 1982; Minuchin, 1974).

The Family Routines Inventory (FRI; Boyce et al., 1983; Jensen et al., 1983) and the Family Ritual Questionnaire (FRQ; Fiese & Kline, 1993; Fiese, 2006), for example, are two well-researched measures that could be employed to assess these meso level contextual influences. The FRI is a theoretically based measure that assesses family routines on the assumption that such behaviors are intended to provide stability for family members during stressful periods. Sample FRI items include "Whole family eats together almost every night" and "Parent(s) have some time each day for just talking to the children" (Jensen et al., 1983, p. 204). Similarly, the FRQ measures family rituals across settings (e.g., dinnertime and religious celebrations) and dimensions (e.g., roles, symbolic significance) that have been found to be related to adolescents' anxiety.

Micro-level biopsychosocial competencies, primary attachments, the therapist-client relationship, and emotional processing. At the micro level, our systems-contextual integrative model (Fig. 3.1, Table 3.1) includes the biopsychosocial competencies of the individual, primary attachment relationships, and the therapeutic alliance (which we consider as a primary relationship in adulthood that can restore attachment security). At the meso-micro interface, these positive attachment relationships facilitate intrapersonal cognitive-affective change processes (emotional processing), instill positive expectations about psychotherapy specifically (e.g., Constantino et al., 2012) and about life in general, and establish / restore trust, secure attachment, and social competence / generalized self-efficacy.

The dynamic for this micro-level emotional processing, both within the therapy relationship and in primary attachment relationships outside of therapy, may be Mergenthaler's (1996) Therapeutic Cycle that involves four phases: Relaxing, Experiencing, Connecting, and Reflecting. In the Relaxing phase, emotional processing is minimal as is cognitive abstraction. In the Experiencing phase, the psychotherapist assists the client in activating emotional structures and emotional processing becomes intense. Then in the Connecting phase, there are heightened efforts for meaning making and cognitive abstracting along with the heightened emotional experiencing. Finally, after the cognitive abstraction or insights are obtained, in the Reflecting phase emotions decrease while cognitive abstracting remains high to consolidate meanings, after which cognitive abstraction activity also decreases to baseline. The more that the therapeutic cycle, which we renamed the Healing Cycle (HC),[3] recurs the more likely that success in therapy occurs, including a decrease in shame, and an increase in moments of presence (Stern, 2004), emotional and experiential awareness, faith, hope, and love, and increased self-coherence in client narratives. Another older measure of depth of emotional processing, the Experiencing Scales (Klein et al., 1986), has been widely used in humanistic-experiential psychotherapy research studies.[4]

---

[3] We renamed Mergenthaler's (1996) "Therapeutic Cycle" the "Healing Cycle" because contextually the term "healing" has ancient cultural and religious origins. In this spiritual/religious sense, the trauma cycle would be the external and internal perturbations of evil and sickness while the healing cycle would be healing by the Holy Spirit in early Christianity as described by Kelsey (1973), with restoration to "sofron" (Greek term meaning restored to one's right mind or sanity). We should point out that Mergenthaler's (1996) therapeutic cycle was derived through computer text analysis of psychodynamic psychotherapy sessions. We do not consider the healing cycle to be equivalent to person-centered therapy's assumptions of the organismic valuing process and the unconditional positive regard (Rogers, 1962), because in the healing cycle, negative affect and defenses, such as pride and self-justification, are focused upon as much as are low self-esteem and self-contempt (Cooper, 2003). The therapeutic "journey" from predominance of the negative affect and images and maladaptive behaviors of the trauma cycle to symptom decrease, prosocial behaviors, and improved well-being via the healing cycle may thus involve a Dantean like descent into the "infernal dimension'"i.e., the "dark depths of the soul" before an ascent into the "unity of the future" and "true being" can take place (Feld, 2011, pp. 182–183).

[4] The Experiencing Scales (Klein et al., 1986) measure emotional experiencing, which involves both emotional awareness and reflective meaning-making, also referred to as depth of emotional processing (Greenberg & Pascual-Leone, 2006; Pascual-Leone & Greenberg, 2007). There is evi-

Narrative / qualitative change methods and measures. We believe that the HC is a process that unfolds like a story. Meier (2012a) described a narrative-based theory of change for individuals in counseling and psychotherapy (see Fig. 3.2) that typically involves multiple, converging pathways of affective, cognitive, and behavioral effort (Anderson, 2004). Individuals recall, relate, and generate one or more stories that contain people, events, and situations with associated emotional elements. Much of the initial stage of psychotherapy involves identifying those emotions and the extent to which clients can tolerate their expression and experience. All these processes take place in social contexts; in psychotherapy, these contexts include the

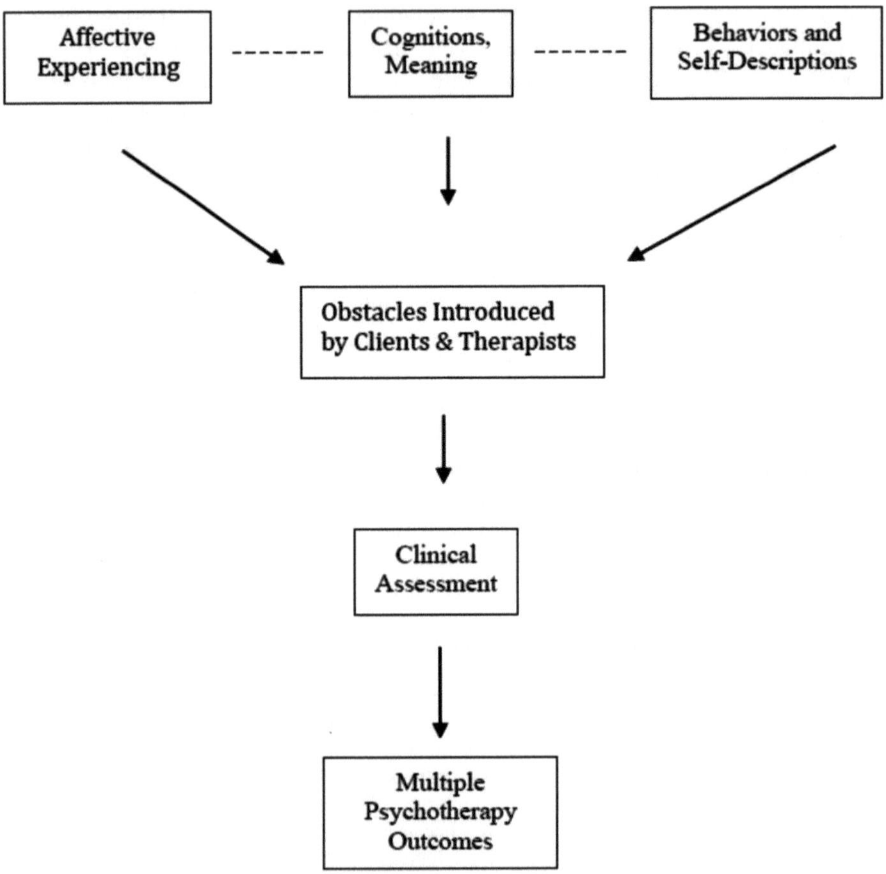

Fig. 3.2 Narrative theory of change

dence for the moment to moment affective-cognitive change events distinguishing good outcome from poor outcome cases (Pascual-Leone, 2009). Although Mergenthaler's (1996) therapeutic cycle has also been replicated (e.g., LoVerde et al., 2012; McCarthy et al., 2011), its time course is across sessions rather than moment by moment, and its linguistic analysis may not actually be measuring emotional experiencing per se, merely the talking about emotions (Pascual-Leone, 2009).

client-therapist relationship and relationships among clients in settings with couples, families, and groups.

Identifying emotions and the accompanying content about persons and events creates an agenda for processing and resolving the client's psychological difficulties in psychotherapy. Samoilov and Goldfried (2000), p. 382) indicate that emotional arousal lays the foundation for reorganization of underlying emotional themes, assimilation of new information, and formation of new implicit meaning structures. Next, individuals create meaning in their psychotherapy-related stories to solve or resolve the distress-causing situation. Often a change in self-description around personal agency is part of this process, and here a focus on behavior change can be beneficial. Formal clinical assessment can provide feedback to therapist and client about the degree and direction of therapeutic progress, allowing for an indication of progress and the need to alter current treatment approaches. This clinical process is seldom straightforward, however, as many individuals struggle with obstacles to processing content containing strong emotion as well as changing problem-related behaviors in social contexts.

Empirical support for narrative therapies and these specific symptom level and interpersonal change components has been found in numerous studies (e.g., Silver et al., 1998; Vromans & Schweitzer, 2010; Weber et al., 2006). Vromans and Schweitzer (2010), for example, examined depression and interpersonal outcomes for 47 adults with major depression who received manualized narrative therapy (i.e., where therapists had a written set of narrative-related procedures to employ in a particular sequence). Results indicated significant improvement for both depressive symptoms and interpersonal functioning. Researchers have also found that writing about emotional upheavals can positively affect psychological and physical health (Pennebaker et al., 2003). In these studies, individuals typically write about an emotionally disturbing topic for 15 to 30 min per day over 3 to 5 days. Such writing can lead to long-term improvement in psychological and physical health but may also produce short-term increases in emotional distress (Smyth, 1998). Other research has found that facilitating emotional processing and verbalization of affect is associated with positive outcomes (Diener et al., 2007).

Summary and Implications for Research and Practice

Here we have introduced our systems-contextual integrative model (SCIM, Part 1. In the next chapter, we will present Part 2 of the SCIM, the dynamics of the Healing Cycle and the Trauma Cycle and its implication for integrative psychotherapy process theories, evidence-based assessment, and outcomes.

References

Albee, G. W. (1998). Fifty years of clinical psychology: Selling our soul to the devil. *Applied & Preventive Psychology, 7*, 189–194. https://doi.org/10.1016/S0962-1849(05)80021-6

Anderson, H. (2004). Collaborative relationships and dialogic conversations: Ideas for a relationally responsive practice. In L. E. Heatherington & G. Friedlander (Eds.), *Family psychology: Science-based interventions* (pp. 399–415). American Psychological Association.

Angyal, A. (1965). *Neurosis & treatment: A holistic theory*. Wiley.

Antony, M. (2001). *Practitioner's guide to empirically based measures of anxiety*. Kluwer. https://doi.org/10.1007/b108176

Baer, R. A. (2006). *Assessing mindfulness and acceptance processes in clients*. New Harbinger.

Bakan, D. (1966). *The duality of human existence: Isolation and communion in modern man*. Rand McNally.

Bandura, A. (2006). Guide for constructing self-efficacy scales. In F. Pajares & T. D. Urdan (Eds.), *Self-efficacy beliefs of adolescents*. IAP.

Barkham, M., Margison, F., Leach, C., et al. (2001). Service profiling and outcomes benchmarking using the CORE-OM: Towards practice-based evidence in the psychological therapies. *Journal of Consulting and Clinical Psychology, 69*, 184–196. https://doi.org/10.1037/0022-006X.69.2.184

Barlow, D. H. (2021). *Clinical handbook of psychological disorders: A step-by-step treatment manual* (6th ed.). Guilford. https://doi.org/10.1093/oxfordhb/9780199328710.001.0001

Benjamin, L. S. (1996). *Interpersonal diagnosis and treatment of personality disorder* (2nd ed.). Guilford.

Benjamin, L. S. (2003). *Interpersonal reconstructive therapy: An integrative personality-based treatment for complex cases*. Guilford.

Benjamin, L. S. (2006). The use of structural analysis of social behavior (SASB) as an assessment tool. *Annual Review of Psychology, 2*, 83–109. https://doi.org/10.1146/annurev.clinpsy.2.022305.095337

Biglan, A., Flay, B. R., Embry, D. D., & Sandler, I. N. (2012). The critical role of nurturing environments for promoting human Well-being. *American Psychologist, 67*, 257–271. https://doi.org/10.1037/a0026796

Blair, C., & Raver, C. C. (2012). Child development in the context of adversity: Experiential canalization of brain and behavior. *American Psychologist, 67*, 309–318. https://doi.org/10.1037/a0027493

Bolger, N., Davis, A., & Rafaeli, E. (2003). Daily methods: Capturing life as it is lived. *Annual Review of Psychology, 54*, 579–616. https://doi.org/10.1146/annurev.psych.54.101601.145030

Bond, F. W., Hayes, S. C., Baer, R. A., Carpenter, K. M., Guenole, N., Orcutt, H. K., Waltz, T., & Zettle, R. D. (2011). Preliminary psychometric properties of the acceptance and action Questionniare—II: A revised measure of psychological flexibility and experiential avoidance. *Behavior Therapy, 42*, 676–688. https://doi.org/10.1016/j.beth.2011.03.007

Bornas, X., Riera del Amo, A., Tortella-Feliu, M., & Llabres, J. (2012). Heart rate variability profiles and exposure therapy treatment outcome in flight phobia. *Applied Psychophysiology and Biofeedback, 37*, 53–62. https://doi.org/10.1007/s10484-011-9179-5

Boyce, W. T., Jensen, E. W., James, S. A., & Peacock, J. L. (1983). The family routines inventory: Theoretical origins. *Social Science and Medicine, 17*(4), 193–200. https://doi.org/10.1016/0277-9536(83)90116-8

Brofenbrenner, U. (1979). *The ecology of human development: Experiments by nature and design*. Harvard Press. https://doi.org/10.4159/9780674028845

Bruch, H. (1973). *Eating disorders: Obesity, anorexia nervosa, and the person within*. Basic Books.

Castonguay, L. G. (2011). Psychotherapy, psychopathology, research, and practice: Pathways of connections and integration. *Psychotherapy Research, 21*(2), 125–140. https://doi.org/10.1080/10503307.2011.563250

Castonguay, L. G., & Beutler, L. E. (2005). *Principles of therapeutic change that work*. Oxford University Press. https://doi.org/10.1093/med:psych/9780195156843.001.0001

Chen, E. (2012). Protective factors for health among low-socioeconomic-status individuals. *Current Directions in Psychological Science, 21*, 189–193. https://doi.org/10.1177/0963721412438710

Conner, T. S., Tennen, H., Fleeson, W., & Barrett, L. F. (2009). Experience sampling methods: A modern idiographic approach to personality research. *Social and Personality Psychology Compass, 3*(3), 292–313. https://doi.org/10.1111/j.1751-9004.2009.00170.x

Constantino, M. J., Ametrano, M. R., & Greenberg, R. P. (2012). Clinician interventions and participant characteristics that foster adaptive patient expectations for psychotherapy and psychotherapeutic change. *Psychotherapy (Chicago, Ill.), 49*, 557–569. https://doi.org/10.1037/a0029440

Cooper, T. D. (2003). *Sin, pride, and self-acceptance: The problem of identity in theology and psychology*. InterVarsity Press.

Dahlke, R. (1999). *Everyday initiations: How to solve crises using rituals*. Woodside, CA: Bluestar Communications.

deShazer, S. (1982). *Patterns of brief family therapy*. Guilford.

Devilly, G. J., & Borkovec, T. D. (2000). Psychometric properties of the credibility /expectancy questionnaire. *Journal of Behavior Therapy and Experimental Psychiatry, 31*, 73–86. https://doi.org/10.1016/S0005-7916(00)00012-4

Diener, M. J., Hilsenroth, M. J., & Weinberger, J. (2007). Therapist affect focus and patient outcomes in psychodynamic psychotherapy: A meta-analysis. *American Journal of Psychiatry, 164*, 936–941.

Doehrmann, O., et al. (2012). Predicting treatment response in social anxiety disorder from functional magnetic resonance imaging. *Archives of General Psychiatry*, Online First, E1–E11. https://doi.org/10.1001/2013.jamapsychiatry.5

Duncan, B. L., Miller, S. D., Sparks, J. A., Cloud, D. A., et al. (2003). The session rating scale: Preliminary psychometric properties of a "working" alliance measure. *Journal of Brief Therapy, 3*(1), 3–12.

Epstein, S. (2014). *Cognitive-experiential theory: An integrative theory of personality*. Oxford. https://doi.org/10.1093/acprof:osobl/9780199927555.001.0001

Evans, C., Connell, J., Barkham, M., et al. (2002). Towards a standardized brief outcome measure: Psychometric properties and utility of the CORE-OM. *British Journal of Psychiatry, 180*, 51–60. https://doi.org/10.1192/bjp.180.1.51

Fahrenberg, J., Myrtek, M., Pawlik, K., & Perrez, M. (2007). Ambulatory assessment: Monitoring behavior in daily life settings. *European Journal of Psychological Assessment, 23*(4), 206–213. https://doi.org/10.1027/1015-5759.23.4.206

Feld, A. (2011). *Melancholy and the otherness of god: A study of the hermeneutics of depression*. Lexington Books. https://doi.org/10.5040/9781666999730

Fiese, B. H., & Kline, C. A. (1993). Development of the family ritual questionnaire: Initial reliability and validation studies. *Journal of Family Psychology, 6*, 1–10. https://doi.org/10.1037/0893-3200.6.3.290

Fiese, B.H. (2006). *Family routines and rituals*. New Haven, CT: Yale University Press.

Ford, D. L., & Lerner, R. M. (1992). *Developmental systems theory: An integrative approach*. Sage.

Fraley, R. C., Waller, N. G., & Brennan, K. A. (2000). An item-response theory analysis of self-report measures of adult attachment. *Journal of Personality and Social Psychology, 78*, 350–365. https://doi.org/10.1037/0022-3514.78.2.350

Frank, J.D., & Frank, J.B. (1991). *Persuasion and healing: A comparative study of psychotherapy*. Baltimore: The Johns Hopkins University Press.

George, C., & West, M. L. (2012). *The adult attachment projective system*. Guilford.

Grant, R.D. Jr, Miller, A.W., & Wells, A. (1992). Recovering connections. : Harper Collins.

Greenberg, L. S., & Pascual-Leone, A. (2006). Emotion in psychotherapy: A practice friendly review. *Journal of Consulting and Clinical Psychology: In Session, 62*, 611–630. https://doi.org/10.1002/jclp.20252

Hansen, N. E., & Freimuth, M. (1997). Piecing the puzzle together: A model for understanding the theory-practice relationship. *The Counseling Psychologist, 25*(4), 654–673. https://doi.org/10.1177/0011000097254008

Hawkins, C. A., & Hawkins, R. C. II (2012). Family systems and chemical dependency. In C. A. McNeese & D. M. Dinitto (Eds.), *Chemical dependency: A systems approach* (4th ed.). Pearson.

Hawkins, R. C., II. (1992). Substance abuse and stress-coping resources: A life contextual and clinical viewpoint. In B. C. Wallace (Ed.), *The chemically dependent: Phases of treatment recovery*. Brunner/Mazel.

Hawkins, R. C., II, & Clement, P. F. (1980). Development and construct validation of a self-report measure of binge eating tendencies. *Addictive Behaviors, 5*, 219–226. https://doi.org/10.1016/0306-4603(80)90042-8

Hawkins, R. C., II, Fremouw, W. J., & Clement, P. F. (Eds.). (1984). *The binge-purge syndrome: Diagnosis, treatment, and research*. Springer.

Hawkins, R. C. II & Meier, S. T. (2015). Psychotherapeutic theories of change and measurement: An integrative model. *Journal of Unified Psychotherapy and Clinical Science, 3*(1), 80–119.

Hopwood, C. J., & Bornstein, R. F. (2014). *Multimethod clinical assessment*. Guilford.

Horowitz, L. M. (2004). *Interpersonal foundations of psychopathology*. American Psychological Association. https://doi.org/10.1037/10727-000

Horowitz, L. M., Alden, L. E., Wiggins, J. S., & Pincus, A. L. (2000). *Inventory of interpersonal problems manual*. The Psychological Corporation.

Horowitz, M. (2005). *Understanding psychotherapy change: A guide to configural analysis*. Washington, D.C.: American Psychological Association.

Horowitz, L. M., Strupp, H. H., Lambert, M. J., & Elkin, I. (1997). *Measuring patient changes in mood, anxiety, and personality disorders: Toward a core battery*. American Psychological Association.

Horvath, A. O., & Greenberg, L. S. (1989). Development and validation of the working Alliance inventory. *Journal of Counseling Psychology, 36*(2), 223–233. https://doi.org/10.1037/0022-0167.36.2.223

Howard, K. I., Kopta, S. M., Krause, M. S., & Orlinsky, D. E. (1986). The dose-effect relationship in psychotherapy. *American Psychologist, 41*, 159–164. https://doi.org/10.1037/0003-066X.41.2.159

Howard, K. I., Lueger, R. J., Maling, M. S., & Martinovich, Z. (1993). A phase model of psychotherapy: Causal mediation of outcome. *Journal of Consulting and Clinical Psychology, 61*, 678–685. https://doi.org/10.1037/0022-006X.61.4.678

Howard, K. I., Moras, K., Brill, P. L., Martinovich, Z., & Lutz, W. (1996). The evaluation of psychotherapy: Efficacy, effectiveness, and patient progress. *American Psychologist, 51*, 1059–1064. https://doi.org/10.1037/0003-066X.51.10.1059

Jensen, E. W., James, S. A., Boyce, W. T., & Hartnett, S. A. (1983). The family routines inventory: Development and validation. *Social Science and Medicine, 17*(4), 201–211. https://doi.org/10.1016/0277-9536(83)90117-X

Jinkerson, J. D., Masilla, A., & Hawkins, R. C., II. (2014). Narrow and wide band relationships between the MBTI psychological type and DSM diagnoses. *Journal of Psychological Type, 74*(3), 29–48.

Jinkerson, J. D., Masilla, A., & Hawkins, R. C., II. (2015). Can Myers-Briggs dimensions predict therapy outcome? Differences in the thinking-feeling function pair in cognitive therapy for depression/anxiety. *Research in Psychotherapy: Psychopathology, Process and Outcome, 18*(1), 21–31. https://doi.org/10.4081/ripppo.2015.167

Johnson, M. D. (2012). Healthy marriage initiatives: On the need for empiricism in policy implementation. *American Psychologist, 67*, 296–308. https://doi.org/10.1037/a0027743

Kelsey, M. (1973). *Healing and Christianity*. Harper & Row.

Kiesler, D. J. (1996). *Contemporary interpersonal theory and research: Personality, psychopathology, and psychotherapy*. Wiley.

Klein, M. H., Mathieu-Coughlin, P., & Kiesler, D. J. (1986). The experiencing scales. In L. S. Greenberg & W. S. Pinsof (Eds.), *The psychotherapeutic process: A research handbook*. Guilford Press.

Kraus, D. R., Seligman, D. A., & Jordan, J. R. (2005). Validation of a behavioral healthcare outcome and assessment tool designed for naturalistic settings: The treatment outcome package. *Journal of Clinical Psychology, 61*(3), 285–314. https://doi.org/10.1002/jclp.20084

Lambert, M. J. (2007). What we have learned from a decade of research aimed at improving psychotherapy outcome in routine care. *Psychotherapy Research, 17*, 1–14. https://doi.org/10.1080/10503300601032506

Lambert, M. J., Burlingame, G. M., Umphress, V., Hansen, N. B., Yancher, S. C., Vermeersch, D., & Clouse, G. C. (1996). The reliability and validity of a new psychotherapy outcome questionnaire. *Clinical Psychology and Psychotherapy, 3*(4), 249–258. https://doi.org/10.1002/(SICI)1099-0879(199612)3:4<249::AID-CPP106>3.0.CO;2-S

Lambert, M. J., Hansen, N. B., & Finch, A. E. (2001). Patient-focused research: Using patient outcome data to enhance treatment effects. *Journal of Consulting and Clinical Psychology, 69*, 159–172. https://doi.org/10.1037/0022-006X.69.2.159

Leary, T. (1957). *Interpersonal diagnosis of personality: A functional theory and methodology for personality evaluation*. Wiley.

LoVerde, R., Sarracino, D., & Vigorelli, M. (2012). Therapeutic cycles and referential activity in the analysis of the therapeutic process. *Research in Psychotherapy: Psychopathology, Process and Outcome, 15*(1), 22–31. https://doi.org/10.4081/ripppo.2012.99

Luborsky, L., & Crits-Christoph, P. (1997). *Understanding transference: The core conflictual relationship theme method*. American Psychological Association. https://doi.org/10.1037/10250-000

Lueger, R. J., Howard, K. I., Martinovich, Z., Lutz, W., Anderson, E. E., & Grissom, G. (2001). Assessing treatment progress of individual patients using expected treatment response models. *Journal of Consulting and Clinical Psychology, 69*, 150–158. https://doi.org/10.1037/0022-006X.69.2.150

Magnavita, J. J., & Anchin, J. C. (2013). *Unifying psychotherapy: Principles, methods, and evidence from clinical science*. Springer.

Maling, M., Gertman, M., & Howard, K. (1995). The response of interpersonal problems to varying doses of psychotherapy. *Psychotherapy Research, 5*(1), 63–75. https://doi.org/10.1080/10503309512331331146

Mayer, J. D. (2004). How does psychotherapy influence personality? A theoretical integration. *Journal of Clinical Psychology, 60*, 1291–1315. https://doi.org/10.1002/jclp.20076

Mayer, J. D. (2005). A tale of two visions: Can a new view of personality help integrate psychology? *American Psychologist, 60*, 294–307. https://doi.org/10.1037/0003-066X.60.4.294

McAdams, D. P., & Pals, J. L. (2006). A new big five: Fundamental principles for an integrative science of personality. *American Psychologist, 61*, 204–217. https://doi.org/10.1037/0003-066X.61.3.204

McCarthy, K. Y., Mergenthaler, E., Schneider, S., & Grenyer, B. (2011). Psychodynamic change in psychotherapy: Cycles of patient–therapist linguistic interactions and interventions. *Psychotherapy Research, 21*(6), 722–732. https://doi.org/10.1080/10503307.2011.615070. Epub 2011 Sep 29. PMID: 21955173.

McCrae, R. R., & Costa, P. T. (1987). Validation of the five-factor model of personality across instruments and observers. *Journal of Personality and Social Psychology, 52*, 81–90. https://doi.org/10.1037/0022-3514.52.1.81

McCrae, R. R., & Costa, P. T. (2010). *NEO inventories. Professional manual*. PAR.

McEwen, B. S., & Stellar, E. (1993). Stress and the individual: Mechanisms leading to disease. *Archives of Internal Medicine, 153*(18), 2093–2101. https://doi.org/10.1001/archinte.1993.00410180039004

McKay, D. (Ed.). (2008). *Handbook of research methods in abnormal and clinical psychology*. Sage.

Mehl, P. E., & Conner, T. S. (2011). *Handbook of research methods for studying daily life*. Guilford.

Meier, S. T. (2012a). Nomothetic outcome assessment in counseling and psychotherapy: Development and preliminary psychometric analyses of the depression/anxiety negative affect scale. *Psychological Test and Assessment Modeling, 54*, 343–362. https://doi.org/10.1037/t25540-000

Meier, S. T. (2012b). *Language and narratives in counseling and psychotherapy*. Springer.
Meier, S. T., & Davis, S. (2011). *The elements of counseling* (7th ed.). Brooks/Cole.
Melchert, T. P. (2013). Beyond theoretical orientations: The emergence of a unified scientific framework in professional psychology. *Professional Psychology: Research and Practice, 44*, 11–19. https://doi.org/10.1037/a0028311
Mergenthaler, E. (1996). Emotion-abstraction patterns in verbatim protocols: A new way of describing psychotherapeutic processes. *Journal of Consulting and Clinical Psychology, 64*, 1306–1315. https://doi.org/10.1037/0022-006X.64.6.1306
Miller, S. D., Duncan, B. L., Brown, J., Sparks, J. A., & Claud, D. A. (2003). The outcome rating scale: A preliminary study of the reliability, validity, and feasibility of a brief visual analog measure. *Journal of Brief Therapy, 2*(2), 91–100.
Minuchin, S. (1974). *Families and family therapy*. Harvard University Press. https://doi.org/10.4159/9780674041127
Moos, R., & Moos, B. (1994). *Family environment scale manual: Development, applications, research* (3rd ed.). Consulting Psychologist Press.
Moos, R. H. (1994). *Work environment scale manual*. Consulting Psychologists Press.
Moss, D. (2005). Psychophysiological psychotherapy: The use of biofeedback, biological monitoring, and stress management principles in psychotherapy. *Psychophysiology Today, 2*(1), 13–18.
Myers, I. B. (1980). *Gifts differing*. Consulting Psychologists Press.
Myers, I. B., McCaulley, M. H., Quenk, N. I., & Hammer, A. L. (1998). *MBTI manual: A guide to the development and use of the Myers-Briggs type indicator* (3rd ed.). Consulting Psychologists Press.
Nezu, A. (2000). *Practitioner's guide to empirically based measures of depression*. Kluwer.
Norberg, M. M., Wetterneck, C. T., Sass, D. A., & Kanter, J. W. (2011). Development and psychometric evaluation of the Milwaukee psychotherapy expectations questionnaire. *Journal of Clinical Psychology, 67*, 474–490. https://doi.org/10.1002/jclp.20781
Olff, M., deVries, G., Guzelcan, Y., Assies, J., & Gersons, B. (2007). Changes in cortisol and DHEA plasma levels after psychotherapy for PTSD. Psychoneuroendocrinology, 32, 619–626. doi:https://doi.org/10.1016/j.psyneuen.2007.04.001.
Olson, D. (2011). FACES IV and the circumplex model: Validation study. *Journal of Marital and Family Therapy, 3*(1), 64–80. https://doi.org/10.1111/j.1752-0606.2009.00175.x
Pascual-Leone, A. (2009). Dynamic emotional processing in experiential therapy: Two steps forward, one step back. *Journal of Consulting and Clinical Psychology, 77*(1), 113–126. https://doi.org/10.1037/a0014488
Pascual-Leone, A., & Greenberg, L. S. (2007). Emotional processing in experiential therapy. Why the "only way out is through". *Journal of Consulting and Clinical Psychology, 75*, 875–887. https://doi.org/10.1037/0022-006X.75.6.875
Pennebaker, J. W., Mehl, M. R., & Niederhoffer, K. G. (2003). Psychological aspects of natural language use: Our words, our selves. *Annual Review of Psychology, 54*, 547–577. https://doi.org/10.1146/annurev.psych.54.101601.145041
Pepper, S. C. (1942). *World hypotheses*. University of California Press.
Roefs, A., Fried, E.I., Kindt, M, … & Jansen, A. (2022). A new science of mental disorders: Using personalised, transdiagnostic, dynamical systems to understand, model, and treat psychopathology. *Behaviour Research and Therapy, 153*, 104096.
Rogers, C. (1962). *On becoming a person*. Houghton Mifflin.
Rokeach, M. (1973). *The nature of human values*. Free Press.
Safran, J. D., & Messer, S. B. (1997). Psychotherapy integration: A postmodern critique. *Clinical Psychology: Science and Practice, 4*, 140–152. https://doi.org/10.1111/j.1468-2850.1997.tb00106.x
Salter, D. W. (2000). *SETA manual: A users' guide to the Salter environmental type assessment*. Consulting Psychologists Press.
Samoilov, A., & Goldfried, M. R. (2000). Role of emotion in cognitive-behavior therapy. *Clinical Psychology: Science and Practice, 7*, 373–385. https://doi.org/10.1093/clipsy.7.4.373

Schneider-Corey, M., & Corey, G. (2005). *Groups: Process and practice* (7th ed.). Brooks/Cole.
Shedler, J. (2010). The efficacy of psychodynamic psychotherapy. *American Psychologist, 65*, 98–109. https://doi.org/10.1037/a0018378
Shedler, J., & Westen, D. (2007). The Shedler-Westen assessment procedure (SWAP): Making personality diagnosis clinically meaningful. *Journal of Personality Assessment, 89*, 41–55. https://doi.org/10.1080/00223890701357092
Silver, E., Williams, A., Worthington, F., & Phillips, N. (1998). Family therapy and soiling: An audit of externalizing and other approaches. *Journal of Family Therapy, 20*, 413–422. https://doi.org/10.1111/1467-6427.00096
Smyth, J. M. (1998). Written emotional expression: Effect sizes, outcome types, and moderating variables. *Journal of Consulting and Clinical Psychology, 66*, 174–184. https://doi.org/10.1037/0022-006X.66.1.174
Steel, H., Steel, M., & Murphy, A. (2009). Use of the adult attachment interview to measure process and change in psychotherapy. *Psychotherapy Research, 19*(6), 633–643. https://doi.org/10.1080/10503300802609698
Stern, D. (2004). *The present moment in psychotherapy and everyday life*. Norton.
Sullivan, H. S. (1953). *The interpersonal theory of psychiatry*. Norton.
Szasz, T. S. (1974). *The myth of mental illness: Foundations of a theory of personal conduct*. Harper & Row.
Tausczik, Y. R., & Pennebaker, J. W. (2010). The psychological meaning of words: LIWC and computerized text analysis methods. *Journal of Language and Social Psychology, 29*(1), 24–54. https://doi.org/10.1177/0261927X09351676
Vromans, L. P., & Schweitzer, R. D. (2010). Narrative therapy for adults with a major depressive disorder: Improved symptom and interpersonal outcomes. *Psychotherapy Research, 21*, 4–15. https://doi.org/10.1080/10503301003591792
Wachtel, P. L. (1977). *Psychoanalysis and behavior therapy: Toward an integration*. Basic Books.
Wachtel, P. L. (1997). *Psychoanalysis, behavior therapy, and the relational world*. American Psychological Association. https://doi.org/10.1037/10383-000
Wachtel, P. L. (2014). An integrative relational point of view. *Psychotherapy, 51*(3), 342–349. https://doi.org/10.1037/a0037219
Wampold, B. (2001). *The great psychotherapy debate: Models, methods, and findings*. Lawrence Erlbaum Associates.
Wampold, B. E., & Budge, S. L. (2012). The 2011 Leona Tyler award address: The relationship—And its relationship to the common and specific factors of psychotherapy. *The Counseling Psychologist, 40*(4), 601–623. https://doi.org/10.1177/0011000011432709
Wampold, B. E., & Imel, Z. E. (2015). *The great psychotherapy debate* (2nd ed.). Routledge. https://doi.org/10.4324/9780203582015
Weber, M., Davis, K., & McPhie, L. (2006). Narrative therapy, eating disorders and groups: Enhancing outcomes in rural NSW. *Australian Social Work, 59*, 391–405. https://doi.org/10.1080/03124070600985970
Westen, D. (1991). Clinical assessment of object relations using the TAT. *Journal of Personality Assessment, 56*(1), 56–74. https://doi.org/10.1207/s15327752jpa5601_6
Westen, D., Gabbard, G. O., & Blagov, P. (2006). Back to the future: Personality structure as a context for psychopathology. In R. F. Krueger & J. L. Tackett (Eds.), *Personality and psychopathology*. Guilford.
Westen, D., Schedler, J., Bradley, B., & DeFife, J. A. (2012). An empirically derived taxonomy for personality diagnosis: Bridging science and practice in conceptualizing personality. *American Journal of Psychiatry, 169*, 273–284. https://doi.org/10.1176/appi.ajp.2011.11020274
Wheat, A. L., & Larkin, K. T. (2010). Biofeedback of heart rate variability and related physiology: A critical review. *Applied Psychophysiology and Biofeedback, 35*, 229–242. https://doi.org/10.1007/s10484-010-9133-y
Widiger, T. A., & Costa, P. T. (Eds.). (2013). *Personality disorders and the five-factor model* (3rd ed.). American Psychological Association. https://doi.org/10.1037/13939-000

Wiggins, J. S. (1995). *Interpersonal adjective scales professional manual*. Psychological Assessment Resources.

Wiggins, J. S. (1996). An informal history of the interpersonal circumplex tradition. *Journal of Personality Assessment, 66*, 217–233. https://doi.org/10.1207/s15327752jpa6602_2

Wilson, K. G., & DeFrene, T. (2009). *Mindfulness for two: An acceptance and commitment approach to mindfulness in psychotherapy*. New Harbinger.

Yalom, I., & Leszcz, M. (2005). *The theory and practice of group psychotherapy* (5th ed.). Basic Books.

Yoshikawa, H., Aber, J. L., & Beardslee, W. R. (2012). The effects of poverty on the mental, emotional, and behavioral health of children and youth. *American Psychologist, 67*, 272–284. https://doi.org/10.1037/a0028015

Young, J. E., Klosko, J. S., & Weishaar, M. (2003). *Schema therapy: A practitioner's guide*. Guilford. https://doi.org/10.1007/s11630-003-0064-2

Youngstrom, E. A., Halverson, T. F., Youngstrom, J. K., Lindhiem, O., & Findling, R. L. (2017). Evidence-based assessment as an integrative model for applying psychological science to guide the voyage of treatment. *Clinical Psychology: Science and Practice, 24*(4), 331–363. https://doi.org/10.1111/cpsp.12207

Zilcha-Mano, S., Dinger, U., McCarthy, K. S., & Barber, J. P. (2014). Does alliance predict symptoms throughout treatment, or is it the other way around? *Journal of Consulting and Clinical Psychology, 82*(6), 931–935. https://doi.org/10.1037/a0035141

Chapter 4
A Systems-Contextual Integrative Heuristic Model, Part 2—The Dynamics of the Healing Cycle and the Trauma Cycle

As we described in Chap. 3, Andras Angyal's (1965) holistic theory of personality described a healthy system principle that involves an increased striving for autonomy and homonomy (basically individual development and social interest, respectively)[1] that is inherently dynamic and facilitative of positive life experiences and positive emotion (see also Lester, 1995). Mergenthaler's (1996) therapeutic cycle is the engine for human change processes at the micro level of our model, and we contend that this dynamic, which we call the Healing Cycle (HC), operationalizes the healthy system principle. The healthy system principle as a construct bears similarity to psychoanalytic (specifically Jungian) notions of the positive imago (Hendrix, 1988, 2008) and is distinguished from the unhealthy (neurotic) system principle that Angyal (1965) also postulated and that has been described as the negative imago (an aspect of the Trauma Cycle, TC, in our model). Angyal's (1965) theory of universal ambiguity may be more clearly described and visualized as an ambiguous gestalt, like the popular "faces and/or vases" image. For example, a scene eliciting a perception of independence may be perceived negatively as aloneness or positively as individual mastery. Angyal believed that it was inevitable that every individual will experience some trauma, and that these traumatic experiences will lead to dual encoding of particular psychological–interpersonal qualities (e.g.,

[1] Angyal's (1965) autonomy–homonomy distinction bears resemblance to Bakan's (1966) agency–communion terminology. Formally, it may also be considered an elaboration of Lewin's field theory distinction between the "life space" (person within subjectively perceived environment) and "psychological ecology" (objective environment apart from the life space but in a "boundary zone" to it) (Lewin, 1943, in Cartwright, 1951, pp. 56–59). Epstein's (2014) cognitive-experiential theory (CET) is another dual-process theory, i.e., distinguishing "intuitive-experiential and rational-analytic styles" (Table 8.1, p. 176). However, CET also implicitly postulates a dual continuum of positive and negative attributes of these two styles (Table 8.1, p. 176). Hawkins II and Brown (2014) have described other examples of dual process, dual continua models (i.e., models having socially desirable vs. socially undesirable forms of the dual process traits or styles) (e.g., Hogg & Frank, 1992; Spence et al., 1979).

R. Hawkins, S. Meier, *Healing Outcomes*,
https://doi.org/10.1007/978-3-032-33611-8_4

dependency as clinging, as well as the more positive connotation of being interdependent), such that these qualities are no longer associated just with attachment security.[2] For example, about 60% of men and 50% of women report at least one traumatic event during their lifetime (Kessler et al., 1996). Mahoney (1991, 2003) likewise described oscillation cycles of expansion (opening up, hope, and joy) and contraction (avoidance, worry, and disengagement) that may correspond respectively to the operation of the healthy system principle and the unhealthy system principle.[3]

In our systems-contextual integrative model (SCIM, Fig. 3.1 in Chap. 3), the repetition of the Healing Cycle (HC) within the gestalt of the healthy system principle would foster restoration of secure attachment with decreases in toxic shame and increases in awareness, faith, hope, love, gratitude, virtues, self-efficacy, and self-coherence, while the unhealthy system principle (with its experiential avoidance, decreased awareness and coherence, and increased shame, anxiety, resentment, despair, and dissociation) would be less frequently activated, milder, and more transitory. However, if the unhealthy system predominates, the effects would be seen in the consequences of what we call the Trauma Cycle (TC), which not only disrupts the HC but also activates feeling-toned complexes, negative affect dynamics, and interpersonal enactments of Luborsky's Core Conflictual Relationship Themes (CCRT) (Luborsky & Barrett, 2006; Luborsky & Crits-Christoph, 1997) and Kiesler's (1996) Maladaptive Transaction Cycle that can crystallize and

[2] Angyal's (1965) neurotic (unhealthy) system principle, which we associate with what we call the Trauma Cycle, may nonetheless be linked with insecure attachment that can be strongly maintained by both negative reinforcement (anxiety reduction) and positive reinforcement (identification). Borrowing from Fairburn's object relations theory, Benjamin (2003, p. 331) referred to these internalized representations as "good-bad objects." Merkur (2007) has elaborated upon objections relations theory in describing a root of psychoanalytic psychotherapy in Christian mystical meditation and contemplation of the passion, death, and resurrection of Christ. He distinguishes the transition from self-focus and splitting to interpersonal relational thinking (pp. 83–91), which bears some resemblance to the Trauma Cycle–Healing Cycle dynamic.

[3] Persons are complex adaptive systems (Singer, 2009) interrelated through structural coupling (Magai & Haviland-Jones, 2002), and psychotherapy is a complex nonlinear change process (Schiepak, 2009). The alternation of the gestalt from the healthy system principle to the unhealthy system principle occurs as a sudden qualitative state change, called a phase shift in dynamical systems theory. These phase shifts occur among point attractors or repellors (representing specific negative feeling-toned complexes), periodic limit cycles (as in a cusp catastrophe model), and/or even chaotic attractors when fragmentation and proliferation of complexes occur for dissociative states. The Hayes et al. (2001) relational frame theory may also be applied to the sudden shifts in the dual process in the SCIM in that the healthy system principle frame ("healing cycle") and the neurotic system principle frame ("trauma cycle") conceptually describe the functional contexts within which salutogenic and pathogenic behaviors, thoughts, values, and relationships are ordered (Hawkins II, 2016). Hopes, beliefs, symptom decreases, and commitments to values can occur and be maintained through single-session "walk-in" counseling contexts (Slive & Bobele, 2011) and through controversial "energy psychology" (Feinstein, 2012). We argue that rapid shifts from the unhealthy system principle (trauma cycle) to the healthy system principle (healing cycle) may mediate or at least mirror these changes.

perpetuate as personality disorders.[4] As shown in Table 3.1, important Micro-level measurement tools include Luborsky's CCRT procedure, Mergenthaler's (1996) task analysis computer program (TAS/C), Leary's Interpersonal Checklist (Leary, 1957), Benjamin's (2006) Structural Analysis of Social Behavior (SASB), Young's Schema Questionnaire (Young et al., 2003), the Shedler-Westen Assessment Protocol (SWAP-200; Shedler & Westen, 2007), and the Inventory of Interpersonal Problems (IIP; Horowitz et al., 2000).

The mechanism through which the oscillations of the HC and TC take place needs further study. Are these dual processes independent or are they a bipolar dimension? In theology and depth psychology, there is the belief that "good and evil" are co-present in differing proportions in human souls and motives. Scott Kelso and colleagues (Kelso & Engstrom, 2006; Kelso, 2009, 2013) have theorized that dynamical phase shifts (e.g., between the HC and the TC) indicate the complementary nature of these processes, and they described coordination dynamics as integrating contraries into metastable coordinated states. Apter's (2001, 2007) reversal theory likewise hypothesizes binary pairs of opposing metamotivational states or modes that can shift ("reverse") suddenly as determined by the person's meaning (which Apter called "structural phenomenology"). These modes generate positive or negative emotions resulting from these reversals. Our SCIM is a type of reversal theory wherein the shift to the unhealthy TC becomes too frequent and even locked in unless counteracted by repetitions of the HC. Hayes' (2004) Acceptance and Commitment therapy (ACT) increases psychological flexibility and coherence by shifting the functional context and relational frame for a particular behavior and emotion (i.e., from an unhealthy system trauma frame to a healthy system healing frame) (Hawkins, 2016) with increased psychological flexibility being significantly negatively correlated with attachment anxiety, primitive defenses, and identity diffusion (Salande & Hawkins, 2017).

One key aspect of the dynamic systems perspective in our systems-contextual integrative model is that the oscillation from the TC to the HC can be observed in rather rapid shifts from moment to moment within a session as well as across sessions. For example, person-specific rapid symptom changes within major depression episodes have been reported by Nemesure et al. (2024). Abraham et al. (1990) have speculated that oscillations of mood and self-image may be modeled as a bifurcation from a focal point to a chaotic attractor with normal mood and depression as attractor regions, due to increasing grief-related dependency as a rate of change intensifier. Cui et al. (2025) have provided simulations for sudden clinical

[4] The trauma cycle may be on the milder end of a continuum described in the Theory of Structural Dissociation of the Personality (Van der Hart et al., 2006), according to which Dissociative Disorders involve a chronic trauma-induced splitting of the Emotional Parts (EP) of the personality from the Apparently Normal Parts (ANP). EP may be analogous biopsychosocially to the trauma cycle, while ANP may bear similarity to the healing cycle (although with limited cognitive-affective experiencing). Functional MRI studies (e.g., Schumpf et al., 2013) have found evidence that EP and ANP can be distinguished in patients with Dissociative Identity Disorders, but not in matched healthy actors feigning dissociative experiences.

changes. One type of change they describe, bifurcation-induced tipping (R-tipping), is particularly applicable to the biphasic shifts in our SCIM. Hayes and Andrews (2020) have developed a network destabilization and transition model (NDT) that describes a two-attractor scheme for sudden switching from a pathological to a healthier attractor that may apply to the TC to HC shift. Haken and Tschacher (2017) provide computer simulations of how to weaken a maladaptive attractor and develop and strengthen an alternative attractor. Similarly, Zilcha-Mano (2025) has developed "bottom-up" data driven individual-specific animated profiles (which he calls "animaps") to characterize the dynamic multidimensional mental health patterns of individual clients pre-treatment, and he claims that this method will complement "top down" theories of psychotherapeutic process and outcomes: "A dynamic multidimensional understanding of mental health may require transforming our understanding of therapeutic change from a delta (change) in symptoms to a shift from one multidimensional dynamic to a new, more adaptive one" (Zilcha-Mano, 2025, p. 796). Our SCIM with its shifts from the TC to the HC is a dynamic multidimensional theory that is a good candidate for integration with the data driven computer models of Haken and Tschacher (2017) and Zilcha-Mano (2025).

The multimethod clinical assessment of the Healing Cycle, as indicated earlier, would include not only domain-specific measures of functioning but also more general changes in clients' self-perceptions, called generalized self-efficacy by Bandura (1977, 1989), improved social relationships and overall sense of meaning, and purposefulness in life. This purposefulness would entail the restoration of hope (Frank, 1961; Frank & Frank, 1991). Also included in the multimethod clinical assessment would be performance-based measures, such as software-based analysis of language and emotion words (e.g., LIWC, TAS/C). How language, emotions, and behaviors change can be determined by behavioral tasks that CBT recommends, where an individual is able to demonstrate functional capability in situations of threat (e.g., progressive exposures to phobic situations such as heights or closed spaces, or to body sensations of anxiety as in panic disorder). Other performance-based measures could include projective tasks that would reveal the kinds of thinking or symbolizing that would be congruent with healthy optimal functioning (e.g., the Rorschach-Performance Appraisal System and the Thematic Apperception Test).

Originally, the alternation of the Healing Cycle (HC) and Trauma Cycle (TC) within the SCIM was proposed as a heuristic framework to list the various instruments and methods that could be used to measure aspects of each of these dual processes (Hawkins & Meier, 2015). However, after more study and reflection, not only the HC but also the TC involves temporal system dynamics. While the HC has an explicitly interpersonal aspect, namely therapist and client or mother and child, the TC specifies merely that adverse traumatic events have been experienced over the course of one's lifetime, and that these may derive from negative rituals such as abuse, shaming, etc. Of more significance in the current formulation is that while the HC appears to be a positive spiral process (i.e., starting from a point and then gradually expanding and increasing with growth, cf., Garland et al., 2010), the TC appears to be the reverse, a negative spiral. Due to the adverse experiences of the individual the spiral contracts, going from larger interpersonal gyrations to focusing more on the isolated individual, as the individual experiences more fragmentation, shaming, negative affect, and avoidance. Thus, in contrast to the HC, the TC involves a withdrawal into the self in a survival mode that may become fixed and rigid if not counteracted by healing interactions (i.e., the HC). Bar-Kalifa et al. (2024) have pointed out in their overview of recent research on affect dynamics that more studies now are addressing the importance of positive emotions in mental health change rather than restricting focus to negative emotions (e.g., Seligman, 1999, 2011).[5] They suggest that "unlike negative emotions that tend to narrow an individual's thoughts and actions, positive emotions expand these repertoires" (2024, p. 446).

In normal development, the shifting from the HC to the TC may be adaptive, as temporary shifts to the Trauma Cycle may allow some individual consolidation and protection in the face of interpersonal events that may exceed the coping capacity of the child or the adult client. However, if the TC has become locked in, it is metaphorically a "hell", and the only way to provoke a shift to the healing cycle may be through an external perturbation, i.e., a caring interpersonal relationship.

As shown in Fig. 3.1, the Healing Cycle is evoked repeatedly both within psychotherapy sessions and in the clients' relationships outside of therapy to strengthen overall psychotherapy outcomes, which are multiply measured at the three levels of change: micro (intra-individual), meso (interpersonal relational), and macro (societal, cultural) in terms of functionality. As the HC is repeatedly evoked and stabilized, the flexibility of clients to engage in the world and to limit and extricate themselves from the TC occurs more easily and more quickly, with good psychotherapy outcomes (de Felice et al., 2022). These therapeutic changes would be as predicted by the stages of psychotherapy and the dose response theory of psychotherapeutic effectiveness (Howard et al., 1986; Howard et al., 1993; Lueger et al., 2001), including remoralization, decreased symptom distress, improved interpersonal relations, improved social role performance, and systems-structural changes in cognitive-personality organization, individuation, and subsequently increased flourishing and epistemological and values changes generally described by humanistic-existential personality theorists and by the positive psychology school (e.g., Seligman, 2002; Seligman et al., 2006).

It is important also to consider that there will likely be underlying neurocognitive and psychophysiological processes involved that would be another level of intra-individual change and healing. One theory that is particularly of interest is the opponent process theory of Solomon and Corbit (1974). Opponent process theory hypothesizes that neurocognitively and emotionally a stimulus that would be

[5] An older and simplified formulation of the balance of positive and negative emotions in personality is the positivity ratio (i.e., P/ P + N, where P is the number of positive emotions and N is the number of negative emotions; Schwartz & Grice, 2022). "Flourishing" persons have higher positivity ratios while "languishing" persons have lower positivity ratios (e.g., Fredrickson, 2013; Fredrickson & Losada, 2005), although these findings have been disputed on mathematical grounds (Brown et al., 2014) but then supported (Schwartz & Grice, 2022). The SCIM goes beyond positivity ratios, as the HC and the TC are complex dynamic systems wherein change occurs across micro, meso, and macro contextual levels.

experienced as unpleasant or painful would activate an opposing process that would restore homeostasis (Cabanac, 2009). Cabanac coined the term "alliesthesia," which means changed perception, to describe this shift in the opponent processes. Thus, for example, an individual who is physiologically cold stressed and experiencing a lowered core temperature would, according to alliesthesia, seek out warm stimuli to restore homeostasis by raising core body temperature to normal (e.g., Cabanac, 1969; Hawkins, 1975). In terms of emotional and social functioning, to counteract certain urges (such as the urge to overeat) and to correct certain kinds of anxiety and other aversive affective states, alliesthesia may be facilitated by subcortical brain systems in conjunction with the bilateral functioning of the left and right cerebral brain hemispheres. The left hemisphere would be associated more with linguistic rational processing and the right hemisphere more with non-verbal emotional processing (Hawkins & Brown, 2014).

Transtheoretical aspects. The importance of the SCIM is that it is heuristically both integrative and transtheoretical. This model can describe broadly the core processes in the major theories of personality and psychotherapy, and it may also suggest specific links to underlying physiological and neurological mechanisms.[6] Following Angyal's (1965) holistic model of personality, particularly the ambiguous gestalt and alternation of the healthy system principle and the unhealthy system principle, we can accommodate the core dynamic in classical psychoanalytic drive theory, i.e., the ego's mediating the demands of the id, the superego, and external reality, and the HC's mediating emotional processing and cognitive abstraction phases to help individuals to assimilate previously unconscious threatening experi-

[6] Our systems-contextual integrative model, although being a theory that is quite molar rather than molecular, may potentially be linked to physiological / neurological events and theoretical models, in at least two respects. First, the operation of the healing cycle and its phases of emotional experiencing alternating with (and being joined by) cognitive abstraction may involve in a broad sense the synchronous balanced operation of the right hemisphere and left hemisphere of the brain and their distinctive kinds of information processing (i.e., right hemisphere emotional experiencing and pattern recognition, and left hemisphere verbal-linguistic processing) (see Schore, 2013, 2014, for an overview of the implications for psychotherapy of brain lateralization and integration); alternatively, the prefrontal lobes, particularly the ventrolateral unit, orbital unit, medial / ACC unit, and the dorsolateral unit (Soper et al., 2017) need to work in synchrony as in a concert, but these processes may become desynchronized and dysfunctional from trauma. The WAIS-IV, WIAT-III, and WMS-IV may be used to examine differential neurocognitive abilities that may underlie personality and interpersonal behavior (Krauskopf, 1998) with implications for neurocognitive-behavioral remediation and improved functioning (Stiffey Jr. & Hawkins II, 2011). Second, the interaction between the healing cycle and the trauma cycle may be translatable into opponent process mechanisms (Solomon, 1980) in terms of right-hemisphere–left-hemisphere–neural circuits (Comer et al., 2015) and subcortical neural connections that underlie core emotional processes (e.g., Panksepp et al., 2014). For example, Carver et al. (2008) have proposed a two-factor serotonergic model for depression and impulsive aggression that postulates one mode mediating approach seeking / impulsive behavior and a second mode for inhibitory control and higher order reflection / planning. Emotion regulation would be facilitated by repeated practice of the fluid and well-synchronized operation of the interpersonal healing cycle and its correlates at the autonomic nervous system level and in terms of brain circuits hypothesized by Carver et al. (2008) and by Comer et al. (2015) to tune the brain–mind–person–environment interplay.

ences or impulses related to trauma into an integrated cognitive-affective experience that can be shared consciously with others (i.e., insight). This cognitive-affective processing is open to further elaboration rather than remaining a shame-based contraction or repression-based system.[7]

The SCIM can also incorporate contemporary relational psychoanalytic theory in that the HC in particular and the healthy system principle in general, along with the macro, meso, and micro levels of analysis, are explicitly interpersonal, relational processes involving intersubjectivity and transference-countertransference phenomena (e.g., Andersen & Chen, 2002; Andersen & Przybylinski, 2012).[8] Jungian analytic psychotherapy can be included as well, in that the unfolding of the healthy system principle and integration of the unhealthy system principle-based Core Conflictual Relationship Themes, negative effects, and personality fragments (feeling-toned complexes) related to trauma are given conscious meaning within an interpersonal field and thus integrated in an individuation process involving the appreciation of differences in Psychological Type dynamics (discussed later in this chapter, as well as in Chap. 6). Humanistic-existential theories of personality and psychotherapy are embraced within our model because the operation of the healthy system principle is inherently purposive. It is oriented toward growth, individuation, and, in contemporary positive psychology terms, human flourishing, with a full engagement in meaningful life experiences that Mahoney (1991, p. 410) called "teleonomic" (i.e., direction without a final goal).

In terms of cognitive-behavioral theories, the systems-contextual integrative model, and particularly the Healing Cycle, have embedded emotional experiencing that involves inherently reinforcing interactions with the therapist (and with significant others) that are marked by eventual decreases in negative affect and increases

[7] Defense mechanisms may be regarded as cognitive avoidance maneuvers (Epstein, 2014) at varying levels of adaptiveness and maturity which may be differentially related to particular personality disorders (Perry et al., 2009) or styles (McWilliams, 2011, 2014).

[8] Transference-countertransference phenomena may be addressed in our model at the micro contextual level in terms of interpersonal affective dynamics that can be illustrated via Control Mastery Theory (CMT) (e.g., Silberschatz, 2005). CMT may be viewed as an organized set of plans for therapist-client transactions to reinstate the healing cycle and thereby restore healthy intrapsychic and interpersonal functioning. CMT pathogenic beliefs are shorthand notations of trauma cycle affect dynamics, scenes, and scripts, just as secure attachment, empathy, and trust are applicable to the healing cycle. CMT "pro-plan" exchanges facilitate the healing cycle while "anti-plan" exchanges maintain the trauma cycle. A CMT "passive-to-active" test may invoke a countertransference reaction wherein the therapist is in the uncomfortable position of experiencing what the client experienced when traumatized, a mutual activation of the trauma cycle within both the therapist and the client. The test is passed when the therapist, becoming aware of the countertransference, empathically enacts the healing cycle to activate a reciprocal healing response in the client. Benjamin's (2003) Interpersonal Reconstructive Therapy likewise distinguishes therapeutic empathy that enhances the "Green Growth Collaborator" ("pro-plan" and analogous to the healing cycle but more specifically attuned to correcting pathogenic beliefs stemming from "Important Persons and their Internalized Relations" which Benjamin calls the "Red Regressive Loyalist") from good intentioned but misguided empathy that would be "anti-plan" and thus might strengthen the "Red Regressive Loyalist" or trauma cycle in terms of our model.

in positive affect. These cycles of negative affect and cognitive distortions connected with contemporaneous and past trauma-based relationship experiences are given meaning (i.e., cognitively restructured) with the result that symptom distress is decreased (i.e., decreased anxiety and depression as measured by CBT self-report questionnaires). Experiential awareness and cognitive defusion, as postulated by ACT (Hayes et al., 1999), as well as self-efficacy expectations (Bandura, 1977, 2006), are increased.[9] In addition, the contextual macro, meso, and micro levels, moderate the HC to allow the specification of antecedent factors both external to the person in the social and physical environment (e.g., adverse experiences or rituals and routines) as well as the cognitive self-statements (automatic negative thoughts, tacit core beliefs) within the person. The target symptom behaviors, thoughts, and physiological reactions that have been maintained through negative reinforcement consequences (e.g., anxiety reduction) may be modified by repetitions of the Healing Cycle that are enacted within the relationship between the client and the CBT practitioner. These new maintaining factors (interpersonal positive feedback loops) would also include positive alterations in cognitive schema, attributions, and expectations in a manner consistent with triadic reciprocal causation (i.e., reciprocal interactions between person, behavior, and environment) in Bandura's social cognitive theory (Bandura, 1977, 1989). The result is that the client will come to construe experiences in a way which reinforces increased self-efficacy and personal agency.

Finally, we believe the SCIM will encourage novel integrative psychotherapies, such as Willi's (1999; Willi et al., 2000) ecological psychotherapy "niche" model, a hybrid combination of a CBT initial focus on symptom reduction within the context of the client's current relationships and developmental transitions, and a subsequent psychodynamic exploration that provides insight into past traumas and deepens emotional and experiential awareness.

Person-level and event-level measurement. In contrast to variable-based multivariate approaches, this systems-contextual integrative model also specifies observations that can be distinctively and discretely predicted at either the person level or the event level using Observation Oriented Modeling (Grice, 2011; Grice et al., 2012). At the event level and at the person level, in our SCIM, we emphasize patient-focused research (Howard et al., 1996), patient profiling (Kraus et al., 2005; Lambert et al., 2001), and also intensive study of moments of change (e.g., Stern's, 2004, present moments) using observer ratings of Mergenthaler's (1996) therapeutic cycle, emotional experiencing (Klein et al., 1986), and the SWAP-200. Linguistically, if the psychotherapy dialogue is transcribed and analyzed with computer text analyzers such as those developed by Mergenthaler (1996); de Felice et al., 2019, 2020), Pennebaker and colleagues' (e.g., Tausczik & Pennebaker, 2010) Linguistic Inquiry Word Count (LIWC), and Meier's (2012, 2024) Depression/Anxiety Negative Affect (DANA) scale, additional methodological innovations can be

[9] In terms of Bowen's family systems theory (e.g., Gilbert, 1992) cognitive defusion and generalized self-efficacy expectations would correspond to differentiation of self. A testable prediction from our model is that self-differentiation would be a function of repetitions of the healing cycle and decreased frequency of activation of the trauma cycle [i.e., S-D = f (HC − TC)].

further specified for the Healing Cycle and indeed for the entire micro and meso levels of interpersonal psychotherapeutic processes.

Our SCIM's focus on the person level is combined with an emphasis on psychological strengths. We further specify the micro contextual level by describing the unfolding of the ego along a continuum from health to psychopathology, but particularly emphasizing health: the Psychological Type theory (PTT) of Carl Jung (Jung, 1971), and its most popular measurement tool, the Myers-Briggs Type Indicator (MBTI) (Myers, 1980; Myers et al., 1998). Although the MBTI specifically and PTT in general have been criticized, consistency of behaviors of particular individuals within particular situations has been demonstrated, making the construction of psychological types from the "bottom-up" specification of stable individual differences (such as the MBTI 16 Types) in certain situations feasible in principle (Cervone, 2004; Mischel, 2004; Mischel & Shoda, 1995). Within PTT, type dynamics and type development are important integrative concepts. Individuation at midlife and beyond, for example, involves the integration of less conscious, less familiar psychological functions, called the tertiary and inferior functions,[10] into the person's conscious orientation. The biasing and the mutual accommodation within the therapeutic relationship between individuals of different psychological types gives rise to a set of predictable misunderstandings and subsequent understandings that can enhance the experiencing of one's sense of self as having a distinctive personality style, but also that one's psychological type is relative and flexible, as one comes to understand and even to appreciate differences between one's own psychological type and the psychological types of other people (Myers, 1980).[11] Thus type mismatches can give rise to misunderstandings that can activate the trauma cycle, complex affect dynamics, and cyclical conflictual relationship patterns (including the "negative imago"). However, addressing the projections and distortions arising from type differences can be areas for deeper emotional processing via the healing cycle within the therapeutic relationship, promoting mutual understanding, insight, and individuation.

[10] For more information on type dynamics and type development and counseling applications of the MBTI please see Myers (1980), McCaulley (2000), Quenk (2002, 2009), and Jinkerson et al. (2014, 2015). Reynierse's (2012, 2013) data have challenged the validity of type dynamics, instead emphasizing the primacy of individual preferences as complementary opposites (i.e., extraversion or introversion, sensing or intuition, thinking or feeling, judging or perception) and demonstrating preference multidimensionality regarding mapping psychological type to specific situational contexts. Good type development is analogous to good character development (Francis, 2005). MBTI theory may be applied across levels of analysis and contexts in an integrative framework (see Appendix). Kelly and Kelly et al. (2010) have described "personality as a complex system made up of the same kinds of stuff throughout...Each level is characterized by its own form of psychophysical organization and has both interior and exterior aspects that allow it to participate in some form of experienced world appropriate to itself. The activities of these different strata are somehow interconnected and coordinated in a greater or lesser degree" (p. 637).

[11] Psychological type or the FFM trait dimensions have been used to map person-environment fit or misfit in different workplace environments or occupations (e.g., Denissen et al., 2018; Myers et al., 1998; Salter, 2000). See Appendix for a case illustration.

Another methodological innovation involves the measurement of emotional experiencing itself. Emotions and affects are primary motivations and brain mechanisms that are elaborated in humans as scenes and scripts (e.g., Kaufman, 1989; Tomkins, 1978, 2008a, 2008b). These emotions, affects, and scripts can be tracked using several different methods: concurrent subjective phenomenological assessment measures, such as the traditional Thematic Apperception Test (TAT) (Bram, 2014; Westen, 1991); objective psychophysiological measurements (Cacioppo et al., 1991; Hofmann, 1999; Moss, 2005) including hormone levels (Mehta & Josephs, 2011) and fMRI biomarkers (Doehrmann et al., 2012) during psychotherapy, and contemporary cognitive science tools such as the Implicit Attitudes Test (Greenwald et al., 1998; Greenwald & Banaji, 1995; Stieger et al., 2010) that can be used to test reactions to emotional stimuli (such as facial expressions). Heart rate variability (HRV) can be used to map changes in affective arousal and coherence in the autonomic nervous system sympathetic and parasympathetic branches (e.g., HeartMath software, http://www.heartmath.org). An unusual, but potentially rich method is to measure the different emotional expression signatures, called sentic cycles (Clynes, 1977). These emotional signatures, which are partly innate and are evident in EEG patterns that are distinctively different for different emotional states, can be measured with a pressure transducer pad where one is invited to express through one's key pad touch a specified sequence of emotions (each emotion repeatedly named and cued via audio instruction), called a sentic cycle (i.e., anger, fear, hate, grief, sex, love, joy, reverence), such that over time one develops wave form patterns that are distinctive for each emotion expressed and are accompanied by heightened experience of these emotions (i.e., a kind of "emotional biofeedback" that may enhance emotional processing). These sentic forms and associated affects can also be measured over the course of psychotherapy and while the client has various forms of aesthetic experiences (including viewing art or nature or listening to music). Bucci's (1997, 2011) multiple code theory, which integrates psychoanalytic psychotherapy with cognitive science, describes the process by which dissociated emotional schema related to trauma can be elicited, reorganized, and integrated within the therapist-client relationship via a referential process that is like Mergenthaler's (1996) therapeutic cycle (Mergenthaler & Bucci, 1999).

Relatedly, a key therapeutic domain emphasized by many theoretical orientations is avoidance (i.e., of affect, behaviors, and cognitions), along with defensiveness, and resistance. Meier (2012, 2024)) described the development of the Depression / Anxiety Negative Affect Scale (DANA), a brief, clinician-rated method for assessing negative affect for the purposes of progress monitoring and outcome assessment (PMOA). Initial psychometric studies have shown the DANA to be sensitive to detecting change in psychotherapy, particularly when clinicians' estimates of clients' emotional avoidance are included. That is, clients whose therapists rated them as experiencing negative affect during the therapeutic process evidenced effect sizes (ESs) greater than 1, indicating decreases on test scores assessing negative affective intensity across sessions. For clients rated as avoiding negative affect, however, ESs remained stable or decreased over time, indicating no improvement or worsening. Emotional avoidance (as conceptualized and measured by the DANA) and related theoretical constructs (such as experiential avoidance, Hayes et al., 1999) are key pieces of clinical data relevant to therapeutic progress, but they have typically not been integrated into the assessment of therapeutic progress and outcomes.

Summary of the Systems-Contextual Integrative Model and its Measurement Implications

The overall thrust of this chapter is to describe the SCIM dynamic (shown in Fig. 3.1) as a heuristic, conceptual framework to organize examples of specific measures that can be used in a thorough multimethod assessment of the overall process of change toward healing outcomes. These multiple measures are each specifically theoretically linked with a process or level in the SCIM. Table 3.1 elaborates these measures and their linkage to the specific levels in the SCIM.

The operation of the healthy system principle/healing cycle is enhanced and facilitated by its being nested within supportive human relationships where the individual can make meaning of previously meaningless and threatening events (Mahoney, 2003). The individual will also experience oscillation cycles[12] of more frequent and increased expansion and growth (healthy system principle and the Healing Cycle) and less frequent and less prolonged contraction and experiential avoidance (unhealthy system principle and the Trauma Cycle), allowing for individual differences according to Psychological Type, culture, and values. This growth process is also fostered by rituals and routines at the meso level of family, work, and school, as well as at the macro level in terms of social and cultural beliefs, values, and world views.[13]

These three nested levels and the basic ambiguous gestalt (i.e., alternation of control by the healthy system principle and by the unhealthy system principle) have certain philosophical parallels in the world wisdom traditions, and yet we believe that they are more usefully applied to the creation of integrative measurements to tap the change processes. In this model, we talk about a braiding that emphasizes the interweaving of the different strands of system principles, levels, and their corresponding measurement tools specified in our system-contextual integrative model. An example of interweaving or braiding would be practice-research network based comparisons of conventional treatment outcome measures, such as the OQ 45.2 and the Treatment Outcome Package (TOPS; Kraus et al., 2005) for detecting changes in client-reported symptom distress, interpersonal relations, and social role functioning, with more novel alternatives that do not rely upon self-report. Such

[12] Tension between the opposing healthy system principle (healing cycle) and the neurotic system principle (trauma cycle) may give rise to creative will (Rank, 1932, 1936, as cited by Ekenstierma, 2025). However, shifting too long to the trauma cycle would be ego destructive.

[13] Our model should apply to prediction of psychotherapy outcomes for children and adolescents, with the specification of appropriate measures of developmental psychopathology core processes.

alternative approaches might include computer text analysis of emotional activation and cognitive abstraction in therapeutic dialogue narratives (Meier, 2012, 2024; Mergenthaler, 1996; Pascual-Leone, 2009), concurrent psychophysiological monitoring in the client and therapist (Villmann et al., 2008), and revisions of the Rorschach (Rorschach Prognostic Rating Scale, Meyer, 2000; RPAS, Meyer et al., 2011) and the Holtzman Inkblot Technique Revised Brief Forms (Hawkins et al., 2019), which have the potential to measure changes in client's perceptual responses over the course of psychotherapy to tap emergent mature cognitive-affective, interpersonal, and creative processes.[14]

It is important that our heuristic model allows and values client individual differences in choosing healing outcomes, in the form of personality differences and cultural diversity. We also honor therapist and client preferences for theoretical orientation, and for tracing process and progress along different strands at different rates with different end points. This integrated braided framework presupposes that the interconnected whole is bigger than the sum of the parts. Experiential training and processing are part of an expansion or growth oscillation (as in the therapeutic cycle of Mergenthaler, 1996) that generally will allow everyone to unfold according to their nature and yet function within an open system wherein change is facilitated. Collaboration between therapist and client in the assessment and treatment phases of psychotherapy will likely facilitate this attunement. Finn and colleagues, for example, have developed Therapeutic Assessment (TA) (Finn, 2007; Finn et al., 2012; Kopetzki et al., 2025) as a transtheoretical way of reframing psychological testing so that the clients' questions about their presenting problems are addressed in the feedback discussion of the test findings, along with evocation of emotional schemas (e.g., Core Conflictual Relationship Themes) as part of the process. In a sense, TA facilitates deeper emotional processing (Pascual-Leone & Greenberg, 2007) by activating the healthy system principle and thus facilitating subsequent successful therapeutic outcomes.[15][16]

[14] Projective and neurocognitive performance-based assessment of personality and personality changes resulting from psychological interventions may provide an integrative, transtheoretical bridge for measuring outcomes that would be less biased than self-report measures. Multimethod assessment provides construct validity for clinical inferences (Hopwood & Bornstein, 2014). Within our model, a key is to view these performances as enactments, whether these are test-based (e.g., R-PAS) or interpersonal behaviors (e.g., transference, behavioral rehearsal / situational role play exposures).

[15] The MMPI clinical and content scales have not been found to be an important predictor of psychotherapy outcome in a training clinic where standardized measures were used (Harte et al., 2008; Hawkins II et al., 2005), but we have found it helpful to include the MMPI in our standard psychological test battery in conjunction with the MBTI for its value in the collaborative therapeutic assessment dialogue (Finn et al., 2012).

[16] Therapeutic Assessment's immediate therapeutic impact may be because it conveys a felt sense that the collaborative learning can be trusted, i.e., epistemic trust within a context of secure attachment in the therapeutic relationship (Fonagy & Alison, 2014). TA's collaborative trust-building dialogue may help diminish both overly rigid negative moods and overly variable and reactive negative moods through helping clients to make their evaluations of persons and life events more nuanced and flexible.

In this chapter, and in the preceding chapter, we have suggested that two separate traditions in psychology, theories of personality and psychotherapy on the one hand, and measurement in psychological assessment and in treatment process/outcome evaluation on the other, that can be folded together within one unified model for the mutual advantage of each tradition. The advantages of this integration would be (a) to provide a heuristic conceptual framework that would organize the use of currently available measures and encourage the development of new theoretically derived measures, and (b) to offer an assortment of process and outcome measures for clinicians and trainees to use in practice-research networks and evidence-based practices to demonstrate that the therapeutic process described conceptually in our Healing Cycle facilitates positive treatment outcomes. Furthermore, as accountability becomes more important with the implementation of healthcare reform in the United States, unified models such as the systems-contextual integrative model may also help to advance policy and dissemination research related to counseling, psychotherapy, and behavioral healthcare (e.g., Chor et al., 2014).

Appendix: A Case Study to Illustrate the Systems-Contextual Integrated Model (SCIM) and Its Heuristic Use for Measurement in Psychological Assessment and Intervention

Brief Overview: As its name implies, this model integrates both a theory of personality (adapted from Angyal, 1965) and a theory of psychotherapy that embeds individual human change processes in interpersonal and larger social ecological contexts (adapted from Brofenbrenner, 1979). The levels of these contexts (i.e., micro, meso, and macro) should be viewed not as linear statistical mediators or moderators, but instead as fused, permeable coupled systems (as in Ford & Lerner's 1992 model), i.e. person:environment rather than person-environment, or as relational fields (in dyads and larger groups) and imaginal fields (within the individual) as postulated by Hawkins (1993). This model's operation can best be conveyed as the interplay of individual dispositional traits / psychological types and characteristic adaptations to perturbations from social ecological contexts at the micro, meso, and macro levels (as shown in Fig. 3.1 and operationalized with suggested measures in Table 3.1) as these are manifested in the unfolding of each person's unique life narrative (as postulated by McAdams & Pals, 2006). However, the framework for the measurement of the SCIM in terms of the measures is Bandura's (1989) social cognitive theory, more specifically his reciprocal triadic theory.

The "engine" of the SCIM is the unfolding action of a healthy systems principle (with both autonomy and homonomy as aspects) that incorporates a "HC" (Healing Context) involving dyadic transactions with primary attachment persons (e.g., parents, psychotherapist) that increase the child's, or client's, positive emotional expression and cognitive self-awareness. This healthy systems principle may be inborn, but it is sustained by these primary attachment bonds. The primary dyadic nurturance (micro level) is itself maintained by the social surround and positive routines and special rituals of the family, clan, neighborhood, work, or school settings (meso level), and by the "zeitgeist" worldviews and cultural values as these are manifested in political, economic, and religious ideologies (macro level). However, inevitably disappointments and varying degrees of trauma in the form of neglect, enmeshment, abuse, and/or abandonment occur, including the mismatching of the child's (or client's) needs with the vagaries of the supplies of key resources at the micro, meso, and/ macro contextual levels. The neurotic systems principle is the abstract term for the negative process and maladaptive transactions that we call the "TC" (Trauma Cycle) with its reciprocal strengthening of negative affects (particularly fear, shame, and helplessness / hopelessness) which, although adaptive to the survival of the child / client in the short run, cause fragmentation, loss of coherence and interpersonal attunement, behavioral and cognitive avoidance, and decreased self-efficacy attributions over time. The task for the parental figure / psychotherapist is to assist the child / client in recovering attachment security by re-activating the "HC," such that the child's / client's positive affects, motivations, and prosocial behaviors are restored, with attendant increases in coherence, self-efficacy expectations, and positive interpersonal transactions. As Willi described in his ecological model of psychotherapy (Willi, 1999; Willi et al., 2000), the child / client is thereby assisted in reconstructing the "niche" that will better fit his or her personality (healthy type development—individuation) and valued actions in the world (as described in Acceptance and Commitment Therapy).

Case Illustration: The model is best articulated at the level of the child's / client's unique life narrative, which can be viewed, at any given point of time, as a kind of "snapshot" of the dynamical systems interplay of the balance between the TC and the HC within the nested levels of the interpersonal and ecological contexts. Accordingly, we shall present a clinical case study comprising an amalgamation of actual clients' stories and contexts. Consistent with our emphasis upon the operationalization of key theoretical personality / psychotherapy contexts, in this case vignette, we shall also provide the measures from which the clinical inferences about antecedent and maintaining factors are derived.

Fred is a 55-year-old Caucasian divorced male high school English teacher who is requesting individual psychotherapy at the recommendation of his ex-spouse, with presenting problems of sadness (dysthymia, with onset in adolescence), loss of enjoyment, initial insomnia, guilt and shame, low self-esteem, and obsessive concerns about perceived social inadequacies (resulting in cognitive and behavioral avoidance of social encounters outside of work), worries about losing his job and "growing old alone," coupled with irritability / annoyance at the increasing demands of his curriculum planning due to the requirements of standardized testing related to the federal regulations (he states that at his most recent job evaluation he was told that he was "underperforming," a distinct contrast from his job ratings up to the past 2 years). Fred notes that until "No Child Left Behind" and the "failing" performance of his high school in the past 2 years with the resultant pressure on teachers to "teach test taking" he thoroughly enjoyed working with small groups of students or with individual tutorials on mutually enjoyable English novels and poetry. In terms of family of origin and psychosocial context, Fred grew up in New England. Both his parents were of European-American ethnicity. Fred's father died about 5 years ago, just before the time his wife divorced him. His mother is currently residing in an assisted living setting because of mild cognitive impairment. Fred has a younger sister, who is a civil engineer, as was his late father. Fred has one daughter, age 25, reportedly happily married and employed as a high school mathematics teacher. Fred's wife, who is a Texan and second generation Mexican-American, has remarried, but still communicates her concern about Fred's depression and social anxiety disorder. The following are the measures that tap the SCIM model systems and levels:

Individual symptom measures: BDI-II = 24 (moderate); BAI = 20 (moderate); Leighbowitz Social Anxiety Scale Total = 65 (clinically elevated); Automatic Thoughts Questionnaire (Negative) = 75 (clinically elevated); Penn State Worry Questionnaire = 62 (elevated near the clinical range of GAD). The Treatment Outcome Package (TOP) at baseline showed elevations on negative life stressors, medical concerns about prostatitis (but otherwise good health—Fred jogs regularly and is normal weight), and clinical-scale elevations on depression and work problems. Fred does not drink alcohol nor smoke cigarettes, but he admits that he is "somewhat compulsive" about his running. He has a past history of cannabis use, and confesses that he would "smoke weed" currently if he were not a school teacher, because the cannabis is "relaxing socially and mind expanding". Based on the DSM-IV SCID-I and SCID II, Fred's Axis I diagnosis was Dysthymic Disorder (300.4), r/o Major Depression Recurrent, Mild, in Partial Remission (296.35); Social Phobia, Specific Type (fear of interaction with strangers, especially women, at parties) (300.23); r/o Generalized Anxiety Disorder (300.02); on Axis II (r/o Personality Disorder, NOS, with avoidant and obsessive-compulsive traits) (309.9); on Axis III, Prostatitis, by client's self-report (note that Fred has taken Prozac, 40 mg/day for 2 years, and occasional Xanax,.25 mg for anxiety, as needed, both prescribed by his primary care physician); on Axis IV, Occupational Stress, Limited Social Support; and on Axis V: Current and Past GAF = 60.

Micro-level individual intellectual and personality measures: WAIS-IV full scale IQ (FSIQ) in the superior range, but a significant discrepancy between a very superior verbal comprehension index (VCI) and a high average perceptual reasoning index (PRI) of 25 scale score units, with notable strengths in Vocabulary, Information, and Similarities subtests, and weaknesses in Block Design, Visual Puzzles, and Matrix Reasoning; he had a valid MMPI-2 with a defined code type of 2–7-8, with a marginally elevated scale 4; MBTI "best fit" type is INFJ (Introverted Intuition with Feeling); TAT themes (via Westen's SCORES method) revealed high interpersonal valuing, but conflict around achievement and issues with anger. Fred's story to Card 1 (depicting a boy looking at an object that looks like a violin) was illustrative: "This boy likes the beauty of the violin music, but is embarrassed by public recitals and pressure from his parents to 'be the 1st violin' (i.e., the best student). He will likely quit playing the violin publicly but will still play it by himself." Finally, on the Holtzman Inkblot Technique Revised Brief Forms, Fred's responses showed a high percentage of Human Movement, good Form Appropriateness and creativity, but a high percentage of Fear and Morbid content.

Micro-level affective dynamics and governing scenes: Fear and Shame affects predominate, with blocked Anger affect likely. Governing scene: A young boy who is curious and sensitive encounters pressure to perform perfectly at a level above his peers both in school and in sports; Identity scripts: Avoid social pressure, develop introvert interests in reading, poetry, and self reflection.

Meso-level interpersonal measures: On the Inventory of Interpersonal Problems (IIP), Fred scored high on Scale 4 (Socially Inhibited) and Scale 7 (Self-Sacrificing). Fred reports that his wife told him that her MBTI type is ENFJ (she is a school counselor), and that he believes that his mother's MBTI type is ENTP and his late father's type was ISTJ; he is less sure of his sister's type, but suspects she is an ESTJ. He believes that his daughter's psychological type is INTP, and his female therapist, a relational psychoanalyst, whom he has seen for 5 years, told him her MBTI type is INFP. Fred was asked to take the Salter Environmental Type Assessment with respect to his high school setting, which he described as "ESTJ", which is the same as the MBTI type of the school principal that he disliked. Fred did note, however, that his main support at work comes from two other English teachers who he thinks are also "NFs". Fred noted that his "ideal environment" to work in would be a library where he could pursue his literary interests in mythology and depth psychology, and perhaps share this knowledge with a few "bright and motivated" students who shared his interests. On the ECR, and through the psychosocial history obtained in the clinical interview, Fred's likely attachment style is "anxious, pre-occupied" although he notes that he has learned to avoid attachments for fear of being hurt. This interpersonal avoidance reportedly leaves him feeling anxious and very lonely. Notable history includes Fred's report that his father self-medicated with alcohol, and that his maternal grandfather was a "chronic alcoholic" who physically abused his mother when she was a girl. As a boy, Fred described feeling that he disappointed his father by not trying out for the school football team. He stated that ever since he was teased in gym class by more athletic boys, he has eschewed team sports and does not even watch them. He did report faithfully attending his daughter's soccer games, however, in which she excelled. He noted that his sister was also an award winning swimmer in college. Fred reported that he had loved his wife who initially was so "warm and supportive" of him, but that later he came to resent and try to avoid her anger at his passivity. Yet Fred noted that he was "devastated' when she announced that she was divorcing him and dating another man. Finally, with respect to his feelings about his psychoanalyst, Fred describes her very positively, although he notes that recently he has been disappointed and a bit annoyed that she has not been praising his efforts as much as he perceived that she once did earlier in the psychotherapy.

Macro-level measures: From the clinical diagnostic interview, Fred described himself as a "progressive Democrat," and a Catholic who no longer attends Mass due to his disagreement with the Catholic Church's stance on abortion and masturbation. Economically he described himself as not being one of the "one percent". He noted that his father and mother were both Republicans and "did not like FDR" (whom Fred idealizes). His world view is contextualist, and he notes that he is "depressed" about the presidential candidates, both of whom he regards as "controlled by Wall Street Bankers". On the Valued Actions Questionnaire, he described social life and recreation as less important, and work, education, exercise, spirituality / purpose in life, and citizenship as more important.

In this model, the effects of the contextual relational fields (mismatches with both his parents' psychological types, the "bureaucratic" work setting, his social avoidance and social support limited to just his fellow English teachers and his psychotherapist), his political and religious disenchantment, and his alienation, all fail to ameliorate the developmental "TC" (with dysthymia, social anxiety, and personal / social alienation) and do not promote the "HC."

Treatment Plan: Based on this diagnostic assessment and psychological testing the following treatment recommendations were developed and collaboratively discussed in the therapeutic assessment feedback session (Finn, 2007):

1. Continue with relational psychoanalysis with his current psychotherapist with whom Fred has a strong therapeutic alliance (explore and encourage Fred's recent expression of anger in the therapeutic relationship, decrease shame, and increase self-compassion);
2. With the support of his therapist, encourage Fred to pursue concurrent short-term CBT for social phobia (manualized group or individual treatment) with graded situational exposures (e.g., to social encounters with strangers, including women) and cognitive restructuring of negative anxiety related and depressogenic thoughts;
3. Psychiatric consultation to evaluate the effectiveness of his current psychotropic medications, especially to consider his initial insomnia and current levels of depression and anxiety;
4. Recommend to Fred that he seek spiritual direction with regard to his conflicts with his Catholic faith, with the goal of his eventually returning to regular religious practice;
5. After the CBT for social phobia and depression, consider encouraging Fred to join a men's group to further increase self-efficacy expectations, positive social comparisons, and masculine self-identity (a Robert Bly type mythopoetic themed group would be ideal, in that it would resonate with Fred's introverted intuitive type preference);
6. Assist Fred in developing his ecological "niche" (Willi, 1999) by inviting him to explore alternative private school teaching positions more congruent with his preference for more intensive small group and one-on-one tutoring; an interim plan would be for Fred to "moonlight" by tutoring disadvantaged children in reading, poetry, and theater;
7. Help Fred strengthen his tertiary and inferior functions (introverted thinking and extraverted sensation) by supplementing jogging with weight training in a gym setting, and gradual participation in organized competitive sports (e.g., soccer, bowling, racquetball) where Fred could practice strategizing and visual-motor

coordination skills, as well as connecting with his daughter's interest in soccer, and meeting women (in coed soccer and bowling leagues);

8. Refer for further evaluation for cognitive remediation training for possible non-verbal learning disorder, and encourage Fred on his own to practice daily on the Lumosity "brain games" website (www.lumosity.com);
9. To increase Fred's range of emotional expression (particularly with anger and grief), encourage him to read Manfred Clynes' (1977) book on "Sentics" and practice "sentic cycles" on a daily basis.

Outcome Measures: The TOP clinical symptom scales would be the primary general outcome measure (administered every 2 sessions), along with the following CBT domain-specific self-report measures: BDI-II, BAI, LSAS, and PSWQ (also every 2 sessions). Improved interpersonal functioning would be assessed with the IIP and cognitive-affective-perceptual changes with the HIT Revised Brief Forms (each re-administered every eight sessions).

Additional Hypotheses for Research: In this case study, the client has experienced numerous mismatches between his individual temperament and the available social environmental resources (Chess & Thomas, 1999), and these mismatches have begun early in life. The duration of this client's therapy is therefore likely to be long term, although if Fred can create a favorable "niche" his personal resources may enable him to show more rapid progress. The therapeutic hypotheses that can be tested from the SCIM are the following: (1) the length of the therapy will depend upon the number of mismatches between the individual and his / her context (presuming a base level of need and security satisfaction, economically and in terms of health); (2) the impact of this mismatching will be greater at the lower contextual levels of the system (i.e., micro-level primary dyadic mismatches are weighted heavier than meso-level mismatches and meso-level mismatches are weighted heavier than macro-level mismatches).

References

Abraham, F. D., Abraham, R. H., & Shaw, C. D. (1990). *A visual introduction to dynamical systems theory for psychology*. Aerial Press.

Andersen, S. M., & Chen, S. (2002). The relational self: An interpersonal-cognitive theory. *Psychological Review, 109*(4), 619–645. https://doi.org/10.1037/0033-295X.109.4.619

Andersen, S. M., & Przybylinski, E. (2012). Experiments on transference in interpersonal relations: Implications for treatment. *Psychotherapy, 49*(3), 370–383.

Angyal, A. (1965). *Neurosis & treatment: A holistic theory*. Wiley.

Apter, M. J. (Ed.). (2001). *Motivational styles in everyday life. A guide to reversal theory*. American Psychological Association. https://doi.org/10.1037/10427-000

Apter, M. J. (2007). *Reversal theory: The dynamics of motivation, emotion and personality* (2nd ed.). Oneworld.

Bakan, D. (1966). *The duality of human existence: Isolation and communion in modern man*. Rand McNally.

Bandura, A. (1977). Self-efficacy: Toward a unifying theory of behavioral change. *Psychological Review, 84*, 191–215. https://doi.org/10.1037/0033-295X.84.2.191

Bandura, A. (1989). Human agency in social cognitive theory. *American Psychologist, 44*, 1175–1184. https://doi.org/10.1037/0003-066X.44.9.1175
Bandura, A. (2006). Guide for constructing self-eficacy scales. In F. Pajares & T.D. Urdan (Eds.) *Self-efficacy beliefs of adolescents*. Greenwich, CT: IAP.
Bar-Kalifa, E., Bringmann, L. F., & Zilcha-Mano, S. (2024). The role of affect dynamics as mechanisms of change in mental health interventions: Integrating applied and basic science. *Journal of Consulting and Clinical Psychology, 92*(8), 445–453. https://doi.org/10.1037/ccp0000905
Benjamin, L. S. (2003). *Interpersonal reconstructive therapy: An integrative personality-based treatment for complex cases*. Guilford.
Benjamin, L. S. (2006). The use of structural analysis of social behavior (SASB) as an assessment tool. *Annual Review of Psychology, 2*, 83–109. https://doi.org/10.1146/annurev.clinpsy.2.022305.095337
Bram, A. D. (2014). Object relations, interpersonal functioning, and health in a non-clinical sample: Construct validation and norms for the TAT SCORS-G. *Psychoanalytic Psychology, 31*(3), 314–342. https://doi.org/10.1037/a0036286
Brown, N. J. L., Sokal, A. D., & Friedman, H. L. (2014). Positive psychology and romantic scientism. *American Psychologist, 69*(6), 636–637. https://doi.org/10.1037/a0037390
Brofenbrenner, U. (1979). *The ecology of human development: Experiments by nature and design*. Cambridge, MA: Harvard Press. https://doi.org/10.4159/9780674028845.
Bucci, W. (1997). *Psychoanalysis and cognitive science: A multiple code theory*. Guilford.
Bucci, W. (2011). The role of subjectivity and intersubjectivity in the reconstructionof dissociated emotional schemas: Converging perspectives from psychoanalysis, cognitive science, and affective neuroscience. *Psychoanalytic Psychology, 28*, 247–266. https://doi.org/10.1037/a0023170
Cabanac, M. (1969). Pleasantness or unpleasantness of a thermal sensation and homeothermia. *Physiology & Behavior, 4*(3), 359–364. https://doi.org/10.1016/0031-9384(69)90189-9
Cabanac, M. (2009). *The fifth influence or the dialectics of pleasure*. iUniverse. https://doi.org/10.1093/oso/9780195331028.003.0009
Cacioppo, J. T., Berntson, C. G., & Andersen, B. L. (1991). Psychophysiological approaches to the evaluation of psychotherapeutic process and outcome: Contributions from social psychophysiology. *Psychological Assessment, 3*, 321–336. https://doi.org/10.1037/1040-3590.3.3.321
Carver, C. S., Johnson, S. L., & Joorman, J. (2008). Serotonergic function, two-mode models of self-regulation, and vulnerability to depression: What depression has in common with impulsive aggression. *Psychological Bulletin, 134*, 912–943. https://doi.org/10.1037/a0013740
Cervone, D. (2004). The architecture of personality. *Psychological Review, 111*, 183–204. https://doi.org/10.1037/0033-295X.111.1.183
Chess, S., & Thomas, A. (1999). *Goodness of fit: Clinical applications from infancy through adult life*. Brunner / Mazel.
Chor, K. H. B., Olin, S. S., & Hoagwood, K. E. (2014). Training and education in clinical psychology in the context of the patient protection and affordable care act. *Clinical Psychology: Science and Practice, 21*(2), 91–105. https://doi.org/10.1111/cpsp.12068
Clynes, M. (1977). *Sentics: The touch of emotions*. Anchor Press / Doubleday.
Comer, C. S., Harrison, P. K., & Harrison, D. W. (2015). The dynamic opponent relativity model: An integration and extension of capacity theory and existing theoretical perspectives on the neuropsychology of arousal and emotion. *SpringerPlus, 4*, 345. https://doi.org/10.1186/s40064-015-1120-6
Cui, J., Hasselman, F., Olthof, M., & Lichtwarck-Aschoff, A. (2025). Understanding types of transitions in clinical change: An introduction from the complex dynamic systems perspective. *Journal of Psychopathology and Clinical Science, 134*(4), 469–482. https://doi.org/10.1037/abn0000991
de Felice, G., Giuliani, A., Gelo, O., Mergenthaler, E., De Smet, M., Meganck, R., Paoloni, G., Andreassi, S., Schiepek, G., Scozzari, A., & Orsucci, F. (2020). What differentiates poor and

good outcome psychotherapy? A statistical-mechanics-inspired approach to psychotherapy research, part two: Network analyses. *Frontiers in Psychology, 11*, 788.

de Felice, G., Giuliani, A., Pincus, D., et al. (2022). Stability and flexibility in psychotherapy process predict outcome. *Acta Psychologica, 227*, 103323. https://doi.org/10.1016/j.actpsy.2022.103604

de Felice, G., Orsucci, F., Scozzari, A., Gelo, O., Serafini, G., Andreassi, S., Vegni, N., Paoloni, G., Lagetto, G., Mergenthaler, E., & Giuliani, A. (2019). The misleading dodo bird verdict. How much of the outcome variance is explained by common and specific factors? *New Ideas in Psychology, 54*, 50–55.

Denissen, J. J. A., Bleidorn, W., Hennecke, M., Luhmann, M., Orth, U., Specht, J., & Zimmermann, J. (2018). Uncovering the power of personality to shape income. *Psychological Science, 29*(1), 3–13. https://doi.org/10.1177/0956797617724435

Doehrmann, O., et al. (2012). Predicting treatment response in social anxiety disorder from functional magnetic resonance imaging. *Archives of General Psychiatry*, Online First, E1–E11. https://doi.org/10.1001/2013.jamapsychiatry.5

Epstein, S. (2014). *Cognitive-experiential theory: An integrative theory of personality*. Oxford. https://doi.org/10.1093/acprof:osobl/9780199927555.001.0001

Feinstein, D. (2012). Acupoint stimulation in treating psychological disorders: Evidence of efficacy. *Review of General Psychology, 16*(4), 1–17. https://doi.org/10.1037/a0028602

Finn, S. E. (2007). *In our client's shoes: Theory and techniques of therapeutic assessment*. Taylor & Francis.

Finn, S. E., Fischer, C. T., & Handler, L. (2012). *Collaborative / therapeutic assessment: A casebook and guide*. Wiley.

Ford, D. L., & Lerner, R. M. (1992). *Developmental systems theory: An integrative approach*. Newbury Park, CA: Sage.

Fonagy, P., & Alison, E. (2014). The role of mentalization and epistemic trust in the therapeutic relationship. *Psychotherapy, 51*(3), 372–380. https://doi.org/10.1037/a0036505

Frank, J. D. (1961). *Persuasion and healing*. The Johns Hopkins Press.

Frank, J. D., & Frank, J. B. (1991). *Persuasion and healing: A comparative study of psychotherapy*. The Johns Hopkins University Press.

Francis, L.J. (2005). *Faith and psychology: Personality, religion, and the individual*. London: Darton, Longman, & Todd.

Fredrickson, B. L. (2013). Updated thinking on positivity ratios. *American Psychologist, 68*(9), 814–822. https://doi.org/10.1037/a0033584

Fredrickson, B. L., & Losada, M. F. (2005). Positive affect and the complex dynamics of human flourishing. *American Psychologist, 60*(7), 678–686. https://doi.org/10.1037/0003-066X.60.7.678

Garland, E. L., Fredrickson, B., Kring, A. M., Johnson, D. P., Meyer, P. S., & Penn, D. L. (2010). Upward spirals of positive emotions counter downward spirals of negativity: Insights from the broaden-and-build theory and affective neuroscience on the treatment of emotion dysfunctions and deficits in psychopathology. *Clinical Psychology Review, 30*(7), 849–864. https://doi.org/10.1016/j.cpr.2010.03.002

Gilbert, R. M. (1992). *Extraordinary relationships: A new way of thinking about human interactions*. Wiley.

Greenwald, A. G., & Banaji, M. R. (1995). Implicit social cognition: Attitudes, self-esteem, and stereotypes. *Psychological Review, 102*, 4–27. https://doi.org/10.1037/0033-295X.102.1.4

Greenwald, A. G., McGhee, D. E., & Schwartz, J. K. L. (1998). Measuring individual differences in implicit cognition: The implicit association test. *Journal of Personality and Social Psychology, 74*, 1464–1480. https://doi.org/10.1037/0022-3514.74.6.1464

Grice, J. W. (2011). *Observation-oriented modeling: Analysis of cause in behavioral sciences*. Elsevier.

Grice, J. W., Barrett, P. T., Schlimgen, L. A., & Abramson, C. I. (2012). Toward a brighter future for psychology as an observation oriented science. *Behavioral Science, 2*, 1–22. https://doi.org/10.3390/bs2010001

Haken, H., & Tschacher, W. (2017). How to modify psychopathological states? Hypotheses based on complex systems theory. *Nonlinear Dynamics in Psychology, and Life Sciences, 21*(1), 19–34.

Harte, C., Lopez, M., & Hawkins, R. C., II. (2008, November). *Predictive validity of the MMPI-2: Clinical scale disturbance as an indicator of cognitive behavioral therapy treatment outcome.* Presented at the Association for Behavioral and Cognitive Therapy convention.

Hawkins, R. C., II. (1975). Human temperature regulation and the perception of thermal comfort. Unpublished Ph.D. dissertation, University of Pennsylvania. Available from *Dissertation Abstracts, Proquest*.

Hawkins, R. C., II. (2016). Biofeedback and the illusion of control: A functional contextual perspective. *Biofeedback, 44*(4), 225–228. https://doi.org/10.5298/1081-5937-44.4.05

Hawkins, R. C., II, & Brown, D. (2014, November). *Nonverbal learning disorder as a neurocognitive endophenotype for anxiety in adults: Implications for CBT assessment and intervention.* Poster presented at the annual convention of the Association for Behavioral and Cognitive Therapy.

Hawkins, R. C., II, Chapman, K. S., & Nieuviarts, N. (2019, March). *Development and preliminary construct validation of the Holtzman Inkblot Technique-Brief Revised Forms in students and clients*. Poster presented at the annual meeting of the Society for Personality Assessment.

Hawkins, R. C., II, & Meier, S. T. (2015). Psychotherapeutic theories of change and measurement: An integrative model. *Journal of Unified Psychotherapy and Clinical Science, 3*(1), 80–119.

Hawkins, R. C., II, Spriggs, M., Lee, H., & Lopez, M. (2005, November). *Can the MMPI-2 predict outcomes from cognitive-behavioral treatments for anxiety disorders?* Presented at the Association for Behavioral and Cognitive Therapy Convention.

Hayes, A. M., & Andrews, L. A. (2020). A complex systems approach to the study of change in psychotherapy. *BMC Medicine, 18*(1), 197. https://doi.org/10.1186/s12916-020-01662-2

Hayes, S. C. (2004). Acceptance and commitment therapy, relational frame theory, and the third wave of behavioral and cognitive therapies. *Behavior Therapy, 35*(4), 639–665. https://doi.org/10.1016/S0005-7894(04)80013-3

Hayes, S. C., Barnes-Holmes, D., & Roche, B. (Eds.). (2001). *Relational frame theory: A post-Skinnerian account of human language and cognition*. Kluwer. https://doi.org/10.1007/b108413

Hayes, S. C., Strosahl, K. D., & Wilson, K. G. (1999). *Acceptance and commitment therapy: An experiential approach to behavioral change*. Guilford.

Hendrix, H. (1988, 2008). *Getting the love you want: A guide for couples*. Holt.

Hofmann, S. (1999). The value of psychophysiological data for cognitive behavioral treatment of panic disorder. *Cognitive and Behavioral Practice, 6*, 244–248. https://doi.org/10.1016/S1077-7229(99)80082-0

Hogg, J. A., & Frank, M. L. (1992). Toward an interpersonal model of codependence and contradependence. *Journal of Counseling and Development, 70*, 371–375. https://doi.org/10.1002/j.1556-6676.1992.tb01618.x

Hopwood, C. J., & Bornstein, R. F. (2014). *Multimethod clinical assessment*. Guilford.

Horowitz, L. M., Alden, L. E., Wiggins, J. S., & Pincus, A. L. (2000). *Inventory of interpersonal problems manual*. The Psychological Corporation.

Hawkins, R. C. II. (1993). *Psychopathology emerging within a relational field: Insights from Jungian theory, type development, and cognitive science*. Paper presented at the 10th biennial convention of the Association for Psychological Type, Newport Beach, CA.

Howard, K. I., Kopta, S. M., Krause, M. S., & Orlinsky, D. E. (1986). The dose-effect relationship in psychotherapy. *American Psychologist, 41*, 159–164. https://doi.org/10.1037/0003-066X.41.2.159

Howard, K. I., Lueger, R. J., Maling, M. S., & Martinovich, Z. (1993). A phase model of psychotherapy: Causal mediation of outcome. *Journal of Consulting and Clinical Psychology, 61*, 678–685. https://doi.org/10.1037/0022-006X.61.4.678

Howard, K. I., Moras, K., Brill, P. L., Martinovich, Z., & Lutz, W. (1996). The evaluation of psychotherapy: Efficacy, effectiveness, and patient progress. *American Psychologist, 51*, 1059–1064. https://doi.org/10.1037/0003-066X.51.10.1059

Jinkerson, J. D., Masilla, A., & Hawkins, R. C., II. (2014). Narrow and wide band relationships between the MBTI psychological type and DSM diagnoses. *Journal of Psychological Type, 74*(3), 29–48.

Jinkerson, J. D., Masilla, A., & Hawkins, R. C., II. (2015). Can Myers-Briggs dimensions predict therapy outcome? Differences in the thinking-feeling function pair in cognitive therapy for depression/anxiety. *Research in Psychotherapy: Psychopathology, Process and Outcome, 18*(1), 21–31. https://doi.org/10.4081/ripppo.2015.167

Jung, C. G. (1971). *Psychological types*. Princeton University Press.

Kaufman, G. (1989). *The psychology of shame: Theory and treatment of shame-based systems*. Springer.

Kelly, E. F., Kelly, E. W., et al. (2010). *Irreducible mind: Toward a psychology for the 21st century*. Rowman & Littlefield.

Kelso, J. A. S. (2009). Synergies: Atoms of brain and behavior. *Advances in Experimental Medicine and Biology, 629*, 83–91. https://doi.org/10.1007/978-0-387-77064-2_5

Kelso, J. A. S. (2013). Coordination dynamics. In R. A. Meyers (Ed.), *Encyclopedia of complexity and system science* (pp. 1537–1564). Springer. https://doi.org/10.1007/978-0-387-30440-3_101

Kelso, J. A. S., & Engstrom, D. A. (2006). *The complementary nature*. The MIT Press. https://doi.org/10.7551/mitpress/1988.001.0001

Kessler, R. C., Sonnega, A., Bromet, E., Hughes, M., & Nelson, C. B. (1996). Posttraumatic stress disorder in the National Comorbidity Survey. *Archives of General Psychiatry, 52*, 1048–1060. https://doi.org/10.1001/archpsyc.1995.03950240066012

Kiesler, D. J. (1996). *Contemporary interpersonal theory and research: Personality, psychopathology, and psychotherapy*. Wiley.

Klein, M. H., Mathieu-Coughlin, P., & Kiesler, D. J. (1986). The experiencing scales. In L. S. Greenberg & W. S. Pinsof (Eds.), *The psychotherapeutic process: A research handbook*. Guilford Press.

Kopetzki, A., Blais, M., de Saeger, H., Finn, S. E., Lewis, K. C., & Hopwood, C. (2025). Test selection in psychoanalytically informed assessment. *Psychoanalytic Psychology, 42*(4), 247–258. https://doi.org/10.1037/pap0000547

Kraus, D. R., Seligman, D. A., & Jordan, J. R. (2005). Validation of a behavioral healthcare outcome and assessment tool designed for naturalistic settings: The treatment outcome package. *Journal of Clinical Psychology, 61*(3), 285–314. https://doi.org/10.1002/jclp.20084

Krauskopf, C. J. (1998). The personality assessment system: A radical hypothesis. *Applied and Preventive Psychology, 7*(4), 235–245. https://doi.org/10.1016/S0962-1849(98)80027-9

Lambert, M. J., Hansen, N. B., & Finch, A. E. (2001). Patient-focused research: Using patient outcome data to enhance treatment effects. *Journal of Consulting and Clinical Psychology, 69*, 159–172. https://doi.org/10.1037/0022-006X.69.2.159

Leary, T. (1957). *Interpersonal diagnosis of personality: A functional theory and methodology for personality evaluation*. Wiley.

Lester, D. (1995). *Theories of personality: A systems approach*. Taylor & Francis.

Lewin, K. (1943, 1951). Defining the "field at a given time". In D. Cartwright (Ed.), *Field theory in social science* (pp. 56–59). Harper & Row.

Luborsky, L., & Barrett, M. S. (2006). The history and empirical status of key psychoanalytic concepts. *Annual Review of Clinical Psychology, 2*, 1–19. https://doi.org/10.1146/annurev.clinpsy.2.022305.095328

Luborsky, L., & Crits-Christoph, P. (1997). *Understanding transference: The core conflictual relationship theme method*. American Psychological Association. https://doi.org/10.1037/10250-000

Lueger, R. J., Howard, K. I., Martinovich, Z., Lutz, W., Anderson, E. E., & Grissom, G. (2001). Assessing treatment progress of individual patients using expected treatment response models. *Journal of Consulting and Clinical Psychology, 69*, 150–158. https://doi.org/10.1037/0022-006X.69.2.150

Magai, C., & Haviland-Jones, J. (2002). *The hidden genius of emotion: Lifespan transformations of personality*. Cambridge University Press. https://doi.org/10.1017/CBO9780511509575
Mahoney, M. J. (1991). *Human change processes: The scientific foundations of psychotherapy*. Basic Books.
Mahoney, M. J. (2003). *Constructive psychotherapy: A practical guide*. Guilford.
McAdams, D. P., & Pals, J. L. (2006). A new Big Five: Fundamental principles for an integrative science of personality. *American Psychologist, 61*, 204–217. https://doi.org/10.1037/0003-066X.61.3.204.
McCaulley, M. (2000). The Myers-Briggs type indicator in counseling. In E. Watkins Jr. & V. L. Campbell (Eds.), *Trends in counseling practice* (2nd ed.). Lawrence-Erlbaum Associates, Publishers.
McWilliams, N. (2011). *Psychoanalytic diagnosis: Understanding personality structure in the clinical process* (Rev. ed.). Guilford.
McWilliams, N. (2014). Psychodynamic therapy. In L. S. Greenberg, N. McWilliams, & A. Wenzel (Eds.), *Exploring three approaches to psychotherapy*. American Psychological Association.
Mehta, P.H., & Josephs, R.A. (2011). Social endocrinology. In D. Dunning (Ed.), *The handbook of social motivation* (pp. 171–190). New York, NY: Psychology Press.
Meier, S. T. (2012). Nomothetic outcome assessment in counseling and psychotherapy: Development and preliminary psychometric analyses of the depression/anxiety negative affect scale. *Psychological Test and Assessment Modeling, 54*, 343–362. https://doi.org/10.1037/t25540-000
Meier, S. T. (2024). Initial evaluation of an AI-augmented progress monitoring and outcome assessment. *Counselling and Psychotherapy Research, 26*, 66. https://doi.org/10.1002/capr.12869
Mergenthaler, E. (1996). Emotion-abstraction patterns in verbatim protocols: A new way of describing psychotherapeutic processes. *Journal of Consulting and Clinical Psychology, 64*, 1306–1315. https://doi.org/10.1037/0022-006X.64.6.1306
Mergenthaler, E., & Bucci, W. (1999). Linking verbal and nonverbal representations: Computer analysis of referential activity. *British Journal of Medical Psychology, 72*, 339–354. https://doi.org/10.1348/000711299160040
Merkur, D. (2007). *Crucified with Christ: Meditations on the passion, mystical death, and the medieval invention of psychotherapy*. SUNY Press.
Meyer, G. (2000). Incremental validity of the Rorschach prognostic rating scale over the MMPI ego strength scale and IQ. *Journal of Personality Assessment, 74*(3), 356–370. https://doi.org/10.1207/S15327752JPA7403_2
Meyer, G. J., Viglione, D. J., Mihura, J. L., Erard, R. E., & Erdberg, P. (2011). *Rorschach performance assessment system (RPAS): Administration, coding, interpretation, and technical manual*. Rorschach Performance Assessment System.
Mischel, W. (2004). Toward an integrative science of the person. *Annual Review of Psychology, 55*, 1–22. https://doi.org/10.1146/annurev.psych.55.042902.130709
Mischel, W., & Shoda, Y. (1995). A cognitive-affective system theory of personality: Reconceptualizing situations, dispositions, dynamics, and invariance in personality structure. *Psychological Review, 102*, 246–268. https://doi.org/10.1037/0033-295X.102.2.246
Moss, D. (2005). Psychophysiological psychotherapy: The use of biofeedback, biological monitoring, and stress management principles in psychotherapy. *Psychophysiology Today, 2*(1), 13–18.
Myers, I. B. (1980). *Gifts differing*. Consulting Psychologists Press.
Myers, I. B., McCaulley, M. H., Quenk, N. I., & Hammer, A. L. (1998). *MBTI manual: A guide to the development and use of the Myers-Briggs type indicator* (3rd. ed.). Consulting Psychologists Press.
Nemesure, M. D., Collins, A. C., Price, G. D., Griffin, T. Z., Pillai, A., Nepal, S., Heinz, M. V., Lekkas, D., Campbell, A. T., & Jacobson, N. C. (2024). Depressive symptoms as a heterogeneous and constantly evolving dynamical system: Idiographic depressive symptom networks of rapid symptom changes among persons with major depressive disorder. *Journal of Psychopathology and Clinical Science, 133*(2), 155–166. https://doi.org/10.1037/abn0000884

Panksepp, J., Wright, J. S., Dobrossy, M. D., Schlaepfer, T. E., & Coenen, V. A. (2014). Affective neuroscience strategies for understanding and treating depression: From preclinical models to three novel therapeutics. *Clinical Psychological Science, 2*(4), 472–494. https://doi.org/10.1177/2167702614535913

Pascual-Leone, A. (2009). Dynamic emotional processing in experiential therapy: Two steps forward, one step back. *Journal of Consulting and Clinical Psychology, 77*(1), 113–126.

Pascual-Leone, A., & Greenberg, L. S. (2007). Emotional processing in experiential therapy. Why the "only way out is through". *Journal of Consulting and Clinical Psychology, 75*, 875–887. https://doi.org/10.1037/0022-006X.75.6.875

Perry, J. C., Beck, S. M., Constantinides, P., & Foley, J. E. (2009). Studying change in defensive functioning in psychotherapy using the defense mechanism rating scales: Four hypotheses, four cases. In R. A. Levy & J. S. Ablon (Eds.), *Handbook of evidence-based psychodynamic psychotherapy: Bridging the gap between science and practice*. Humana Press. https://doi.org/10.1007/978-1-59745-444-5_6

Quenk, N. (2002). *Was that really me?: How everyday stress brings out our hidden personality*. Davies-Black Publishing.

Quenk, N. (2009). *Essentials of Myers-Briggs type indicator assessment* (2nd ed.). Wiley.

Rank, O. (1932). *Art and artist: Creative urge and personality development*. A.A. Knopf.

Rank, O. (1936). *Will therapy: An analysis of the therapeutic process in terms of relationship*. A.A. Knopf.

Reynierse, J. H. (2012). Toward an empirically sound and radically revised typetheory. *Journal of Psychological Type, 72*(1), 1–25.

Reynierse, J. H. (2013). Type theory revisited: Implications of complementary opposites for the five-factor model of personality and organizational interventions. In N. D. Christensen & R. P. Tett (Eds.), *Handbook of personality at work*. Brunner / Routledge.

Salande, J. D., & Hawkins, R. C. II. (2017). Psychological flexibility, attachment style, and personality organization: Correlations between constructs of differing approaches. Journal of Psychotherapy Integration, 27(3), 365–380. https://doi.org/10.1037/int0000037

Salter, D. W. (2000). *SETA manual: A users' guide to the Salter environmental type assessment*. Consulting Psychologists Press.

Schore, A. N. (2013). Introduction. In J. J. Magnavita & J. C. Anchin (Eds.), *Unifying psychotherapy: Principles, methods, and evidence from clinical science*. Springer.

Schore, A. N. (2014). The right brain is dominant in psychotherapy. *Psychotherapy, 51*(3), 388–397. https://doi.org/10.1037/a0037083

Schiepak, G. (2009). Complexity and nonlinear dynamics in psychotherapy. *European Review, 17*(2), 331–356.

Schumpf, Y. R., Eijenhuis, E. R. S., Chalavi, S., et al. (2013). Dissociative part-whole biopsychosocial reactions to backward masked angry and neutral faces: An fMRI study of dissociative identity disorder. *NeuroImage: Clinical, 3*, 54–64. https://doi.org/10.1016/j.nicl.2013.07.002

Schwartz, R. M., & Grice, J. (2022). Positive ratios revisited: Reports of the theory's death have been greatly exaggerated. *The Journal of Positive Psychology, 17*(1), 1–9. https://doi.org/10.1080/17439760.2020.1832245

Seligman, M. E. P. (1999). Positive Social Science. *Journal of Positive Behavior Interventions, 1*(3), 181–182.

Seligman, M. E. P. (2002). *Authentic happiness: Using the new positive psychology to realize your potential for lasting fulfillment*. Free Press.

Seligman, M. E. P. (2011). *Flourish: A visionary new understanding of happiness and Well-being*. Free Press.

Seligman, M. E. P., Rashid, T., & Parks, A. C. (2006). Positive psychotherapy. *American Psychologist, 61*, 774–788. https://doi.org/10.1037/0003-066X.61.8.774

Shedler, J., & Westen, D. (2007). The Shedler-Westen assessment procedure (SWAP): Making personality diagnosis clinically meaningful. *Journal of Personality Assessment, 89*, 41–55. https://doi.org/10.1080/00223890701357092

Silberschatz, G. (Ed.). (2005). *Transformative relationships: The control mastery theory of psychotherapy*. Guilford.

Singer, W. (2009). The brain, a complex adaptive system. *European Review, 17*(2), 321–329. https://doi.org/10.1017/S1062798709000751

Slive, A., & Bobele, M. (Eds.). (2011). *When one hour is all you have: Effective therapy for walk-in clients*. Zeig, Tucker, & Theisen.

Solomon, R. L., & Corbit, J. D. (1974). An opponent-process theory of motivation: I. Temporal dynamics of affect. *Psychological Review, 81*(2), 119–145. https://doi.org/10.1037/h0036128

Solomon, R. S. (1980). The opponent process theory of acquired motivation: The costs of pleasure and the benefits of pain. *American Psychologist, 35*(8), 691–712. https://doi.org/10.1037/0003-066X.35.8.691

Soper, H.V., Comstock, T., Kissinger, R., & Gaines, D. (2017). Understanding the frontal lobe of the brain: Fractioning the prefrontal lobes and associated executive functions. *Fielding Monograph Series, Volume 11*. Santa Barbara, CA: Fielding University Press.

Spence, J. T., Helmreich, R. L., & Holahan, C. A. (1979). Negative and positive components of psychological masculinity and femininity and their relationship to self-reports of neurotic and acting out behavior. *Journal of Personality and Social Psychology, 37*, 1673–1682. https://doi.org/10.1037/0022-3514.37.10.1673

Stern, D. (2004). *The present moment in psychotherapy and everyday life*. Norton.

Stieger, S., Göritz, A. S., & Burger, C. (2010). Personalizing the IAT and the SC-IAT: Impact of idiographic stimulus selection in the measurement of implicit anxiety. *Personality and Individual Differences, 48*, 940–944. https://doi.org/10.1016/j.paid.2010.02.027

Stiffey, D., Jr., & Hawkins, R. C., II. (2011). *Neurocognitive behavioral assessment and treatment: A case study*. Invited Lecture to the University of Texas at Austin Clinical Psychology Program.

Tausczik, Y. R., & Pennebaker, J. W. (2010). The psychological meaning of words: LIWC and computerized text analysis methods. *Journal of Language and Social Psychology, 29*(1), 24–54. https://doi.org/10.1177/0261927X09351676

Tomkins, S.S. (1978). Script theory: Differential magnification of affects. In H.E. Howe, Jr. (Ed.), *Nebraska Symposium on Motivation*, 1978. Lincoln, NB: University of Nebraska Press.

Tomkins, S.S. (2008a). *Affect, imagery, consciousness: The complete edition* (Volume I and Volume II). New York: Springer.

Tomkins, S.S. (2008b). *Affect, imagery, consciousness: The complete edition* (Volume III and Volume IV). New York: Springer.

Van der Hart, O., Eijenhuis, E. R. S., & Steele, J. (2006). *The haunted self: Structural dissociation and the treatment of chronic traumatization*. Norton.

Villmann, T., Liebers, C., Bergmann, B., Gumze, A., & Geyer, M. (2008). Investigation of psychophysiological interactions between patient and therapist during a psychodynamic therapy and their relation to speech using in terms of entropy analysis using a neural network approach. *New Ideas in Psychology, 26*, 309–325.

Westen, D. (1991). Clinical assessment of object relations using the TAT. *Journal of Personality Assessment, 56*(1), 56–74. https://doi.org/10.1207/s15327752jpa5601_6

Willi, J. (1999). *Ecological psychotherapy: Developing by shaping the personal niche*. Hogrefe & Huber.

Willi, J., Frei, R., & Gunther, E. (2000). Psychotherapy of panic syndrome: Focusing on ecological aspects of relationships. *American Journal of Psychotherapy, 54*(2), 226–242. https://doi.org/10.1176/appi.psychotherapy.2000.54.2.226

Young, J. E., Klosko, J. S., & Weishaar, M. (2003). *Schema therapy: A practitioner's guide*. Guilford.

Zilcha-Mano, S. (2025). Individual-specific animated profiles of mental health. *Perspectives on Psychological Science, 20*(4), 787–805. https://doi.org/10.1177/17456916231226308

Chapter 5
Individual Client-Level Differences and Treatment Outcome: Idiographic Assessment of Patterns and Types

The purpose of this chapter is to explore how client-level factors shape the therapeutic process. As background, it is important to note that within the history of personality science, nomothetic traits have been the emphasis of individual differences research. "Nomothetic" refers to continuously distributed traits, which exist along a normal curve for a general population, with most individuals scoring in the middle of the distribution and fewer at either tail. From the nomothetic trait conception in personality, parametric statistics emphasizing variable-based analysis became the standard practice. Unfortunately, variable-based measurements, and changes in mean levels of hypothetical outcome measures, are relatively poor predictors of overall psychotherapy outcomes. The reason for this is that mean-level differences, although statistically significant, do not necessarily describe the outcomes of the individual clients in experiments or randomized controlled trials (e.g., Grice, 2015; Lamiell, 2019; Lamiell & Slaney, 2021; Michell, 2009, 2011; Molenaar & Campbell, 2009; Speelman & McGann, 2013). Grice developed Observation Oriented Modeling (OOM; Grice, 2011, 2015; Grice et al., 2020), which provides an alternative non-parametric correction for this limitation of parametric statistical analyses of variable-based trait measures of continuously distributed domain specific measures.

Aside from nomothetic personality traits and individual differences across persons, there has always been an alternative approach that emphasizes client level or person-centered idiographic process measures, focused on the individuals in personality studies within the normal population (Allport, 1937, 1968; Beck & Jackson, 2020; Grisso & Springstein, 2025; Stern, 1938) and particularly in clinical samples (Beltz et al., 2016; von Eye & Wiedermann, 2025; Wright et al., 2019; Wright & Woods, 2020). Thus, individuals may show different networks of characteristics over time that do not necessarily result from nomothetic traits (Levinson et al., 2024). This approach to emphasize idiographic analyses of individuals rather than aggregating them into groups in psychotherapy outcome studies is an important

R. Hawkins, S. Meier, *Healing Outcomes*,
https://doi.org/10.1007/978-3-032-33611-8_5

step; however, analytical approaches for doing this have been rather limited, as they violate those assumptions used in variable-based parametric statistics (Grice, 2015).

Evidence-Based Idiographic Assessment of Treatment Outcomes and Treatment Mediators

Explicit in the presentation of our systems-contextual integrated model (SCIM) is that it involves the restoration of the healthy system principle (i.e., the Healing Cycle, HC). The SCIM implies that there are multi-level mechanisms for shifting clients from the Trauma Cycle (TC) to the HC. At the client-level (micro, person-centered level), in this chapter, we discuss mechanisms of change that impact the individual. These mechanisms of change also will include some discussion at the meso level; namely, the effect of the social and physical environmental contexts on target problem behaviors.

The treatment outcomes for anxiety disorders and affective disorders have been studied at the Clinical Psychology Training Clinic at the University of Texas at Austin, where Hawkins was practicum training director from 1998 to 2001. The formation of the UT Austin Clinical Psychology Training Clinic stems from the development of the Laboratory for the Study of Anxiety Disorders by Michael J. Telch, PhD, in 1988. Dr. Telch, who was mentored by Albert Bandura, PhD, at Stanford University, became the Director of Clinical Training in the Psychology Dept. in 1993 and then systematized evidence-based assessment and case formulation within the Training Clinic along the lines of cognitive behavioral psychology, especially Bandura's Social Cognitive Theory (SCT; Bandura, 1977, 1986) involving triadic reciprocity. Dr. Bandura (1986) proposed triadic reciprocity theory in which behavior is reciprocally influenced by "person factors" (e.g., attitudes, values, personality, self-efficacy) as well as "environment factors" (e.g., actions of others, social context). Thus, person factors interact with environment factors which interact with behavior factors in reciprocal fashion. SCT was adopted in the UT Austin Training Clinic where the person factors and environment factors were conceived of as mechanisms of change or maintaining factors for the target problem behaviors, as well as for changes to normal functioning. It is important to note that Telch's case formulation model can be applied transtheoretically to other evidence-based assessment approaches.

Consider, for example, the target problem of panic disorder (PD). For PD, conditions within the client (e.g., fear of body sensations and anxiety sensitivity) as well as behavioral avoidance strategies for certain environmental situations where the client rated the likelihood of panic as high, influence the development of PD. The problem pattern is also maintained through a reciprocal process of strengthening the client's catastrophic misinterpretation and fear of body sensations as threatening and the client's safety maneuvers for avoiding situations where panic attacks had occurred in the past. An innovation in the Training Clinic was to provide student therapists with a manual of empirically supported assessment and outcome measures to guide CBT, as well as to identify potential mediators of specific treatment outcomes. This unpublished manual (Schmidt et al., 1998) provided guidelines for which instruments to administer for which target problems.

To continue the example of panic disorder, the outcome measure for panic disorder effects would be the Panic Disorder Severity Scale (PDSS; Houck et al., 2002; Shear et al., 1997) or simply a frequency count of panic attacks' occurrence in a week's time and avoidance of certain situations, whereas the underlying mechanism for the treatment effect (the mediator) would be the Anxiety Sensitivity Index (Reiss et al., 1986; Taylor et al., 2007) and/or Dr. Telch's his own instrument, the Panic Appraisal Inventory (Telch et al., 1989). The validity of the idiographic assessment strategy with these measures of treatment outcome and core process measures of mediators for treatment outcome for specific target problems would be empirically tested through case formulation of this triadic relationship between the target behavior problem and these person and environmental maintaining factors. The emphasis of the treatment is that the intervention should impact the problem through first impacting the factors maintaining the problem (i.e., the mediators).

The utility of this case formulation is data-based and is tested through systematic interventions to impact the mediator or maintaining factors. For panic disorder Dr. Telch and his students developed a panic inoculation treatment (Telch et al., 1993) involving interoceptive exposures in a graded hierarchical fashion, wherein the client with PD would be given tasks to bring about increasingly strong body sensations to help the client to habituate to these sensations, rather than to catastrophically misinterpret or misclassify them as threats or alarms for panic. Example exercises would include rapid breathing, slow spinning in a chair to induce feelings of dizziness, running up a flight of stairs to raise heart rate, and eventually culminating in an exposure producing intense body sensations, namely inhalation of a 30% carbon dioxide air mixture, which would induce breath-hunger that has been shown in normal populations of students to increase anxiety sensitivity and even to trigger mild panic attacks in some cases.

To summarize, students in the UT Austin Training Clinic were shown how to conduct panic inoculation treatments and to systematically gather data on their effectiveness. The outcome measure would be the PDSS, the core process mediating measure would be the Anxiety Sensitivity Index or the PAI. Dr. Telch and his colleagues have conducted formal randomized controlled trials to test this mediation of panic attacks and panic disorder (e.g., Smits et al., 2004). In the Smits et al. study, individuals were randomized to waitlist control or to panic inoculation treatment, and then their outcomes were assessed and compared. The treated group showed significantly improved scores on agoraphobic avoidance. Moreover, of particular importance, the core process measures (the Anxiety Sensitivity Index and the Body Sensations Questionnaire; Chambless et al., 1984) were shown to significantly mediate the treatment effect.

What shall we do in the training of our graduate student therapists besides having them conduct controlled trials research? One way is to teach them in clinical practicum to administer both the treatment outcome measure (s) and the core process mediator measure (s) on a regular session-by-session basis throughout the treatment to show to the therapist and to the client that the treatment impacts the mediator and then the outcome is improved. Thus, interceptive exposure would target the fear of body sensations (the anxiety sensitivity). Changes on the PAI associated with the exposure sessions should show PAI scores improving and these PAI improvements preceding improvements on the treatment outcome measure (the PDSS). However, Desmet et al. (2021) have challenged reliance upon client self-report treatment outcome measures, describing some cases where clinical improvement as determined by clinicians was discrepant from clients' self-report measures. It is therefore important for therapists using evidence-based assessments to ask clients for their interpretation of the meaning of scores on self-report measures (Youngstrom et al., 2017).

To summarize the topic of client level effects on treatment, we can say that evidence-based assessment (Youngstrom et al., 2017) involving careful specification of maintaining factors as well as treatment outcomes has been an important demonstration. Hawkins (unpublished) has listed core process mediator measures for most of the anxiety and affective disorders. There are other client level assessments which should also be considered in addition to the problem focused measures. These alternative strength-based measures include person-centered factors as well as situational social context factors. We can look at ways of describing client-level characteristics (e.g., using the Five-Factor Model or the Myers-Briggs Type Indicator), and social support or quality of life contextual influences in the domains of work, social, family, and leisure activities (e.g., Sheehan Disability Scale; Leon et al., 1992; Sheehan et al., 1996).

Next, we will consider personality traits as a treatment moderator. Use of the Five Factor Model (Extraversion, Openness, Conscientiousness, Agreeableness, Neuroticism; McCrae & Costa Jr., 1999) in diagnostics and psychotherapy has been limited, aside from research on how the personality disorders can be mapped as maladaptive FFM facets (e.g., Saulsman & Page, 2004; Widiger & Mullins-Sweatt, 2009). A meta-analytic review by Bucher et al. (2019) found that mental health positive outcomes were related to lower levels of neuroticism and higher levels of extraversion, agreeableness, conscientiousness, and openness. It is important to control for baseline symptoms, as FFM personality did not predict treatment outcome in one study that used this baseline control (Steinert et al., 2014). A scoping review (Fletcher & Delgadillo, 2022) revealed that psychotherapists' FFM traits were associated with their choice of therapeutic orientation and interpersonal skills but were not consistently correlated with treatment outcome. What would be the mechanism of action for clients' and/or therapists' personality predicting psychotherapy outcomes? An obvious candidate would be the therapeutic alliance. Clients' FFM agreeableness scores were significantly positively correlated with their ratings of the therapeutic alliance (Bucher et al., 2019), and therapists' FFM agreeableness scores were also significantly related to clients' ratings of the therapeutic alliance (Mendez et al., 2018). It is important to note that clients' ratings of the therapeutic alliance are generally higher than therapists' ratings (Lev Ari et al., 2025). Complex dynamic systems theories help us understand how iterations of alliance states within sessions and trait alliance across sessions are specific to personality, diagnosis, and/or treatment effects (e.g., CBT for Panic Disorder; Hoffart et al., 2025) or generalizable as a common factor of treatment outcome (e.g., Bordin, 1979).

In his research and practice over the past 40 years (at the UT Austin Clinical Psychology Training Clinic and at the Fielding Practice Research Network at New Life Institute) Hawkins has used the Myers-Briggs Type Indicator (MBTI) for idiographic assessment of Psychological Type. This is not the place to give a full background on the MBTI (see Isabel Briggs-Myers' book *Understanding Differences*, 1980). The MBTI is a well-validated psychometric self-report instrument which yields a Psychological Type score for each individual in addition to the individual's scores on continuously distributed dimensions. The four dimensions in the MBTI are arranged as opposites: Extravert versus Introvert (E—I), Sensing versus Intuitive (S—N), Thinking versus Feeling (T—F), and Judging versus Perceiving (J—P). The E—I dimension indicates the preference for extraversion (focus on the outer world of people) or for introversion (focus on the inner world of impressions or ideas). The S—N dimension indicates the preference for Sensing (focus on the present, concrete facts) or Intuition (focus on future possibilities). The T—F dimension indicates the preference for Thinking (decision-making based on logic and objective analysis) or Feeling (making decisions based on values and how decisions affect other people). The J—P dimension indicates a preference for Judging (liking things structured and planned) or for Perceiving (liking spontaneity and keeping options open). For each of these contrasts, an individual will choose on forced choice items one preference pole or its opposite (preference dichotomies). So, one prefers either Extravert or Introvert, Sensing or Intuitive, Thinking or Feeling, Judging or Perceiving. The combination of these four preference dichotomies yields a four-letter psychological type. There are thus 16 types of combinations (i.e., ISTJ, ISFJ, INFJ, INTJ, ISTP, ISFP, INFP, INTP, ESTP, ESFP, ENFP, ENTP, ESTJ, ESFJ, ENFJ, and ENTJ). Descriptive vignettes of the characteristics for each of these 16 types have been published (see MBTI Form M Manual; Myers et al., 1998), and these have shown utility for occupational and counseling applications. Moreover, the MBTI psychological types provide healthy personality descriptions available for use in the clinical context.

Note that the dimensions of the MBTI do not include neuroticism (emotional instability). The MBTI thus is framed in terms of positive socially desirable characteristics. There are advanced methods for interpreting the MBTI that can be used to explore some socially undesirable characteristics (e.g., MBTI Form M, Step 2, and Step 3). Type theory allows one to characterize individuals in terms of their "best fit" psychological type. Type verification is a carefully described ethical process in which the individual is shown the four preference dichotomies and asked to choose which pole for each dichotomy is preferred. After the Type verification process is completed, that client-verified psychological type can be used to enhance the client's self-esteem and, very important in the healing outcomes framework, to restore a sense of purpose or hope for the client's individual development toward greater fulfillment. In the case study included in the Chap. 4 Appendix, there is an example of how the MBTI is used in conjunction with measures of psychopathology to track client progress through therapy toward "good type development" with a decrease in symptoms and an increase in purposefulness and functionality in relationships and in work. Jinkerson et al. (2015) have reported that MBTI Type is related to treatment outcome in a clinical study.

To measure these Type related changes and their contribution as moderators of the trajectories of overall outcomes of psychotherapy consider that verified MBTI type can provide a frame or a template for a client to use for self-esteem building (in this way reminiscent of George Kelly's fixed-role therapy). Kelly (1955) did not use the Myers-Briggs Type Indicator but instead used an idiographic formulation of the client's strengths. We present this MBTI psychological type feedback to clients as a framework for them to act as if they already possess these healthy characteristics. For example, a client preferring INTJ would be shown the vignette "portrait" of the INTJ type, and the client would then use that thumbnail sketch to guide his or her behavior through therapy and in the outer world to understand and appreciate Type differences among people and their value orientations. The MBTI results for a group of clients can be summarized using the Selection Ratio Type Table (SRTT; McCaulley, 1985), a chi-square 4x4 matrix, to discern whether a particular Type (or Types) is overrepresented for a particular disorder (Hawkins, 1989a), or whether a particular disorder can show different Type related patterns in its manifestation (Hawkins, 1989b). SRTTs can also estimate differences in preferences related to culture, race, gender, and even political views (Hawkins, 2020; Wang & Hawkins, 2021).

Of particular interest is whether MBTI type preferences are related to expectations about seeking counseling in times of personal crisis. The Center for the Application of Psychological Type was a non-profit foundation in Gainesville, Florida, that provided MBTI assessment and archived the data. In 2023 CAPT merged with the Myers & Briggs Foundation. Hawkins was granted permission to analyze the CAPT MBTI Databank archives for 2010–2013 (Hawkins et al., 2017). For many years, the former CAPT Research Director, Gerald P. Macdaid, presented "Facts from the CAPT Databank" (e.g., Macdaid, 1999), which included optional questions inquiring about whether the respondent would be more likely to: "want to be alone" or "want to be with someone"; "tell at least one person" or "tell no one"; "seek counseling" or "not seek counseling." Table 5.1 summarizes the responses of

Table 5.1 CAPT MBTI Databank archives for 2010–2013 (Hawkins et al., 2017) responses to optional questions (N = 2778 males, 3701 females)

ISTJ	ISFJ	INFJ	INTJ
MALES			
*TELL NO ONE #NOT SEEK COUNSELING *BE ALONE		#SEEKCOUNSELING	#BE ALONE
FEMALES			

(continued)

Table 5.1 (continued)

ISTJ	ISFJ	INFJ	INTJ
#TELL NO ONE *BE ALONE		#SEEKCOUNSELING	
ISTP	**ISFP**	**INFP**	**INTP**
MALES			
*TELL NO ONE *NOT SEEK COUNSELING *BE ALONE	#BE ALONE		*NOT SEEK COUNSELING
FEMALES			
#TELL NO ONE *BE ALONE			#TELL NO ONE *BE ALONE
ESTP	**ESFP**	**ENFP**	**ENTP**
MALES			
*NOT SEEK COUNSELING		*SEEKCOUNSELING *BE WITH SOMEONE	
FEMALES			
	#NOT SEEK COUNSELING	#TELLSOMEONE #SEEKCOUNSELING *BE WITH SOMEONE	
ESTJ	**ESFJ**	**ENFJ**	**ENTJ**
MALES			
*TELL1 PERSON #BE WITH SOMEONE		#SEEKCOUNSELING #BE WITH SOMEONE	
FEMALES			
	*TELLSOMEONE #SEEK COUNSELING	#TELLSOMEONE #SEEKCOUNSELING *BE WITH SOMEONE	*TELL1 PERSON *SEEKCOUNSELING *BE WITH SOMEONE

the 2778 males and 3071 females to these questions. Both females and males who preferred INFJ, ENFP, or ENFJ would "seek counseling", as would ESFJ females and ENTJ males. Males preferring ISTJ, ISTP, INTP, and ESTP would "not seek counseling" nor would ESFP females. How do these preferences for counseling under personal crisis align with the actual engagement of the 16 MBTI types in counseling? Tables 5.2a and 5.2b below show the SRTT proportions of therapy clients in Hawkins' private practice archival database from 1993 to 2023. Of the 574 female clients, the proportions of those preferring INFP, ENFP, ENFJ, and INTJ were significantly overrepresented, while those preferring ISTJ, ISTP, ESTP, ISFJ, ESFP, and ESFJ were significantly underrepresented.

Of the 413 male clients, the proportions of those preferring INFP, ENFP, INTJ, and INTP were significantly overrepresented, while those preferring ISTJ, ESTP, ESTJ, and ESFJ were significantly underrepresented. There is thus some congruence between the CAPT databank expectations of "seeking counseling" when in personal crisis (e.g., ENFP, ENFJ) and the proportions of clients with these MBTI

Table 5.2a shows the SRTT proportions of female therapy clients (n = 574) in Hawkins' private practice archival database from 1993 to 2023.

Source of data

Hawkins Clinical Database Females (N=574)

Group tabulated:

Hawkins Clinical Database Females (N=574) (12/25)

N = 574

MBTI Type Table
Center for Applications of Psychological Type

Legend: % = percent of total choosing this group who fall into this type.
I = Self-selection index: Ratio of percent of type in group to % in sample.

SENSING types with THINKING	SENSING types with FEELING	INTUITIVE types with FEELING	INTUITIVE types with THINKING
ISTJ " N= 46 %= 8.01 I= 0.65	ISFJ " N= 65 %= 11.32 I= 0.70	INFJ N= 30 %= 5.23 I= 1.66	INTJ # N= 33 %= 5.75 I= 2.56
ISTP " N= 13 %= 2.26 I= 0.52	ISFP N= 26 %= 4.53 I= 0.70	INFP * N= 60 %= 10.45 I= 2.49	INTP N= 21 %= 3.66 I= 0.91
ESTP " N= 10 %= 1.74 I= 0.48	ESFP " N= 24 %= 4.18 I= 0.58	ENFP * N= 75 %= 13.07 I= 1.98	ENTP N= 22 %= 3.83 I= 1.35
ESTJ N= 35 %= 6.10 I= 0.83	ESFJ " N= 59 %= 10.28 I= 0.73	ENFJ # N= 44 %= 7.67 I= 2.23	ENTJ N= 11 %= 1.92 I= 0.91

			N	%	I
J		E	280	48.78	1.03
U		I	294	51.22	0.97
D	I	S	278	48.43	0.68 *
G	N	N	296	51.57	1.80 *
I	T	T	191	33.28	0.86 "
N	R	F	383	66.72	1.09 "
G	O	J	323	56.27	0.93
	V	P	251	43.73	1.11
P	E	IJ	174	30.31	0.90
E	R	IP	120	20.91	1.10
R	T	EP	131	22.82	1.13
C	S	EJ	149	25.96	0.96
E		ST	104	18.12	0.66 *
P		SF	174	30.31	0.69 *
T		NF	209	36.41	2.10 *
I	E	NT	87	15.16	1.35 "
V	X	SJ	205	35.71	0.72 *
E	T	SP	73	12.72	0.59 *
S	R	NP	178	31.01	1.76 *
	A	NJ	118	20.56	1.88 *
J	V	TJ	125	21.78	0.91
U	E	TP	66	11.50	0.78
D	R	FP	185	32.23	1.32 #
G	T	FJ	198	34.49	0.94
I	S	IN	144	25.09	1.84 *
N		EN	152	26.48	1.77 *
G		IS	150	26.13	0.67 *
		ES	128	22.30	0.69 *

Note concerning symbols following the selection ratios:
" implies significance at the .05 level, i.e., Chi-square >3.8;
implies significance at the .01 level, i.e., Chi-square > 6.6;
* implies significance at the .001 level, i.e., Chi-square > 10.8.
_ (underscore) indicates Fisher's exact probability used instead Chi-square.

Base population used in calculating selection ratios:
CPP Adult Norms Females (N=668) (Hammer & Mitchell, 1996)
Base total N = 668. Sample and base are independent.

Note concerning symbols following the selection ratios:
" implies significance at the.05 level, i.e., Chi-square >3.8
implies significance at the.01 level, i.e., Chi-square > 6.6
* implies significance at the.001 level, i.e., Chi-square > 10.8
_ (underscore) indicates Fisher's exact probability used instead Chi-square
Base population used in calculating selection ratios:
CPP Adult Norms Females (N=668) (Hammer & Mitchell, 1996)
Base total N = 668. Sample and base are independent

Table 5.2b shows the SRTT proportions of male therapy clients (n = 413) in Hawkins' private practice archival database from 1993 to 2023.

Source of data	Group tabulated:	MBTI Type Table
Hawkins Clinical Database Males (N=413)	Hawkins Clinical Database Males (N=413) (12/25)	Center for Applications of Psychological Type
	N = 413	Legend: % = percent of total choosing this group who fall into this type. I = Self-selection index: Ratio of percent of type in group to % in sample.

	SENSING types with THINKING	SENSING types with FEELING	INTUITIVE types with FEELING	INTUITIVE types with THINKING
JUDGING INTROVERTS	ISTJ " N= 57 %= 13.80 I= 0.71	ISFJ N= 22 %= 5.33 I= 0.84	INFJ N= 14 %= 3.39 I= 1.69	INTJ # N= 37 %= 8.96 I= 1.85
PERCEPTIVE INTROVERTS	ISTP N= 27 %= 6.54 I= 0.75	ISFP N= 16 %= 3.87 I= 1.66	INFP * N= 41 %= 9.93 I= 2.20	INTP * N= 54 %= 13.08 I= 2.01
PERCEPTIVE EXTRAVERTS	ESTP # N= 8 %= 1.94 I= 0.31	ESFP N= 8 %= 1.94 I= 0.48	ENFP " N= 39 %= 9.44 I= 1.57	ENTP N= 26 %= 6.30 I= 0.94
JUDGING EXTRAVERTS	ESTJ # N= 29 %= 7.02 I= 0.55	ESFJ " N= 7 %= 1.69 I= 0.36	ENFJ N= 6 %= 1.45 I= 0.97	ENTJ N= 22 %= 5.33 I= 1.52

	N	%	I
E	145	35.11	0.77 #
I	268	64.89	1.19 #
S	174	42.13	0.65 *
N	239	57.87	1.63 *
T	260	62.95	0.92
F	153	37.05	1.18
J	194	46.97	0.85 "
P	219	53.03	1.18 "
IJ	130	31.48	0.97
IP	138	33.41	1.52 *
EP	81	19.61	0.86
EJ	64	15.50	0.69 #
ST	121	29.30	0.62 *
SF	53	12.83	0.74 "
NF	100	24.21	1.73 *
NT	139	33.66	1.56 *
SJ	115	27.85	0.64 *
SP	59	14.29	0.67 #
NP	160	38.74	1.63 *
NJ	79	19.13	1.61 #
TJ	145	35.11	0.87
TP	115	27.85	0.99
FP	104	25.18	1.49 #
FJ	49	11.86	0.82
IN	146	35.35	1.98 *
EN	93	22.52	1.27
IS	122	29.54	0.80 "
ES	52	12.59	0.45 *

Note concerning symbols following the selection ratios:
" implies significance at the .05 level, i.e., Chi-square >3.8;
implies significance at the .01 level, i.e., Chi-square > 6.6;
* implies significance at the .001 level, i.e., Chi-square > 10.8.
_ (underscore) indicates Fisher's exact probability used instead Chi-square.

Base population used in calculating selection ratios:
CPP Adult Norms Males (N=599) (Hammer & Mitchell, 1996)
Base total N = 599. Sample and base are independent.

Note concerning symbols following the selection ratios:
" implies significance at the.05 level, i.e., Chi-square >3.8
implies significance at the.01 level, i.e., Chi-square > 6.6
* implies significance at the.001 level, i.e., Chi-square > 10.8
_ (underscore) indicates Fisher's exact probability used instead Chi-square
Base population used in calculating selection ratios:
CPP Adult Norms Males (N=599) (Hammer & Mitchell, 1996)
Base total N = 599. Sample and base are independent

types who actually participated in counseling. Likewise, there is agreement between the CAPT respondents' MBTI types expecting not to seek counseling and the underrepresentation of clients with those types in therapy with Hawkins (e.g., ISTP, ESTP, ESFP, ESTJ). An interesting discrepancy is that INTP and INTJ types were overrepresented in therapy, but CAPT respondents with these MBTI types expected "not to seek counseling" in times of personal crisis. Is this discrepancy related to differential referrals to Hawkins whose MBTI type preference is INTJ? Obviously, resolution of the relationship between the expectation to seek counseling and the actual engagement in counseling needs to be obtained from more research.

For purposes of psychotherapy outcome prediction, a more longitudinal person-centered idiographic approach is needed. James Grice's Observation Oriented Modeling (OOM, Grice, 2011; Grice et al., 2017) provides one way of doing this. For individuals of a given Type, psychotherapy outcome measures at the micro, meso, and/or macro level can be recorded across sessions and compared with known or hypothesized trajectories to determine the extent to which a clinician researcher's hypotheses about the shape of the trajectory (e.g., the proportion of clients showing improvement in level of depression or anxiety or improvement in self-efficacy) are confirmed. Comparisons can be made between the mean-level changes as determined through variable-based statistics, but also separately for individuals within the group, so that one can determine the proportion of individuals who display or conform to the hypothesized pattern. This allows one to count clients showing successful outcomes and to determine if there are moderating influences of, for example, the therapeutic relationship or to matches versus mismatches with the psychological types of individuals in the client's life in terms of marriage, family, workplace, cultural values, etc. The use of OOM and in conjunction with MBTI Type theory can provide a tool to visualize and assess individual and relational change processes.

Conclusions

This mapping of healthy or healing processes in addition to psychopathology is congruent with the overall emphasis within the SCIM approach to emphasize goal directed, positive strengths as outcomes in the psychotherapeutic process. In addition, the MBTI can be used to illustrate relationship issues that can impact the client's improvement in therapy (i.e., issues in the Type dynamics of client and therapist, client and mate, client and boss, etc.), which is the focus of Chap. 6 ("Healing as collaboration"). This kind of idiographic client-level outcome measurement is very congruent with utilizing an approach to clinical research called practice research integration, which is the focus of Chap. 10. Practice research networks (PRNs) can be used in translational research to implement theory and hypothesized types of intervention to all clients within the PRN and then to examine in a client-level, person-centered way which assessment and outcome measures change over the course of psychotherapy as predicted by the therapeutic model (such as the

SCIM). In Chap. 10, on practice research integration, we also provide the results of two clinical research studies that investigated how clients with panic disorder or with social phobia in a practice research network were followed using OOM to determine outcomes and the proportion of clients that achieved these outcomes in their healing process.

References

Allport, G. W. (1937). *Personality: A psychological interpretation*. Holt.

Allport, G. W. (1968). *The person in psychology: Selected essays*. Beacon Press.

Bandura, A. (1977). Self-efficacy: Toward a unifying theory of behavioral change. *Psychological Review, 84*, 191–215. https://doi.org/10.1037/0033-295X.84.2.191

Bandura, A. (1986). *Social foundations of thought and action: A social cognitive theory*. Prentice-Hall.

Beck, E. D., & Jackson, J. J. (2020). Idiographic traits: A return to Allportian approaches to personality. *Current Directions in Psychological Science, 29*(3), 301–308. https://doi.org/10.1177/0963721420915860

Beltz, A. M., Wright, A. G. C., Sprague, B. N., Molenar, P. C. M., et al. (2016). Bridging the nomothetic and idiographic approaches to the analysis of clinical data. *Assessment, 23*(4), 447–458. https://doi.org/10.1177/1073191116648209

Bordin, E. S. (1979). The generalizability of the psychoanalytic concept of the working alliance. *Psychotherapy: Theory, Research & Practice, 16*(3), 252–260. https://doi.org/10.1037/h0085885

Bucher, M. A., Suzuki, T., & Samuel, D. B. (2019). A meta-analytic review of personality traits and their associations with mental health treatment outcomes. *Clinical Psychology Review, 70*, 51–63. https://doi.org/10.1016/j.cpr.2019.04.002

Chambless, D. L., Caputo, C. G., Bright, P., & Gallagher, R. (1984). Assessment of fear of fear in agoraphobics: The body sensations questionnaire and the agoraphobic cognitions questionnaire. *Journal of Consulting and Clinical Psychology, 52*(6), 1090–1097. https://doi.org/10.1037/0022-006X.52.6.1090

Desmet, M., Van Nieuwenhove, K., De Smet, M., Meganck, R., Deeren, B., Van Huele, I., Decock, E., Raemdonck, E., Cornelis, S., Truijens, F., Zeuthen, K., & Schiepek, G. (2021). What too strict a method obscures about the validity of outcome measures. *Psychotherapy Research, 35*(2), 118–135. https://doi.org/10.1080/10503307.2020.1865584

Fletcher, A. C., & Delgadillo, J. (2022). Psychotherapists' personality traits and their influence on treatment processes and outcomes: A scoping review. *Journal of Clinical Psychology, 78*(7), 1267–1287. https://doi.org/10.1002/jclp.23310

Grice, J. W. (2011). *Observation-oriented modeling: Analysis of cause in behavioral sciences*. Elsevier.

Grice, J. W. (2015). From means and variances to persons and patterns. *Frontiers in Psychology, 6*, 1007. https://doi.org/10.3389/fpsyg.2015.01007

Grice. J.W., Barrett, P., Cota, L. …, & Vest, A. (2017). Four bad habits of modern psychologists. *Behavioral Sciences, 7*(3), 1–21.

Grice, J. W., Medelin, E., Jones, I., et al. (2020). Persons as effect sizes. *Advances in Methods and Practices in Psychological Science, 3*(4), 443–455.

Grisso, M. K., & Springstein, T. (2025). Generalizing across people or capturing unique personal experiences? Nomothetic to idiographic ways of assessing self-reported emotions in daily life. *Translational Issues in Psychological Science.*. Advance online publication. https://doi.org/10.1037/tps0000484

Hawkins, R. C., II. (2020). Discovering your gifts, appreciating differences: Therapeutic use of psychological type and the MBTI. *PsychCentral*. Retrieved on August 19, 2020, from https://psychcentral.com/lib/discovering-your-gifts-appreciating-differences-therapeutic-use-of-psychological-type-and-the-mbti/

Hawkins, R. C., II, et al. (2017, July). INACS MBTI CAPT databank (2010–2013) presentation. In *Institute of Neuroscience and Consciousness Studies (INACS)*.

Hawkins, R. C., II. (1989a, June). *In sickness as in health: Type and psychopathology*. Paper presented at the biennial convention of the Association for Psychological Type (APTVIII).

Hawkins, R. C., II. (1989b, August). *Psychological type and anxiety disorders: Preliminary findings*. Paper presented at the annual convention of the American Psychological Association.

Hoffart, A., Helmich, M. A., Vrabel, K., Ebrahimi, O. V., & Johnson, S. U. (2025). From a latent variable to a complex dynamic system conceptualization of the therapeutic alliance. *Journal of Psychotherapy Integration, 35*(3), 163–179. https://doi.org/10.1037/int0000357

Houck, P. R., Spiegel, D. A., Shear, K., & Rucci, P. (2002, June 05). Reliability of the self-report version of the Panic Disorder Severity Scale. *Depression and Anxiety*. https://doi.org/10.1002/da.10049

Jinkerson, J. D., Masilla, A., & Hawkins, R. C., II. (2015). Can Myers-Briggs dimensions predict therapy outcome? Differences in the thinking-feeling function pair in cognitive therapy for depression/anxiety. *Research in Psychotherapy: Psychopathology, Process and Outcome, 18*(1), 21–31. https://doi.org/10.4081/ripppo.2015.167

Kelly, G. A. (1955). The psychology of personal constructs. Vol. 1. A theory of personality. Vol. 2. Clinical diagnosis and psychotherapy. W. W. Norton.

Lamiell, J. (2019). *Psychology's misuse of statistics and persistent dismissal of its critics*. Palgrave Macmillan. https://doi.org/10.1007/978-3-030-12131-0

Lamiell, J., & Slaney, K. (2021). *Problematic research practices and inertia in scientific psychology: History, sources, and recommended solutions*. Routledge. https://doi.org/10.4324/9781003124757

Leon, A. C., Shear, M. K., Portera, L., & Klerman, G. L. (1992). Assessing impairment in patients with panic disorder: The Sheehan disability scale. *Social Psychiatry and Psychiatric Epidemiology, 27*(2), 78–82. https://doi.org/10.1007/BF00788510

Lev Ari, H. S., Tuval-Mashiach, R., Hay, D. E., Bernstein, Z. L., Kagan, L., Kivity, Y., & Gilboa-Schechtman, E. (2025). A meta-analysis of client-therapist perspectives on the therapeutic alliance: Examining the moderating role of eating disorders versus anxiety disorders, treatment orientation, and measurement time points. *Journal of Psychotherapy Integration, 35*(3), 180–195. https://doi.org/10.1037/int0000355

Levinson, C., Christian, C., & Becker, C. B. (2024). How idiographic methodologies can move the clinical-science field forward to integrate personalized treatment into everyday clinical care and improve treatment outcomes. *Clinical Psychological Science, 13*, 1–14. https://doi.org/10.1177/21677026231217316

Macdaid, G. P. (1999, February). *Facts from the CAPT Databank*. Presented at the 2nd Biennial Clinical Conference of the Center for the Applications of Psychological Type.

McCaulley, M. H. (1985). The selection ratio type table: A research strategy for comparing type distributions. *The Journal of Psychological Type, 10*, 49–56.

McCrae, R. R., & Costa, P. T., Jr. (1999). A five-factor theory of personality. In L. A. Pervin & O. P. John (Eds.), *Handbook of personality: Theory and research* (2nd ed., pp. 139–153). Guilford Press.

Mendez, A., Finlay, M. B., & Vermeersch, D. (2018). Higher levels of agreeableness are associated with higher ratings of therapeutic alliance. *Journal of the American Academy of Child and Adolescent Psychiatry, 57*(10), S195. https://doi.org/10.1016/j.jaac.2018.09.200

Michell, J. (2009). The psychometricians' fallacy: Too clever by half? *British Journal of Mathematical and Statistical Psychology, 62*(1), 41–55. https://doi.org/10.1348/000711007X243582

Michell, J. (2011). Qualitative research meets the ghost of Pythagoras. *Theory & Psychology, 21*(2), 241–259. https://doi.org/10.1177/0959354310391351

Molenaar, P. C. M., & Campbell, C. G. (2009). The new person-specific paradigm in psychology. *Current Directions in Psychological Science, 18*(2), 112–117. https://doi.org/10.1111/j.1467-8721.2009.01619.x

Myers, I.B., McCaulley, M.H., Quenk, N. I., & Hammer, A.L. (1998). *MBTI manual: A guide to the development and use of the Myers-Briggs Type Indicator* (3rd. ed.). Palo Alto, CA: Consulting Psychologists Press.

Reiss, S., Peterson, R. A., Gursky, D. M., & McNally, R. J. (1986). Anxiety sensitivity, anxiety frequency and the prediction of fearfulness. *Behavior Research and Therapy, 24*(1), 1–8. https://doi.org/10.1016/0005-7967(86)90143-9

Saulsman, L. M., & Page, A. C. (2004). The five-factor model and personality disorder empirical literature: A meta-analytic review. *Clinical Psychology Review, 23*(8), 1055–1085. https://doi.org/10.1016/j.cpr.2002.09.001. Erratum in: *Clinical Psychology Review, 2005, 25*(3), 383–394.

Schmidt, N. B., Jaimez, T. L., Mick, M., Murphy, J., Shapiro, E., & Hawkins, R. C., II. (1998). *Handbook of cognitive behavioral assessment and self-monitoring instruments*. Department of Psychology Clinical Psychology Training Clinic, The University of Texas at Austin (unpublished).

Shear, M. K., Brown, T. A., Barlow, D. H., Money, R., Sholomskas, D. E., Woods, S. W., Gorman, J. M., & Papp, L. A. (1997). Multicenter collaborative panic disorder severity scale. *American Journal of Psychiatry, 154*(11), 1571–1575. https://doi.org/10.1176/ajp.154.11.1571

Sheehan, D. V., Harnett-Sheehan, K., & Raj, B. A. (1996). The measurement of disability. *International Clinical Psychopharmacology, 11*(Suppl 3), 89–95. https://doi.org/10.1097/00004850-199606003-00015

Smits, J. A., Powers, M. B., Cho, Y., & Telch, M. J. (2004). Mechanism of change in cognitive-behavioral treatment of panic disorder: Evidence for the fear of fear mediational hypothesis. *Journal of Consulting and Clinical Psychology, 72*(4), 646–652. https://doi.org/10.1037/0022-006X.72.4.646

Speelman, C. P., & McGann, M. (2013). How mean is the mean? *Frontiers in Psychology, 4*, 451. https://doi.org/10.3389/fpsyg.2013.00451

Steinert, C., Hofmann, M., Kruse, J., & Leichsenring, F. (2014). Relapse rates after psychotherapy for depression—stable long-term effects? A meta-analysis. *Journal of Affective Disorders, 168*, 107–118. https://doi.org/10.1016/j.jad.2014.06.043

Stern, W. (1938). *General psychology from a personalistic standpoint*. Macmillan. https://doi.org/10.1037/11642-000

Taylor, S. E., Welch, W. T., Kim, H. S., & Sherman, D. K. (2007). Cultural differences in the impact of social support on psychological and biological stress responses. *Psychological Science, 18*(9), 831–837. https://doi.org/10.1111/j.1467-9280.2007.01987.x

Telch, M. J., Broillard, M., Telch, C. F., et al. (1989). Role of cognitive appraisal in panic related avoidance. *Behavior Research and Therapy, 27*(4), 373–383.

Telch, M. J., Lucas, J. A., Schmidt, N. B., Hanna, H., Jaimez, T. L., & Lucas, R. A. (1993). Group cognitive behavioral treatment of panic disorder. *Behavior Research and Therapy, 31*(3), 279–287. https://doi.org/10.1016/0005-7967(93)90026-Q

von Eye, A., & Wiedermann, W. (2025). Moving from statistical to hypothesis-driven outliers. *Integrative Psychological and Behavioral Science, 59*(2), 43. https://doi.org/10.1007/s12124-025-09908-5

Wang, Q., & Hawkins, R. C., II. (2021, November). *Relationship between MBTI types of immigrants and the stereotype MBTI type of the United States*. Poster presented at the annual convention of the Texas Psychological Association.

Widiger, T. A., & Mullins-Sweatt, S. N. (2009). Five-factor model of personality disorder: A proposal for DSM-V. *Annual Review of Clinical Psychology, 5*, 197–220. https://doi.org/10.1146/annurev.clinpsy.032408.153542

Wright, A. G. C., & Woods, W. C. (2020). Personalized models of psychopathology. *Annual Review of Clinical Psychology, 16*, 49–74. https://doi.org/10.1146/annurev-clinpsy-102419-125032

Wright, C. D., Tiani, A. G., Billingsley, A. L., Steinman, S. A., Larkin, K. T., & McNeil, D. W. (2019). A framework for understanding the role of psychological processes in disease development, maintenance, and treatment: The 3p-disease model. *Frontiers in Psychology, 10*, 2498. https://doi.org/10.3389/fpsyg.2019.02498

Youngstrom, E. A., Halverson, T. F., Youngstrom, J. K., Lindhiem, O., & Findling, R. L. (2017). Evidence-based assessment as an integrative model for applying psychological science to guide the voyage of treatment. *Clinical Psychology: Science and Practice, 24*(4), 331–363. https://doi.org/10.1111/cpsp.12207

Chapter 6
Healing as a Collaboration: Development, Culture, Ethics, and Client-Defined Success

In Chaps. 3 and 4, we introduced our systems-contextual integrative model (SCIM). The SCIM was presented as a heuristic framework for choosing measures to track health and psychopathology within three contextual levels: the micro level (which includes the primary attachment relationship with the parents and the psychotherapeutic relationship), the meso level (comprising family, school, work, and other group influences), and the macro level (the contribution of values, culture, and larger social system influences). However implicit it is in this model, given the SCIM's derivation from Bronfenbrenner's social ecological theory of human development (Brofenbrenner, 1979), it is important for us to consider healing and psychopathology within a developmental psychology framework. Besides Bronfenbrenner, developmental psychologists such as Arnold Sameroff have proposed unified models for human development (e.g., Sameroff, 2010).

Our purpose here is not to provide an overall account of human development or of measures for assessing health or psychopathology in children. For this background, the reader can read general texts such as *Development through Life: A Psychosocial Approach* (Newman & Newman, 2015). Given our integration of systems theory, chaos theory, and other aspects of complex dynamical systems analysis thus far, we need to consider how influential developmental cascades in a clients' formative years of childhood are relevant for healing in adults in general and particularly for the Healing Cycle.

Developmental cascades refer to events or psychological processes which will have subsequent effects on later developmental outcomes such as adult maturity and psychological health. These outcomes may be measurable decades later. For example, Tang et al. (2020) showed that behavioral inhibition (i.e., cautiousness or fearfulness in unfamiliar situations; Kagan, 1994) observed in infancy predicted introversion and internalizing disorder tendencies (anxiety, depression) in adulthood three decades later.

An early theory of some influence which is popular again currently is Waddington's (1957) "epigenetic landscapes," also known as his "chreode" theory.

R. Hawkins, S. Meier, *Healing Outcomes*,
https://doi.org/10.1007/978-3-032-33611-8_6

Chreodes are analogous to the old game wherein an individual would bet on the final endpoint of a metal ball that would be dropped into the top of a vertical maze-like structure and would then fall down any one of several potential paths to reach any one of several potential outcomes. This shows a developmental cascade process. It is not the case that each branch path is independent of the preceding path.

One consideration of developmental cascade theory that is relevant to amplifying the SCIM is to study how the parent–child attachment relationship and family relationships (including those with siblings and other important persons in the proximal environment of the child) are moderated or influenced by subsequent meso-level relationships, particularly the peer group. Judith Rich Harris in 1995 proposed a theory of adolescent peer groups, which described their influence as being more important than the earlier contribution of parents for the subsequent development of character and personality in adolescence. This theory was at first dismissed by personality and developmental theorists because Harris lacked a PhD in developmental psychology. However, this proposal of peer groups' influence is very important for our consideration in understanding the impact of this meso-level process upon the alternation of the HC and the TC at the micro level in abused children. The investigators of the important Minnesota Longitudinal Study of Risk and Adaptation have admitted that unstable social context and difficult life experiences may contribute to discontinuity in attachment security stability (e.g., van Ryzin et al., 2011; Sroufe, 2021; Weinfield et al., 2000).

One way to illustrate the Harris (1995) model would be to consider the potency of the cascade from sexual abuse to subsequently developing unconventional peer group identities in later adolescence, including "trans" gender identity. It is informative to look at such events case by case. One case that was discussed in a *YouTube* video by Glenn Beck (2025) is the case of Claire Abernathy, a de-transitioner who was asked to describe the development of her trans identity and the reasons why she de-transitioned. Our perspective here is to consider Harris's peer group influence theory as a counterbalance for the media attention placed on the role of either political process in general or parental shortcomings and errors specifically. As Claire described to Glenn Beck, as a teenager she had experienced sexual abuse, and as a result, she had wished that she could change her gender identity to become male to feel safe from further attacks. She began to associate online with a trans peer group which became very influential and suggested that she undergo medical sex change procedures. Her mother, wanting to support Claire, became influenced by this same ideology, and then Claire had a double mastectomy. She adopted the male role for a time but then experienced regret and remorse at losing her breasts and had doubts about her transition. This resulted in her de-transitioning efforts.

Does this case example suggest how parents as well as the preteen or teen child are influenced by the peer group and the larger social media controversy about gender fluidity and about victimization of individuals? Obviously, many more studies will need to be undertaken, essentially life history stories from people who have experienced gender change surgery and subsequently have had good developmental outcomes or who have wanted to detransition as Claire Abernathy did. Careful attention to initial sample characterization, having clear definitions of outcomes, waiting long enough for de-transitioning to occur, and preventing attrition in the follow-up sample will be needed (Cohn, 2023). The outcomes are diverse, and the pathways to transition and detransition are heterogeneous and nonlinear (Bosse, 2025; Pullen-Sansfaçon et al., 2024). Ethical care needs to be taken when surveying and interviewing transitioners and de-transitioners.

This Abernathy case is a poignant example of how healthy development and process at the micro level in the SCIM can be disrupted by a triggering event (i.e., sexual abuse), which then leads the teen to experience dysphoria and a desire for a sex change after interacting with a peer group of trans individuals who provided social support and encouragement for this transition. Claire and her mother were influenced by this trans ideology, such that Claire had her surgery, developed a trans male identity, but then experienced regret and wanted to detransition.

As this case study illustrates, the SCIM needs to be expanded developmentally to include case examples of the interaction of these multiple contextual levels as this influences the shifting from the HC to the TC and back to the HC. It is not known exactly what kinds of psychotherapeutic supports can be provided for such individuals who go through this cascading sequence of events. However, it seems imperative that mental health specialists and clinical and developmental scientists should consider such complex interactions across these contextual levels for real-world outcomes that include instances of abuse and trajectories of development which are painful, and for which support and care are needed.

Next, let us consider the impact of the meso level and macro level of change in the SCIM on the psychotherapeutic process. First, however, we need to discuss the important ethical criterion of including the clients' own definitions of successful outcomes. If only the therapist or persons outside of therapy determine the goals of treatment, then there may be some discrepancy with what the clients' own preferred outcomes would be. This is indeed a sine qua non of therapeutic assessment (TA) feedback (Finn, 2007) in which each client's self-defined goals for successful outcomes are given considerable emphasis. Finn and colleagues, for example, developed TA as a transtheoretical way of reframing psychological testing so that the clients' questions about their presenting problems (e.g., "Why do I keep on having romantic relationships that do not last?") are addressed in the feedback discussion of the test findings (Finn, 2007; Finn et al., 2012).

We note the importance of the therapeutic alliance. The Myers-Briggs Type Indicator (MBTI) can be used as a way of visualizing and assessing individual and relational change processes, as mentioned in Chap. 5. To take a case example, the same one that will be used later and elaborated upon in more detail, consider a White male client whose preferred psychological type was INFP. This client, whose psychological type Carl Jung described as Introverted Feeling with Intuition, was in psychotherapy with a White male therapist whose preferred Type was INTJ (i.e., an Introverted Intuitive with Thinking preferences). Although one might on the surface conclude that having two of the MBTI letters in common would facilitate treatment, this is not a proper way of interpreting the degree of matching between the therapist and the client in this case. Indeed, it took a while for the therapeutic alliance to jell because the therapist wanted to utilize a rational CBT approach (Extraverted

Thinking). The client, however, preferred Introverted Feeling, and he wanted to focus on his emotions, particularly his feelings and thoughts of being victimized and how this victimization affected him. Eventually the INTJ therapist became more of a listener and a helper for the client to experience his feelings more deeply, then not only to uncover the negative feelings but also to utilize his intellect to reframe these negative meanings and come up with some more positive goals for himself in his life (e. g., to collect and read old books and thereby to explore the philosophical and religious values in them).

Thus, therapeutic relationship obstacles can be discerned by looking at the degree of matching of the MBTI Types of the therapist and the client. Carl Jung recommended that psychotherapists rotate their psychological type "compass" to align with their client's preferred dominant and auxiliary functions, as illustrated in the previous example. One of the interesting aspects of using the MBTI within the SCIM is that the MBTI can be used as a kind of fractal lens, in that the same 16 Type framework can be applied across the levels of change within the SCIM.

At the meso level, besides the looking at the degree of matching of the client's and the therapist's preferred Types, we can consider the alignment or misalignment of clients' psychological types with those of their significant others outside of therapy. An important "significant other" is the client's spouse or partner. Within Hawkins' practice archive the partner's MBTI type was known, regardless of whether that partner was included in the couples therapy. Considering all combinations of the client's and partner's MBTI types conjointly yields 256 combinations (clients' 16 Types X partners' 16 Types). If mating is non-assortative then for each client of a given Type there would be a 1 in 16 chance that the partner would be of the same Type as the client. For Hawkins' unpublished private practice research database, the chi-square value for this SPSS crosstabs analysis was not statistically significant, meaning that the mating was non-assortative. Nevertheless, the patterns of marital problems or harmonies will be quite different depending on the different type dynamics arising from the different pairings. The fact is that the proportion of females having an MBTI "Feeling" preference is higher than that for males, and conversely more males than females have a "Thinking" preference. So, a female with an ENFP preference may have less difficulty with her ISTJ male partner's "traditional" male sex-role. However, an ENFP male may have more issues with his ISTJ female partner's non-traditional female sex-role. The MBTI's emphasis on "understanding and accepting difference" thus has very important relevance for promoting successful outcomes in couples counseling.

To continue the preceding example, a previous female romantic partner was a source of considerable negative rumination for this INFP client. The ex-partner was described as having a psychological type that was the opposite or near opposite of the client (i.e., ESTJ or ESFJ), and she did not provide validation for the client's Intuitive Feeling perceptions. Moreover, growing up in the South, the client's sensitivity as a male to values considered more socially desirable for women created a mismatch. At the macro level, the client's expectations and preferences were at odds with the military background within which he was raised and, in particular, with his father's espousing ESTJ values characteristic of men in business and/or the military (i.e., Extraverted Thinking with Sensing, the opposite of the INFP client, emphasizing rules, regulations, toughness, etc.), and within a culture that was not accepting of cultural-racial differences (the INFP client in contrast had many friends who were Black, and he was sensitive to those individuals not only at the meso level but also at the macro level). In this case, political, socioeconomic, and racial cultural values were to some degree at a mismatch with the client's values. He also did not have the opportunity to continue his college education due to economic problems and thus lost the opportunity for an environment that was more of a match to his INFP values and goals. Therefore, even at the macro or cultural level, the degree of understanding that this client could gradually develop of the congruence (or lack thereof) of his psychological type with that of others in different levels within the SCIM was a facilitative process in the therapy.

Here is another example of how matches/mismatches moderate healing outcomes, in this case for family therapy of adolescents with attention deficit/hyperactivity disorder (ADHD), inattentive type (Hawkins, 2000). The family therapy was recommended as an adjunct to the individual counseling for the teen with ADHD, to increase parental support and to decrease blaming the teen. For five of six families, the mother's MBTI type was available in addition to that of her teen (all the ADHD teens were male). For these five families, the teens preferred "Perceiving" on the MBTI and four of the five also preferred "Thinking" (i.e., INTP, ENTP, ESTP; the remaining teen was an INFP). In contrast, four of the five mothers had an MBTI preference for "Judging" (i.e., two were ISFJs, one was an ISTJ, and one was an ENFJ; the remaining mother was an INTP). In each instance, the "J" mothers showed the most concern and worry about their ADHD teens. One family was particularly characteristic, in this regard: the INTP ADHD teen's ISFJ mother was anxious and angry with her son, and to an extent also angry with her husband (ENTP) who was not so concerned about his son's ADHD. Utilizing the MBTI as a communication tool to facilitate acceptance of Type differences led to a very good therapy outcome for this family. Aided by the increased parental support (and decreased blaming by the mother), this ADHD teen went on to excel in his college courses.

Can matches/mismatches of MBTI type operate at the cultural level? Wang and Hawkins (2021) explored the possibility that people who immigrate to the United States self-select due to their self-perceived psychological types matching the stereotypical personality type of the United States. The "national" (stereo-) type for the United States has been described as extraverted-sensing-thinking-judging (ESTJ), with some research support (Kise, 2006a, 2006b, 2014). This research was conducted using a large archival database of Myers-Briggs Type Indicator (MBTI) Form F and G scored psychological types provided by the Center for the Application of Psychological Type (CAPT). Of these 13,846 scored protocols, 4583 cases included additional information about gender, race/ethnicity, and immigration status. The number of immigrants to the United States was 267. The Selection Ratio Type Table (SRTT) chi-square software program was used to test whether the observed proportions of immigrants to the United States differed significantly from the base rate expected proportions for non-immigrants of the same race/ethnicity already residing in the United States.

Preliminary analyses were statistically controlled for race and gender as confounding variables. The SRTT analyses revealed that the preference for ESTJ was significantly overrepresented among immigrants to the United States compared to the expected base rate for non-immigrants. That the modal MBTI type of immigrants matched the US stereotype does not prove that immigrants' individual type preferences influenced their decision to immigrate to the United States, given the correlational design of this study. Prospective longitudinal research of intentions to immigrate is needed to make a causal inference that self-selection based upon personality may influence the decision to immigrate to the USA.

Conclusions

The addition of an idiographic measure such as the MBTI 16 Types can facilitate understanding the differing goals and challenges experienced by clients in psychotherapy. By typing the client, the therapist, and the significant others across SCIM levels, including culture, one can treat each of these as individual actors in all combinations of their transactions. The importance of collaboration and of including multimethod assessments and outcome measures that involve strengths and positive values, as well as measures of psychopathology and distress, is hopefully illustrated by the examples just outlined, and by the case study provided in the Appendix to Chap. 4.

In Chap. 10, we talk about practice research integration, the use of practice research networks in translating research findings from the lab to the clinic, and how these can be utilized to test the systems-contextual integrative model's assumptions and predictions.

References

Bosse, J. (2025). When cisnormativity and transnormativity are in bed together: Exposing the underbelly of disinformation-fueled detransition panic. *Canadian Psychology/Psychologie Canadienne, 66*(2), 90–102. https://doi.org/10.1037/cap0000425

Brofenbrenner, U. (1979). *The ecology of human development: Experiments by nature and design*. Harvard Press. https://doi.org/10.4159/9780674028845

Cohn, J. (2023). The detransition rate is unknown. *Archives of Sexual Behavior, 52*(5), 1937–1952. https://doi.org/10.1007/s10508-023-02623-5

Finn, S. E. (2007). *In our client's shoes: Theory and techniques of therapeutic assessment*. Taylor & Francis.

Finn, S. E., Fischer, C. T., & Handler, L. (2012). *Collaborative/therapeutic assessment: A casebook and guide*. Wiley.

Harris, J. R. (1995). Where is the child's environment? A group socialization theory of development. *Psychological Review, 102*(3), 458–489. https://doi.org/10.1037/0033-295X.102.3.458

Hawkins, R. C. II. (2000, March). *Using the MBTI and SSQ in family counseling with teenagers with attention deficit disorder*. Paper presented at CAPT Fourth Biennial Education Conference, Gainesville, FL.

Kagan, J. (1994). *Galen's prophecy: Temperament in human nature*. Basic Books.

Kise, J.A. (2006a). *Differentiated coaching: A framework for helping teachers change*. Corwin Press.

Kise, J. A. (2006b). *Differentiation through personality types: A framework for instruction, assessment, and classroom management*. Corwin Press.

Kise, J.A. (2014). *Unleashing the positive power of differences: Polarity thinking in our schools*. Corwin Press. https://doi.org/10.4135/9781544308630.

Newman, B., & Newman, P. (2015). *Development through life: A psychosocial approach* (13th ed.). Cengage Learning.

Pullen-Sansfaçon, A., Gravel, É., Gelly, M., Planchat, T., Paradis, A., & Medico, D. (2024). A retrospective analysis of the gender trajectories of youth who have discontinued a transition. *International Journal of Transgender Health, 25*(1), 74–89. https://doi.org/10.1080/26895269.2023.2279272

van Ryzin, M. J., Carlson, E. A., & Sroufe, L. A. (2011). Attachment discontinuity in a high-risk sample. *Attachment and Human Development, 13*(4), 381–401. https://doi.org/10.1080/14616734.2011.584403

Sameroff, A. (2010). A unified theory of development: A dialectic integration of nature and nurture. *Child Development, 81*(1), 6–22. https://doi.org/10.1111/j.1467-8624.2009.01378.x

Sroufe, L. A. (2021). Then and now: The legacy and future of attachment research. *Attachment and Human Development, 23*(4), 396–403. https://doi.org/10.1080/14616734.2021.1918450

Tang, A., Crawford, H., Morales, S., Degnan, K. A., Pine, D. S., & Fox, N. A. (2020). Infant behavioral inhibition predicts personality and social outcomes three decades later. *Proceedings of the National Academy of Sciences, 117*(18), 9800–9807. https://doi.org/10.1073/pnas.1917376117

Waddington, C. H. (1957). *The strategy of genes*. Routledge.

Wang, Q., & Hawkins, R. C. II. (2021, November). *Relationship between MBTI types of immigrants and the stereotype MBTI type of the United States*. Poster presented at the annual convention of the Texas Psychological Association, Austin, TX.

Weinfield, N. S., Sroufe, L. A., & Egeland, B. (2000). Attachment from infancy to early adulthood in a high-risk sample: Continuity, discontinuity, and their correlates. *Child Development, 71*(3), 695–702. https://doi.org/10.1111/1467-8624.00178

YouTube video, Glenn Beck. (8/28/2025). Detransitioner: There's NO SUCH THING as a trans child. https://www.youtube.com/watch?v=IODT1PlY6qo

Part II
Applications

Chapter 7
Healing Through Emotion: Emotional Processing, Avoidance, and Measurement

Healing Defined

The word *emotion* derives from a root meaning "movement outward" and shares its origin with *motive*. From a phylogenetic perspective, animals' motives to approach or avoid arise in response to exogenous stimuli (e.g., heat or cold) and endogenous states (e.g., hunger, thirst, and fatigue). In humans, however, emotions encompass not only behavioral responses to stimuli associated with consequences (such as reward or punishment) but also subjective, conscious experiences that are themselves shaped and maintained by those consequences. How individuals deal with their emotions is one of the central themes in psychology and psychotherapy, since difficulties in recognizing, regulating, or expressing emotions are implicated in many forms of psychological distress. Psychotherapeutic work therefore often centers on developing more flexible and adaptive emotional responses.

In terms of measurement of affect and avoidance of affect, few progress monitoring and outcome assessment (PMOA) devices have been created to assess this domain. Because avoidance-related constructs are a transtheoretical factor contributing to treatment failure, feedback that includes systematic information about client avoidance may provide clinicians with an important hypothesis for understanding why clients are failing to improve or worsening. That is, the client may not be improving because she or he is not receiving the full therapeutic intervention, such as experiencing intense negative affect, reflecting on troubling problems, or performing homework. Ongoing assessment, use of feedback-informed methods to track client progress and therapeutic alliance in real time, and outcome monitoring can proactively catch and correct worsening trajectories. Such approaches have been shown to significantly improve retention, reduce deterioration rates by up to 50%, and enhance overall outcomes (Miller et al., 2021; Prescott et al., 2017). This feedback loop, coupled with thorough reassessment when therapy stalls, supports continued progress.

R. Hawkins, S. Meier, *Healing Outcomes*,
https://doi.org/10.1007/978-3-032-33611-8_7

Healing and Emotions

Moderate to high psychological distress is one explanation for why people seek psychotherapy (Howard et al., 1996). Acceptance and Commitment Therapy (ACT) proposes that clinical levels of psychological distress arise not from the presence of negative internal experiences themselves, but from persistent efforts to avoid, suppress, or control them. This process, referred to as *experiential avoidance*, involves attempts to escape unwanted thoughts, emotions, memories, or bodily sensations. This avoidance is subjectively reinforcing even when it interferes with effective functioning or valued life pursuits (Hayes et al., 1996). ACT conceptualizes experiential avoidance as a core pathological process that cuts across diagnostic categories and contributes to the development and maintenance of clinical-level problems.

Theorists have identified avoidance as a core component of specific diagnostic disorders as well as a causal element for a broad range of mental health problems (Gratz et al., 2008; Tull et al., 2004). Kashdan and Breen (2007) observed that excessive social anxiety is related to individuals' "chronic, rigid tendencies to manage and conceal emotional experiences and the situations that elicit them" (p. 2). Avoidance of trauma-related stimuli such as emotions, thoughts, and memories is a major diagnostic criterion for post-traumatic stress disorder (PTSD; American Psychiatric Association, 2022). Hayes et al. (1999) proposed that diverse problem behaviors share a common experiential avoidance function, and research has linked avoidance of negative affect (NA) with the development of problem behaviors (Kingston et al., 2010).

Avoidance of NA is particularly problematic because it tends to produce only short-term relief while increasing long-term distress (Meier, 2014). Efforts to suppress emotions or unwanted thoughts can paradoxically intensify their frequency and emotional impact, a phenomenon supported by research on ironic mental control processes (Wegner, 1994). From an ACT perspective, repeated reliance on avoidance strategies fosters a rigid pattern in which individuals become increasingly preoccupied with controlling their internal experiences rather than engaging adaptively with their environment. Avoidance behaviors are often negatively reinforced because they temporarily reduce distress, but they also prevent emotional learning and adaptation, thereby maintaining symptoms over time.

Experiential avoidance also restricts behavior and reduces access to positive reinforcement. When individuals avoid situations that evoke distress, such as social interactions or challenging tasks, they simultaneously forgo opportunities for connection, achievement, and meaning. Over time, this behavioral narrowing can erode quality of life and contribute to symptoms of depression, anxiety, and related disorders (Kashdan et al., 2006). ACT emphasizes that such patterns reflect a shift away from values-consistent action toward a life organized around the avoidance of discomfort (Hayes et al., 1999). Within ACT, experiential avoidance is a central component of *psychological inflexibility*, a construct that describes behavior governed by attempts to regulate internal experiences rather than by contextual demands or personal values. Psychological inflexibility has been empirically linked to a wide range of clinical problems, including anxiety disorders, depression, substance use disorders, post-traumatic stress disorder, and chronic pain (Chawla & Ostafin, 2007).

Crucially, avoidance appears to have the paradoxical effect of maintaining or even increasing problematic affect, cognitions, and behaviors (Moses & Barlow, 2006). Campbell-Sills and Barlow (2007) reported that thought suppression typically leads to an increase in unwanted thoughts (i.e., a rebound effect). Reviews by Abramowitz et al. (2001) and Wenzlaff and Wegner (2000) concluded that individuals' efforts to suppress unwanted thoughts do indeed produce a larger number of such thoughts. From a behavioral perspective, avoidance behaviors maintain anxiety by preventing individuals from exposure and habituation to what are safe situations (Abramowitz et al., 2012). Peritraumatic dissociation (PD) refers to reactions to traumatic events that include out-of-body experiences, depersonalization, and feeling confused or disoriented. These reactions are thought to be unconscious attempts at regulating affect during traumatic events (Kumpula et al., 2011). Instead of resolution, however, avoidance leads to re-experiencing and hyperarousal around the distressing events long after they occur (Hayes et al., 1999).

The Interplay of Emotion and Reflection

As an alternative to avoidance, ACT promotes acceptance and willingness to experience negative affect as a normal and inevitable part of human life. Acceptance is not resignation, but an active openness to internal experiences as they occur, coupled with committed action guided by personal values. By reducing reliance on avoidance and increasing engagement in meaningful activities, ACT aims to lessen the functional impact of negative affect and enhance psychological flexibility, even in the continued presence of distress (Hayes et al., 1999). To decrease negative affect, we must do the opposite, that is, experience the affect and make sense of it (Hayes et al., 1996; Mergenthaler, 1996).

How might this occur in clinical practice? Mergenthaler's (1996) study of the emotional tone and level of reflection of client statements provides one description of important therapeutic processes that occur as clients move beyond early sessions and engage in psychotherapy. Mergenthaler employed an automated text analysis system to examine therapy transcripts involving (a) a single patient who completed 28 sessions of psychodynamic short-term therapy and (b) 10 improved and 10 non-improved patients in the Penn Psychotherapy Study, using 4 sessions each (2 at the beginning of therapy, 2 at the end) of psychodynamic therapy (Luborsky & Barrett, 2006).

Mergenthaler (1996) found that successful change in therapy depended upon therapeutic cycles that involved shifting between degrees of high and low *emotion* and high and low *abstraction* or *reflection*. As shown in Fig. 7.1, Mergenthaler depicted these combinations as four distinct client states: Therapeutic progress consists of moving in a roughly sequential manner through Relaxing, Experiencing, Connecting, and Reflecting. Clients first build emotion, often by discussing an event

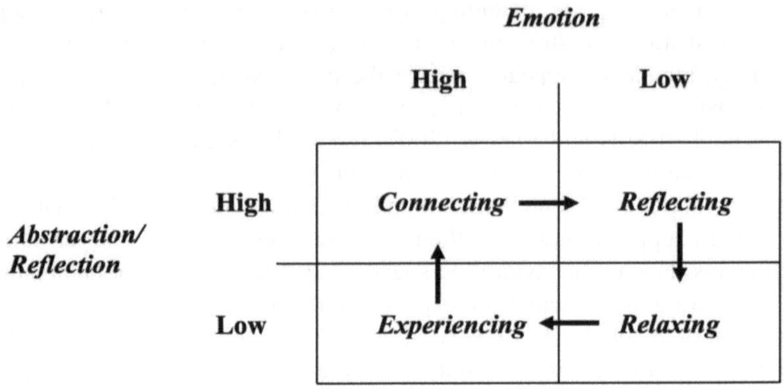

Fig. 7.1 Mergenthaler's sequence of affective–cognitive processing in successful insight-oriented psychotherapy. Progress is characterized by recurring shifts between heightened emotional activation and phases of cognitive reflection and abstraction, allowing emotional material to be integrated into new meanings. Adapted from Mergenthaler (1996), as cited in Meier (2012)

or symptoms, followed by increased reflection, initiated by the therapist or client. Mergenthaler suggested that repeated Connecting states, where clients reflect on emotional material, are particularly important for therapeutic progress. Clients, however, may get caught in intense emotional states or be hindered by defense mechanisms; as noted above, avoidance of intense NA appears to maintain intense NA. Mergenthaler's (1996) analyses of clinical data found that overall, improved clients evidenced a higher proportion of Connecting states and fewer Relaxing states than clients who did not improve. In addition, over the course of therapy, improved clients showed an increasing number of Connecting states, while non-improving clients did not.

Mergenthaler's (1996) research findings also fit with the theory of *affective adaptation*. Wilson and Gilbert (2008) suggested that when experiencing self-relevant, unexplained events that evoke affective reactions, people attempt to understand those events in terms of causes and consequences. Once individuals have such an explanation, they no longer think about the event frequently nor do they have strong affective reactions. Wilson and Gilbert emphasize that by the term "explain," they mean to find meaning in the events, to create an explanation with personal meaning. A major benefit of meaning-making is that it reduces the force of the unexplained event, that is, the individual adapts affectively to the previous troubling event. Once explained, events seem more predictable and controllable in a psychological sense.

As clients deepen and broaden their exploration of emotionally laden content, they begin to make sense of and resolve their problematic situation(s). This exploration and elaboration work is another way of describing a *corrective emotional experience* (Teyber & McClure, 2011) in which clients re-enact and re-experience events in their stories (Anderson, 2004). Greenberg and Angus (2004) reported preliminary results with single therapy cases indicating that "clients' disclosures of emotionally charged personal narratives is foundational to the process of change" (p. 333). When strong feelings are not addressed, however, therapy "stalls and loses meaning" (Teyber & McClure, 2011, p. 186).

Avoidance of Negative Affect

Shifting between affective experiencing and meaning-making can be thwarted by client (and therapist) avoidance. Clients experiencing intense negative affect (NA) may feel like they are surrounded by a consuming fire. Particularly for individuals with high trait NA, describing affectively intense stories about traumas and similar content can feel too intense (Meier, 2019). Client resistance can arise when the therapist leads the client to discuss intense affect when the client feels incapable of doing so. Consequently, avoidance is a pervasive and difficult obstacle to progress in therapy. Psychotherapy approaches describe similar maladaptive methods that individuals employ to regulate emotion, including suppression (i.e., hiding feelings from self or others), social withdrawal, changing situations to alter their impact, use of safety signals (e.g., lucky objects), attention shifting strategies, rationalization, and substance use (Campbell-Sills & Barlow, 2007). Like avoidance, however, these strategies can produce a *rebound effect* (Abramowitz et al., 2001).

The number of avoidance-related constructs described in the psychopathology and psychotherapy literatures attests to its relevance for counseling and psychotherapy processes (Meier, 2014). *Repression*, for example, indicates a desire to avoid processing unpleasant events (Prochaska & Norcross, 2007); similarly, *suppression* refers to efforts to hide one's feelings from oneself and/or others (Campbell-Sills & Barlow, 2007). Shedler (2010) conducted research that identified individuals who consistently deny and repress personal psychological distress; they labeled such individuals *defensive deniers*. Other maladaptive methods employed to regulate emotion include *situational avoidance* and *social withdrawal*, *safety signals* (e.g., lucky objects), *attention shifting strategies*, *rationalization*, and *substance use* (Campbell-Sills & Barlow, 2007). Altering the meaning of threatening or negative events using reinterpretations that are not realistic or evidence-based indicates rationalization (Campbell-Sills & Barlow, 2007). But perhaps the best-known construct is *resistance*, the term many psychotherapists employ to describe a range of phenomena in which clients distract themselves from therapeutic activities and procedures (Beutler et al., 2001; Mitchell, 2013).

Avoidance and Resolving Psychological Problems

Avoidance interferes with the processing of emotional material needed to resolve the psychological consequences of those experiences (Foa & Meadows, 1997). Defensive strategies that individuals use to cope with intrusive memories and intense NA may maintain or increase those processes. Discussing current research on intrusive memories, Berntsen (2010) wrote:

> Any distinctive and highly emotional event will be extraordinarily well encoded and consolidated in memory. This will enhance its accessibility relative to other memories and thus increase the likelihood that it comes to mind involuntarily. (p. 141)

McLaughlin et al. (2007) suggested that "both rumination about past events and worry about potential future events may…play a causal role in the creation of depressed and anxious affect" (p. 24). Depressive rumination, repetitive thoughts that focus on depressive symptoms and their implications, has been found to be related to the development of depression and to increase the length of depressive episodes and intensity of depressive moods (McLaughlin et al., 2007; Nolen-Hoeksema, 1991). In the experimental psychology literature, the cognitive aspect of this phenomenon has been labeled the *Zeigarnik Effect*, the tendency to experience intrusive thoughts about unfinished tasks (Baumeister & Bushman, 2008). Those thoughts are likely to decrease upon completion of an unfinished task, a sequence made more complicated when the task involves processing traumatic events.

Research suggests that avoidance-related factors influence therapeutic outcomes. Foa et al. (1983) found that phobic clients evidenced limited habituation to feared stimuli during treatment sessions, leading to treatment failure. Research has also demonstrated the general efficacy of exposure-related treatments for individuals with PTSD and trauma-related symptoms (e.g., Foa et al., 2009). Deblinger et al. (2011) described a cognitive behavioral therapy employed with sexually abused children that included the development of a therapy narrative to facilitate description and processing of the trauma. In a 16-week program with this component, Deblinger et al. found a reduction of avoidance and reexperiencing symptoms. Andrews et al. (2013) reported the development of the Posttraumatic Avoidance Scale (PAS), a 20-item scale found through factor analysis to measure conscious and unconscious avoidance processes. The PAS may be useful for identifying clients who employ avoidance in therapy as well as the type of avoidance processes, they typically employ.

Detecting Negative Affect and Avoidance of NA

If avoidance is a particularly important impediment to therapeutic progress, then methods of detecting client avoidance, particularly around NA, will be important for adjusting therapeutic processes and improving clinical outcomes. Self-report will be an inappropriate method because clients are unlikely to be fully avoid of their avoidance of negative affect. Consequently, avoidance of NA should be more validly rated by clinicians.

The effects of affective avoidance on therapeutic progress were evaluated during test development studies for a brief measure of NA intensity, the Depression/Anxiety Negative Affect (DANA) scale (Meier, 2012). Designed for PMOA, the clinician-rated DANA is based upon the theoretical and empirically supported idea that as clients improve in therapy, the intensity of their NA decreases (Krampen, 2010; Vermeersch et al., 2000, 2004; Weinstock & Meier, 2003). The DANA includes three scores: (a) the highest intensity level (HIL), the highest NA level endorsed for any NA item for a therapy session; (b) the average intensity level (AIL), the mean intensity for all endorsed items for a session, and (c) total number of NA items (TNA) endorsed in a session.

The DANA's five NA intensity levels scores can range from level 1 (Transient NA) to intensity level 5 (Extreme NA). The rater indicates, by checking any item, that the client has experienced NA at the indicated level. This rating methodology allows the clinician to indicate an intensity level without the need for exact accuracy in terms of the specific NA term chosen (cf. Hesketh et al., 1989). Rather than rate the frequency or intensity of NA terms with a multi-point rating scale (e.g., 1–5), which requires more judgment, DANA raters simply endorse an NA term if observed by the clinician or reported by the client. Raters also complete their NA assessments as soon as possible after a session to minimize memory errors. Paul (1986) noted that *reliability* of an observation decreases when the period between observation of a phenomena and the recording of the observation increases.

Two outpatient samples, with 18 psychotherapists producing a total of 363 session ratings of NA with 81 clients, were employed to evaluate DANA items (Meier, 2012). The clinical samples (i.e., University Counseling Center and Private Practice) consisted of 69% females and 84% Caucasians, with a mean age of 31.5 years. In the Private Practice sample, therapists completed an additional item asking whether the client was "avoiding negative affect" in the rated session. With a possible value of 0 or 1, avoidance ratings were obtained for 151 sessions. A standardized mean difference effect size (ES; Gresham et al., 2010; Rosenthal et al., 2000) was computed for each DANA scale score to assess change from first rated session to last rated session.

Psychometric evaluations indicated that DANA scores demonstrated adequate internal consistency (alpha = 0.76), evidence of convergent and discriminant validity, and sensitivity to change over the course of psychotherapy (Meier, 2012). HIL evidenced the largest ES (0.84), followed by TNA (0.65) and AIL (0.52). Large differences in ES were evident between clients rated them as avoiding or not avoiding NA at their last session. For clients rated as avoiding NA, however, ESs either equaled 0 or decreased, indicating no improvement or worsening (HIL ES = 0, AIL ES = −0.94, and TNA ES = −1.07). In contrast, for clients who did not avoid NA, all ESs were greater than 1, indicating substantial decreases in NA (HIL ES = 1.37, AIL ES = 1.08, and TNA ES = 1.31). Meier (2012) reported that avoidant clients also evidenced high NA levels at their first rated session, with mean scores for HIL above 4 (Intense NA).

More recent research on the working alliance and client distress informed the creation of Version 2 of the DANA. Meier and Seidel (2024) and Meier (2024) found that scores on client alliance and distress measures evidenced different nonlinear relations with client attendance. Rapid increases in alliance scores during initial sessions were associated with larger session counts, while moderate initial distress was associated with greater attendance. Clients whose alliance scores clustered near the top of scale (i.e., a ceiling effect) exhibited most of the observed change over time on the distress measure. Consequently, DANA V2 includes ratings of client distress (highest and lowest within session, on a 0–5 scale) as well as the working alliance (rated as absent, intermittent, or established). To create an unstructured progress note (UPN) for a session, trainee therapists simply entered text at the prompt 'Progress notes' as the last DANA item. Trainee therapists completed the DANA scale immediately after viewing each session.

Can Therapists Detect Avoidance?

Use of the DANA is based upon the assumption that clinicians can provide reliable and valid assessments of NA in their clients. DANA interpretation also assumes that clinicians can provide quality data when assessing NA avoidance as well. The rating task should be facilitated by a relatively high frequency of avoidance expected across diverse client problems, diagnoses, and therapeutic interventions (Campbell-Sills & Barlow, 2007; Mitchell, 2013; Prochaska & Norcross, 2007). If avoidance frequently occurs in psychotherapy, clinicians should notice and report a moderate to high base rate of client avoidance.

Meier (2014) reanalyzed the Meier (2012) avoidance data where eight clinicians provided 151 avoidance ratings (14 missing) with 35 clients. The mean number of sessions rated per therapist in this subsample equaled 20.6 ($SD = 9.2$); 51% of all rated sessions were Sessions 1–5 and 76% of all rated sessions were Sessions 1–10. For all first rated sessions, the mean proportion of sessions where the therapist detected avoidance equaled 0.20 ($SD = 0.41$), indicating that only 20% of first sessions had indications of NA avoidance. For the last rated sessions, the mean equaled 0.19 ($SD = 0.40$). Only one-third (12/35) of clients received at least one avoidance rating across their multiple sessions.

Results suggest an unexpectedly low base rate of reported avoidance. One possibility is that therapists under-reported avoidance in their clients, potentially by failing to detect its occurrence. Congruent with a low rate of clinician-reported NA avoidance, study data evidenced considerable variability in therapists' reports. Of the eight therapists who could have potentially provided an avoidance rating for their client, only five (63%) did so. Of those five, three provided two or more avoidance ratings per client. Almost all therapists (7 of 8, 88%) missed an avoidance rating for at least one client session. Both the avoidance and missed rating ratios display a range of individual differences. Therapists who indicated that their clients never avoided NA also tended to fail to make some avoidance ratings, while therapists who rated clients as more frequently avoiding NA also tended to have the lowest number of missed avoidance ratings. Finally, the total number of DANA items endorsed per session (TNA) was significantly correlated with the presence or absence of an avoidance rating ($r = 0.2$, $p < 0.05$), indicating that a therapist's affirmative avoidance rating for a session was associated with a greater number of DANA terms selected for that session.

Using AI to Improve PMOA

DANA V2.0 included a section for UPNs that were employed to create a *Persistence Table,* a method for representing a matrix of client problems discussed across sessions (Meier, 2024). This table is based on the concept of what Beutler and Hamblin (1986) termed *persistent relevance*, focusing on whether clients' key problem(s) at the beginning of therapy (or whenever they are introduced) remain central to client experience over the subsequent course of therapy. Anecdotally, clinicians have observed that many clients tend to present problems, topics, and themes that they repeatedly discuss across sessions. Clients may also initially present with what they consider more common issues (e.g., trouble studying) and later self-disclose a more sensitive issue (e.g., alcohol abuse or sexual identify).

Emotional reactions to an event increase the likelihood that the event will be remembered (Bowen, 1978). As problems resolve, however, clients stop discussing themes related to people and events that they have processed in therapy (cf. Mergenthaler, 1996). With effective therapy, what may have been a pressing topic when a client began therapy will lose its sense of urgency; other topics may replace the presenting problem, but if the presenting problem has been resolved, the client will be less motivated to discuss it. In general, a decrease in the presentation and length of discussion of a clinically relevant theme, as well as a decrease in negative affect around that theme, suggest that the client is ready for closure on the topic/problem.

Clinical progress notes (from therapist and/or supervisor) can be employed as the source of qualitative data for the tables. Although the content of such notes may vary by therapeutic setting and associated requirements, most therapists include in their notes a summary of key issues per session that can be related to case conceptualization and treatment progress. Using these notes, a persistence table can track the consistency of client themes over time and thus function as a source of data for PMOA. Like self-report PMOA measures, persistence tables should be relatively brief, sensitive to change resulting from psychosocial interventions, and capable of providing treatment feedback relevant to a particular client [Authors]. Because persistence tables depend largely upon the completion of UPNs, their construction should minimize the need for additional time in the PMOA process.

The content in persistence tables should balance (a) parsimony, representing information that can be remembered and acted upon in session, with (b) comprehensiveness, summarizing major clinical issues that should evidence change from therapeutic interventions. If UPNs contain therapeutically relevant information beyond simple documentation of time and attendance, the subsequent persistence table should provide feedback about potential causes of trends observed in progress monitoring and outcome data. Finally, the graphical display in a persistence table offers the advantage of displaying what themes do and do not persist across sessions. Consequently, inspection of a persistence table provides a type of dashboard for a quick summary of important PMOA data.

Meier (2024) evaluated the feasibility and initial results of employing ChatGPT to analyze clinicians' unstructured session progress notes (UPNs) for the purpose of

PMOA. Designed for natural language understanding and generation, ChatGPT has been employed for content creation, code generation, and qualitative analysis (OpenAI, January 31, 2024). In this study, ChatGPT provided qualitative analysis of UPNs produced by 17 graduate therapist trainees for Laila, a simulated client in the HBO series, *In Treatment* (www.hbo.com/in-treatment). ChatGPT performed a content analysis to identify the major themes in UPNs for four psychotherapy sessions. Therapists' session summaries were combined to evaluate the continuation of key clinical themes across the four sessions for this simulated patient. The major themes (and number of cited sessions where the theme occurred) are:

1. **Reluctance to self-disclose and avoidance of negative affect** (4). Because Laila appeared ambivalent about participating in therapy, she frequently avoided expressing or exploring feelings such as anger and hopelessness. This theme was a major topic in all four sessions.
2. **Relationship with grandmother** (4). Laila's grandmother, Rhonda, has been her primary caretaker since Laila was a small child. While deeply caring about Laila, Rhonda has been over-controlling and a source of physical and emotional abuse. This theme was cited in all four sessions.
3. **Girlfriend issues** (4). Laila had a younger girlfriend who was the object of many of her coping fantasies.
4. **Coping strategies** (3). These were methods Laila employed to deal with stress, mostly related to fantasy and escape from her current life.
5. **Racial trauma** (3). Laila and Rhonda described their histories of racism experienced as Black women.
6. **Expressed Negative Affect** (3). While often avoidant, Laila did express NA both verbally and non-verbally.
7. **Therapeutic relationship** (2). UPN content focused on the intermittent quality of the alliance between Laila and Dr. Taylor. While client and therapist appear to experience a bond at times, ruptures also occur. This theme was cited in Session 1 and Session 3.
8. **Suicide** (1). Laila's behaviors raised concerns from her therapist about Laila's potential for suicide at Session 4.

Using DANA V2.0, trainees also provided quantitative ratings per session about the patient's working alliance, negative affect, avoidance of negative affect, and level of distress. Higher alliance ratings were significantly correlated ($p < 0.05$) with less avoidance of NA, higher distress, and higher DANA intensity level. Therapist trainees appeared to interpret Laila's greater expression of NA in later sessions as indicative of improved alliance. Trainees' ratings indicated that Laila evidenced avoidance of NA in initial sessions but expressed more intense NA in Session 3 and Session 4. Working alliance also improved across sessions, moving from initial ratings of absent to intermittent. Based on current research (Meier, 2024; Meier & Seidel, 2024), the alliance data suggest that Laila will continue to attend therapy.

While assessments of lowest distress remained consistent over time, highest distress ratings increased across the four sessions, nearing the top of the scale in Session 3 and Session 4. Similarly, both the total number of endorsed NA descriptors and the highest intensity level (HIL) endorsed increased from Session 1 to Session 4. In previous research, HIL evidenced about a 1 SD improvement (decrease) across an average of 5 sessions, while avoidance of NA also decreased across sessions (Meier, 2012). These quantitative data, at least through Session 4, indicate Laila is not improving in therapy.

The qualitative data in the persistence table and DANA quantitative data indicate convergence and divergence between these sources. Among the provisional conclusions that can be drawn from an examination of the entire set of qualitative and quantitative evidence:

1. Several key themes appear persistent across the four sessions. Laila is beginning to explore and work through these issues and does not appear close to completing her therapeutic work.
2. Laila appeared reluctant to disclose NA and other important content to the therapist in S1–S2 but did express more NA in S3 and S4. Similarly, therapist trainees' DANA ratings of avoidance indicated strong avoidance of NA in S1 and S2, but less avoidance in S3 and S4. Given that NA avoidance is associated with poor therapeutic progress (Meier, 2012), these data suggest that the therapist should continue to help Laila explore, experience, and express clinical material that contains strong NA.
3. As indicated both by persistence table themes and DANA ratings, Laila evidences an intermittent working alliance with her therapist. Within session, she can appear strongly connected to her therapist, while at other times she creates a therapeutic rupture. Given that alliance declines have been associated with early dropout (Mahon et al., 2024), continued attention should be paid to the working alliance.
4. High levels of distress are also associated with early dropout (Meier, 2024; Meier & Seidel, 2024). DANA ratings indicate high distress, but this factor is indirectly mentioned in the UPNs and subsequent persistence table. Laila's discussion of her "Relationship with Grandmother" and "Racial Trauma" reflects her considerable distress, but high distress in general is an important theme for Laila. More attention should be paid in Laila's subsequent therapy to explicitly discussing her intense NA.

In summary, persistent themes related to Laila's reluctance to self-disclose to her therapist and experience negative affect mirrored quantitative data documenting an intermittent working alliance and avoidance of NA. DANA ratings indicating moderate to severe distress, however, were not directly reflected in persistence content. Laila's high distress is particularly important because research indicates that high distress is associated with fewer sessions attended (Meier, 2024; Meier & Seidel, 2024). In Laila's case, she unexpectedly ended therapy after five sessions.

Overall, study results indicate that AI could usefully augment human assessors as part of PMOA. Persistence tables can provide information relevant for clinical feedback, case conceptualization and treatment planning, including readiness for termination. The themes related to Laila's longstanding conflict with her grandmother and her reluctance to self-disclose and experience NA persisted across four sessions. Although few guidelines exist for when to alter a treatment approach, Laila's therapist should begin to consider alternative approaches if these themes persist. In Laila's case, theory and research regarding separation and individuation with adolescents and young adults (Koepke & Denissen, 2012; Moon & Bahn, 2022) may be helpful for understanding Laila's problematic relationship with her grandmother. Consequently, family therapy that includes Laila, her grandmother, and perhaps her father might be a more effective approach (Nichols & Davis, 2020).

The automatic processing of language data (and potentially, nonverbal data) removes major obstacles to the use of PMOA systems. Importantly, ChatGPT and similar applications are accessible to mental health providers in that these programs can process inquiries and provide responses in natural language. While helpful, no statistical or AI expertise is necessary to use ChatGPT. Current PMOA measures primarily employ a self-report methodology, with its limitations related to motivational biases, memory, and varied interpretations of test items, instructions, and response formats (Dohrenwend, 2006; Meier, 2008). Similarly, human coding of psychotherapy-related language and behavior is labor intensive and not feasible in most clinical settings (Atzil-Slonim et al., 2021). In contrast, AI processing is unobtrusive and incidental to the normal discourse that occurs during counseling and psychotherapy. Embedded in an electronic medical record system, for example, AI could provide a low-cost alternative to a human assessor regarding thematic analysis of unstructured progress notes (UPNs). In this study, AI's production of therapy themes also occurred at a more cognitively complex level than the UPNs produced by therapist trainees, which may be related to the quality and utility of assessment interpretations.

Automating the entire set of UPN and persistence table procedures, however, could reduce the reflection component of the PMOA process, including case conceptualization and treatment planning. While analysis of UPNs and persistence tables can be time-consuming, it also provides therapists and assessors an opportunity to reflect on whether provided interventions have influenced client progress. In Laila's case, for example, she prematurely terminated after the fifth session. Attention to Laila's persistence table might have alerted the therapist to this possibility and initiated a review of the case conceptualization and treatment plan. Keeping a human assessor in the analysis process might make the most sense when employing UPNs for case review and supervision, particularly when treatment failure and premature termination are indicated in the assessment feedback.

ChatGPT's production of themes per session reflects clinically relevant information that can be (a) the focus of psychosocial intervention and (b) suggest an approximate time frame for therapy length. Laila's therapy should continue to focus on the "Grandmother Relationship" in the context of her "Reluctance to Self-Disclose" and "Avoidance of NA." Laila's long history of abuse at the hands of her grandmother, as well as Laila's difficulty in talking about these experiences, suggest that a substantial number of additional sessions are likely necessary to make progress. This interpretation also fits with the findings of empirically based psychotherapy phase theories that indicate improving relationships with significant others should be considered long-term goals that typically require a substantial dose of therapy sessions (Howard et al., 1993).

Summary

In the systems-contextual integrative model (SCIM), the Healing Cycle (HC), equivalent to Mergenthaler's (1996) therapeutic cycle as described earlier in this chapter, serves as the core clinical process through which therapists help clients modify dysfunctional patterns across the socio-ecological context, particularly at the micro and meso levels. Each repetition of the HC strengthens therapeutic gains along with greater emotional and experiential awareness, hope, faith, and love, and improved coherence in clients' personal narratives. Clinically, identifying emotions and their associated meanings related to significant people and events helps organize treatment priorities, guides in-session interventions, and supports the resolution of psychological difficulties while activating clients' existing strengths in therapy and daily life.

Given the consistent finding that feedback from progress monitoring (PM) data decreases treatment failure, clinicians should consider incorporating PM measures that provide information about negative affect and avoidance. In addition to relevant psychometric properties (e.g., evidence of reliability and change-sensitivity), clinicians should prefer PM measures that provide theoretical information directly applicable to treatment adjustment such as the DANA (with its avoidance rating) and the Session Rating Scale (which assesses the therapeutic alliance; Miller et al., 2003). Although self-reports may be a brief and efficient method for gathering PM information, they may be influenced by frequent, repeated use; that is, test scores may evidence improvement from practice effects rather than from any intervention. Self-reports also appear to be a poor choice for assessing avoidance-related constructs since avoidance often involves a lack of awareness on the part of the avoidant individual. While clinician ratings may be a more valid method of obtaining some types of clinical data (Shedler, 2010), these require additional clinician time. Clinicians differ in their ability to identify constructs such as avoidance, suggesting a need for training that provides a rationale for performing avoidance assessments.

References

Abramowitz, J. S., Deacon, B. J., & Whiteside, S. P. H. (2012). Exposure therapy for anxiety..

Abramowitz, J. S., Tolin, D. F., & Street, G. P. (2001). Paradoxical effects of thought suppression: A meta-analysis of controlled studies. *Clinical Psychology Review, 21*, 683–703. https://doi.org/10.1016/S0272-7358(00)00057-X

American Psychiatric Association. (2022). *Diagnostic and statistical manual of mental disorders* (5th ed., text rev.). doi:https://doi.org/10.1176/appi.books.9780890425787.

Anderson, H. (2004). Collaborative relationships and dialogic conversations: Ideas for a relationally responsive practice. In L. E. Heatherington & G. Friedlander (Eds.), *Family psychology: Science-based interventions* (pp. 399–415). American Psychological Association.

Andrews, L., Joseph, S., Troop, N., Van Rooyen, T., Dunn, B. D., & Dalgleish, T. (2013). The structure of avoidance following trauma: Development and validation of the Posttraumatic Avoidance Scale (PAS). *Traumatology, 19*(2), 126–135. https://doi.org/10.1177/1534765612455225

Atzil-Slonim, D., Bar-Kalifa, E., Fisher, H., Peri, T., Lutz, W., Rubel, J., & Rafaeli, E. (2021). Emotional congruence between clients and therapists and its effect on treatment outcome. *Journal of Consulting and Clinical Psychology, 89*(4), 341–351. https://doi.org/10.1037/cou0000250

Baumeister, R. F., & Bushman, B. J. (2008). *Social psychology and human nature*. Thomson Wadsworth.

Berntsen, D. (2010). The unbidden past: Involuntary autobiographical memories as a basic mode of remembering. *Current Directions in Psychological Science, 19*, 138–142. https://doi.org/10.1177/0963721410370301

Beutler, L. E., & Hamblin, D. L. (1986). Individualized outcome measures of internal change: Methodological considerations. *Journal of Consulting and Clinical Psychology, 54*, 48–53. doi:10.1037/0022-006X.54.1.48.

Beutler, L. E., Rocco, F., Moleiro, C. M., & Talebi, H. (2001). Resistance. *Psychotherapy, 38*, 431–435. https://doi.org/10.1037/0033-3204.38.4.431

Bowen, M. (1978). *Family therapy in clinical practice*. Aronson.

Campbell-Sills, L., & Barlow, D. H. (2007). Incorporating emotion regulation into conceptualizations and treatments of anxiety and mood disorders. In J. J. Gross (Ed.), *Handbook of emotion regulation* (pp. 542–559). Guilford.

Chawla, N., & Ostafin, B. (2007). Experiential avoidance as a functional dimensional approach to psychopathology: An empirical review. *Journal of Clinical Psychology, 63*(9), 871–890. https://doi.org/10.1002/jclp.20400

Deblinger, E., Mannarino, A. P., Cohen, J. A., Runyon, M. K., & Steer, R. A. (2011). Trauma-focused cognitive behavioral therapy for children: Impact of the trauma narrative and treatment length. *Depression and Anxiety, 28*, 67–75. https://doi.org/10.1002/da.20744

Dohrenwend, B. P. (2006). Inventorying stressful life events as risk factors for psychopathology: Toward resolution of intracategory variability. *Psychological Bulletin, 132*, 477–495. https://doi.org/10.1037/0033-2909.132.3.477

Foa, E. B., Grayson, J. B., Steketee, G. S., Doppelt, H. G., Turner, R. M., & Latimer, P. R. (1983). Success and failure in the behavioral treatment of obsessive-compulsives. *Journal of Consulting and Clinical Psychology, 51*(2), 287–297. https://doi.org/10.1037/0022-006X.51.2.287

Foa, E. B., & Meadows, E. A. (1997). Psychosocial treatments for posttraumatic stress disorder: A critical review. *Annual Review of Psychology, 48*, 449–480. https://doi.org/10.1146/annurev.psych.48.1.449

Foa, E. B., Keane, T. M., Friedman, M. J., & Cohen, J. A. (2009). Effective treatments for PTSD (2nd ed.). New York: Guildford.

Gratz, K. L., Tull, M. T., & Gunderson, J. G. (2008). Preliminary data on the relationship between anxiety sensitivity and borderline personality disorder: The role of experiential avoidance. *Journal of Psychiatric Research, 742*, 550–559. https://doi.org/10.1016/j.jpsychires.2007.05.011

Greenberg, L. S., & Angus, L. E. (2004). The contributions of emotion processes to narrative chance in psychotherapy: A dialectical constructivist approach. In L. E. Angus & J. McLeod (Eds.), *The handbook of narrative and psychotherapy* (pp. 331–364). Sage. https://doi.org/10.4135/9781412973496.d25

Gresham, F. M., Cook, C. R., Collins, T., Dart, E., Rasetshwane, K., Truelson, E., & Grant, S. (2010). Developing a change-sensitive brief behavior rating scale as a progress monitoring tool for social behavior: An example using the social skills rating system-teacher form. *School Psychology Review, 39*, 364–379. https://doi.org/10.1080/02796015.2010.12087758

Hayes, S. C., Strosahl, K. D., & Wilson, K. G. (1999). *Acceptance and commitment therapy: An experiential approach to behavioral change*. Guilford.

Hayes, S. C., Wilson, K. G., Gifford, E. V., Follette, V. M., & Strosahl, K. (1996). Experiential avoidance and behavioral disorders: A functional dimensional approach to diagnosis and treatment. *Journal of Consulting and Clinical Psychology, 64*, 1152–1168. https://doi.org/10.1037/0022-006X.64.6.1152

Hesketh, B., Pryor, R., & Gleitzman, M. (1989). Fuzzy logic: Toward measuring Gottfredson's concept of occupational social space. *Journal of Counseling Psychology, 36*(1), 103–109. https://doi.org/10.1037/0022-0167.36.1.103

Howard, K. I., Lueger, R. J., Maling, M. S., & Martinovich, Z. (1993). A phase model of psychotherapy: Causal mediation of outcome. *Journal of Consulting and Clinical Psychology, 61*, 678–685. https://doi.org/10.1037/0022-006X.61.4.678

Howard, K. I., Moras, K., Brill, P. L., Martinovich, Z., & Lutz, W. (1996). The evaluation of psychotherapy: Efficacy, effectiveness, and patient progress. *American Psychologist, 51*, 1059–1064. https://doi.org/10.1037/0003-066X.51.10.1059

Kashdan, T. B., Barrios, V., Forsyth, J. P., & Steger, M. F. (2006). Experiential avoidance as a generalized psychological vulnerability: Comparisons with coping and emotion regulation strategies. *Behaviour Research and Therapy, 44*(9), 1301–1320. https://doi.org/10.1016/j.brat.2005.10.003

Kashdan, T. B., & Breen, W. E. (2007). Social anxiety and positive emotions: A prospective examination of a self-regulatory model with tendencies to suppress or express emotions as a moderating variable. *Behavior Therapy, 39*, 1–12. https://doi.org/10.1016/j.beth.2007.02.003

Kingston, J., Clarke, S., & Remington, B. (2010). Experiential avoidance and problem behavior: A mediational analysis. *Behavior Modification, 34*(2), 145–163. https://doi.org/10.1177/0145445510362575

Koepke, S., & Denissen, J. J. A. (2012). Dynamics of identity development and separation individuation in parent-child relationships during adolescence and emerging adulthood–A conceptual integration. *Developmental Review, 32*, 67–88. https://doi.org/10.1016/j.dr.2012.01.001

Krampen, G. (2010). Direct measurement of psychotherapeutic outcomes: Experimental construction and validation of a brief scale. *Psychological Test and Assessment Modeling, 52*, 29–47.

Kumpula, M. J., Orcutt, H. K., Bardeen, J. R., & Varkovitzky, R. L. (2011). Peritraumatic dissociation and experiential avoidance as prospective predictors of posttraumatic stress symptoms. *Journal of Abnormal Psychology, 120*, 617–627. https://doi.org/10.1037/a0023927

Luborsky, L., & Barrett, M. S. (2006). The history and empirical status of key psychoanalytic concepts. *Annual Review of Clinical Psychology, 2*, 1–19. https://doi.org/10.1146/annurev.clinpsy.2.022305.095328

Mahon, D., Minami, T., & Brown, J. (2024). Predicting treatment success and failure using routine outcome data: The role of therapist effects in dynamic predictive modeling. *Counselling and Psychotherapy Research*, e12827. https://doi.org/10.1002/capr.12827

McLaughlin, K. A., Borkovec, T. D., & Sibrava, N. J. (2007). The effects of worry and rumination on affect states and cognitive activity. *Behavior Therapy, 38*, 23–38. https://doi.org/10.1016/j.beth.2006.03.003

Meier, S. T. (2008). Measuring change in counseling and psychotherapy. New York: Guilford.

Meier, S. T. (2012). Nomothetic outcome assessment in counseling and psychotherapy: Development and preliminary psychometric analyses of the depression/anxiety negative affect scale. *Psychological Test and Assessment Modeling, 54*, 343–362.

Meier, S. T. (2014). Rediscovering the role of avoidance in counseling and psychotherapy. *Professional Psychology, 45*, 212–217. https://doi.org/10.1037/a0036916

Meier, S. T. (2019). Elevated trait anxiety: Obstacle to progress with female clients? *Professional Psychology: Research and Practice, 50*, 33–38. https://doi.org/10.1037/pro0000211

Meier, S. T. (2024). Initial evaluation of an AI-augmented progress monitoring and outcome assessment. *Counselling and Psychotherapy Research, 25*, e12869. https://doi.org/10.1002/capr.12869

Meier, S. T., & Seidel, J. (2024). A partial test of the early therapeutic environment model: Association of working alliance and distress with client attendance variables. *Journal of Psychotherapy Integration, 34*, 145–160. https://doi.org/10.1037/int0000323

Mergenthaler, E. (1996). Emotion-abstraction patterns in verbatim protocols: A new way of describing psychotherapeutic processes. *Journal of Consulting and Clinical Psychology, 64*, 1306–1315. https://doi.org/10.1037/0022-006X.64.6.1306

Miller, S. D., Duncan, B. L., Brown, J., Sparks, J. A., & Claud, D. A. (2003). The outcome rating scale: A preliminary study of the reliability, validity, and feasibility of a brief visual analog measure. *Journal of Brief Therapy, 2*(2), 91–100.

Miller, S. D., Hubble, M. A., & Chow, D. (2021). *Better results: Using deliberate practice to improve therapeutic effectiveness*. American Psychological Association Press. https://doi.org/10.1037/0000191-000

Mitchell, C. W. (2013). Reducing resistance in psychotherapy. In G. P. Koocher, J. C. Norcross, & B. A. Greene (Eds.), *Psychologists' desk reference* (3rd ed., pp. 258–262). Oxford University Press. https://doi.org/10.1093/med:psych/9780199845491.003.0053

Moon, D-S., & Bahn, G-H. (2022). The concept of synchronization in the process of separation-individuation between a parent and an adolescent. *Journal of the Korean Academy of Child and Adolescent Psychiatry, 33*, 41–47. https://doi.org/ 10.5765/jkacap.220003.

Moses, E. B., & Barlow, D. B. (2006). A new unified treatment approach for emotional disorders based on emotion science. *Current Directions in Psychological Science, 15*, 146–150. https://doi.org/10.1111/j.0963-7214.2006.00425.x

Nichols, M. P., & Davis, S. D. (2020). *Family therapy: Concepts and methods* (12th ed.). Pearson.

Nolen-Hoeksema, S. (1991). Responses to depression and their effects on the duration of depressive episodes. *Journal of Abnormal Psychology, 100*, 569–582. https://doi.org/10.1037/0021-843X.100.4.569

Paul, G. L. (Ed.) (1986). Assessment in residential treatment settings. Champaign, IL: Research Press.

Prescott, D., Maeschalck, C., & Miller, S. D. (Eds.). (2017). *Feedback informed treatment in clinical practice*. American Psychological Association Press. https://doi.org/10.1037/0000039-000

Prochaska, J. O., & Norcross, J. C. (2007). *Systems of psychotherapy*. Thomson.

Rosenthal, R., Rosnow, R. L., & Rubin, D. (2000). *Contrasts and effect sizes in behavioral research: A correlational approach*. Cambridge University Press. https://doi.org/10.1017/CBO9780511804403

Shedler, J. (2010). The efficacy of psychodynamic psychotherapy. *American Psychologist, 65*, 98–109. https://doi.org/10.1037/a0018378

Teyber, E., & McClure, F. H. (2011). *Interpersonal process in therapy: An integrative model* (6th ed.). Brooks/Cole.

Tull, M. T., Gratz, K. L., Salters, K., & Roemer, L. (2004). The role of experiential avoidance in posttraumatic stress symptoms and symptoms of depression, anxiety, and somatization. *Journal of Nervous and Mental Disease, 192*, 754–761. https://doi.org/10.1097/01.nmd.0000144694.30121.89

Vermeersch, D. A., Lambert, M. J., & Burlingame, G. M. (2000). Outcome questionnaire: Item sensitivity to change. *Journal of Personality Assessment, 74*, 242–261. https://doi.org/10.1207/S15327752JPA7402_6

Vermeersch, D. A., Whipple, J. L., Lambert, M. J., Hawkins, E. J., Burchfield, C. M., & Okiishi, J. C. (2004). Outcome questionnaire: Is it sensitive to changes in counseling center clients? *Journal of Counseling Psychology, 51*, 38–49. https://doi.org/10.1037/0022-0167.51.1.38

Wegner, D. M. (1994). Ironic processes of mental control. *Psychological Review, 101*(1), 34–52.

Weinstock, M., & Meier, S. T. (2003). A comparison of two item selection methodologies for measuring change in university counseling center clients. *Measurement and Evaluation in Counseling & Development, 36*, 66–75. https://doi.org/10.1080/07481756.2003.12069082

Wenzlaff, R. M., & Wegner, D. M. (2000). Thought suppression. *Annual Review of Psychology, 51*, 59–91. https://doi.org/10.1146/annurev.psych.51.1.59

Wilson, T. D., & Gilbert, D. T. (2008). Explaining away: A model of affective adaptation. *Perspectives on Psychological Science, 3*, 370–386. https://doi.org/10.1111/j.1745-6924.2008.00085.x

Chapter 8
Measuring Common Factors: Working Alliance, Client Expectations, and Client Distress

Introduction

Our systems-contextual integrative model (SCIM) can be construed as being consistent with the common factor (CF) model in that the Trauma Cycle, the Healing Cycle, and the degree of flexibility in shifting between them are common dynamic systemic processes that cut across psychological disorders and may predict healing outcomes. Moreover, the SCIM requires measurement of specific outcome variables and core process variables in addition to more general outcomes such as improvements in client distress and meaning in life, although more research is needed to discover the mechanisms underlying these processes.

Common Factors Research

Decades of research and clinical practice have suggested that a relatively small group of causal factors influence client progress and outcomes across all types of therapy, therapists, and clients (Bailey & Ogles, 2023; Wampold, 2001). Frank et al. (2025) suggested that the benefits of counseling derive not simply from specific techniques associated with different schools, but from elements common to all therapeutic approaches. These are referred to as common factors (CFs) and are often contrasted with specific factors thought to be operating when therapists apply conceptualizations and interventions from a particular therapeutic school. Proponents of a CF approach point to the findings of psychotherapy outcome studies that indicate that all approaches have approximately equal effects (Smith & Glass, 1977). Studies have also found that clients may evidence improvement even before an active (specific) intervention is introduced (cf., Kelly et al., 2005; Meier, 2026).

R. Hawkins, S. Meier, *Healing Outcomes*,
https://doi.org/10.1007/978-3-032-33611-8_8

While no consensus exists about an exact list of CFs, most theorists propose a small group of process factors thought to influence outcomes (Bailey & Ogles, 2023; Twomey et al., 2023). We describe three common *process* factors: Working alliance, client outcome expectations, and client self-efficacy expectations. The alliance is "the holistic collaborative aspects of the therapist-client relationship" (Flückiger et al., 2018, p. 2). Outcome expectations describe client cognitions about the link between actions and outcomes (Constantino et al., 2018). If clients do not believe that therapy will produce desired outcomes, for example, they are more likely to drop out. Self-efficacy expectations reflect an individual's sense of competence for performing behaviors necessary for desired outcomes (Bandura, 1977, 1989). Each of these elements will be described in this chapter.

Over 30 years of meta-analyses of psychotherapy outcome have found that considerably more of the variance in outcome is attributable to common factors (30%) than to specific treatment effects (15%) (e.g., Lambert, 2005). Cuijpers et al. (2019), however, recently concluded that the current meta-analyses do not substantiate that CFs account for more variance than specific treatment factors, and, more sobering, the evidence for causal mediation by specific treatments is also not well established:

> To date, research on the working mechanisms and mediators of therapies has always been correlational, and in order to establish that a mediator is indeed a causal factor in the recovery process of a patient, studies must show a temporal relationship between the mediator and an outcome, a dose–response association, evidence that no third variable causes changes in the mediator and the outcome, supportive experimental research, and have a strong theoretical framework (Cuijpers et al., 2019, p. 207).

Thus, what is needed are empirical studies showing that changes in the mediator(s), whether a specific core process such as anxiety sensitivity or a common factor such as the therapeutic alliance, occur before changes in the treatment outcome measure.

Therapeutic Alliance

The working alliance is important in CF models because a substantial body of evidence documents the moderate positive effect of the client's perception of the working alliance on subsequent client outcomes in individual psychotherapy (Flückiger et al., 2018). Flückiger et al. (2018) found an effect size (ES) of 0.28 between scores on working alliance and outcome measures. While the link between alliance and outcomes is an important finding, Tilden et al. (2021, p. 1) observed that "the current challenge in our field is to gain a more nuanced understanding of alliance's impact on the progress of treatment over the course of therapy." One of those challenging areas is client attrition, which often occurs at roughly the same time in counseling that when alliance is forming (Sharf et al., 2010).

Researchers have frequently reported ceiling effects with alliance measures (Babatunde et al., 2017; Paap et al., 2020; Reese et al., 2013), although the interpretation of what these signify has remained unclear. Ceiling effects occur when a substantial number of scores cluster near the top of a scale rather than being normally distributed. Meier and Feeley (2021) studied scores on alliance measures reported in two meta-analyses (Flückiger et al., 2020; Harris et al., 2019). Based on a total of 92 estimates of ceiling effects found in 37 studies with 6439 participants, moderate-to-large ceiling effects appeared across multiple measures of client-rated alliance, time administered, and different sample characteristics such as gender, age, and ethnicity.

While the working alliance has typically been defined in terms of theoretical content such as tasks, goals, and bond, based on Bordin's (1979) work, the findings of Meier and Feeley (2021) regarding ceiling effects suggest another key element may be its threshold structure. Here clients shift from initial, neutral interactions with a therapist to a bond that clients experience as established. The distribution of alliance scores reported by Meier and Feeley suggested that alliance development is not gradual or incremental but instead is nonlinear and occurs abruptly and early in therapy for many clients. For at least some clients, this holistic experience does not appear to unfold or develop gradually; instead it functions more like a switch that must be ON before therapy can effectively proceed from the client's perspective.

Meier and Feeley (2021) created displays of ceiling effects evident on scores of a popular alliance measure, the visual analogue Session Rating Scale (SRS; Duncan et al., 2003; Miller et al., 2005). Using 22 ceiling effect estimates from multiple SRS studies, they found a Pearson correlation equal to 0.60 ($p < 0.01$) between ceiling effects and session number. This result indicates that mean SRS scores began near the scale ceiling at initial sessions and increased by small increments over time. Data reported by Owen et al. (2016) best display this relation in comparison to other studies. Owen et al. (2016) reported SRS data in a complete case analysis across seven sessions where data reflect SRS means per session for the same set of clients; the correlation between ceiling effect and session number equaled 0.92 ($p < 0.01$).

Expectations

Outcome expectations and self-efficacy expectations. Researchers have long recognized the potential importance of client expectations in counseling (e.g., Tinsley & Harris, 1976). A well-studied aspect of client cognition (Constantino et al., 2018), client outcome expectations are beliefs about *what* behaviors and actions will lead to desired outcomes, while client self-efficacy expectations refer to beliefs that individuals can *perform* the behaviors and actions that will lead to those desired outcomes. If clients understand what they need to do in therapy to meet their goals and produce desired outcomes (outcome expectations) and believe they can perform those acts (self-efficacy expectations), they experience hope. Hope is a strong motivating factor for clients to persist in counseling even when they encounter internal and external obstacles.

Constantino et al. (2018) examined the relation between early outcome expectations and post-treatment outcomes in a meta-analysis that summarized research results employing 12,722 patients from 81 independent samples. They reported an overall r of 0.18, indicating a small, positive effect for outcome expectations. Testing moderators of this relation, Constantino et al. found an effect for age (i.e., the correlation decreased with increasing age), psychometric evidence for measures used (lower correlation with measures lacking psychometric data), and use of a treatment manual (lower correlation in studies with no manual). Constantino et al. also reviewed studies indicating that (a) outcome expectations can positively influence the working alliance, which then relates to better outcomes, and (b) alliance and expectations can evidence bidirectional influence.

Self-efficacy expectations and outcomes. To the extent that therapeutic participation can be conceptualized in terms of client behaviors necessary to produce desired outcomes, then another potentially important source of client expectations may be individuals' self-efficacy for performing therapy-related activities (Bandura, 1977, 1997). Given that clients must perform psychotherapy-related behaviors that are challenging as well as unfamiliar to many in their daily life, self-efficacy expectations for such behaviors are likely to influence initiation of and persistence in therapy. Depending upon the client and type of therapy, this list of psychotherapy-related behaviors includes disclosing negative characteristics about self and others, experiencing emotionally intense events, verbalizing and processing painful feelings, exposure to feared situations, performing challenging behaviors outside of therapy, questioning long-standing beliefs, and negotiating conflict and disruptions in personal relationships, including the client–therapist relationship.

Some research indicates that self-efficacy expectations are often more potent than outcome expectations for influencing behavior (Bandura, 1977, 1997). Surprisingly few studies, however, have examined client expectations for performing therapeutic activities. Studying 139 undergraduates who sought therapy at a university counseling center, Longo et al. (1992) created 20 items to assess self-efficacy for therapeutic activities in three areas: (a) Ability to perform such in-person behaviors as emotional expression, (b) ability to manage barriers related to therapy attendance, such as schedule conflicts, and (c) ability to take initiative in solving problems. Longo et al. also included a test of outcome expectations about counseling (e.g., "I expect that counseling will help me to be less anxious and tense"). Results indicated that self-efficacy expectations were the primary variable discriminating clients who dropped out of counseling versus those who persisted.

Self-efficacy expectations also indicate how clients can generalize change beyond the therapy setting. A student may understand that she needs to study 20 hours to receive a grade of "A" on an exam. The self-efficacy judgment question in this case is, "Can I study 20 hours for this exam?" Perhaps the student expects that she can only focus her time and attention for 10 hours. Research indicates that *performance accomplishments* are the strongest method for changing self-efficacy (Bandura, 1997). Performance accomplishments refer to successful completion of tasks relevant to the self-efficacy judgment at hand. The student who needs to study 20 hours is likely to perceive high self-efficacy for this task if she has had experience studying 10 hours for multiple periods. Performing the behaviors in question is the most effective approach of changing expectations and narratives in a particular domain.

A second source for influencing self-efficacy expectations is *vicarious experience*: inferring one's self-efficacy based on another's performance on a behavior of interest. Thus, a college student may infer that he may be able to study 20 hours for a test when he observes a roommate do so. The extent to which one infers self-efficacy from observing others, however, depends on the similarity between model and self. Houston et al. (2011), for example, employed culturally appropriate stories of lifestyle changes needed to reduce blood pressure, related by African American individuals on DVDs, and found that such viewing led to statistically significant improvements in Black patients. The performance of persons perceived as very dissimilar from oneself, however, may have little information regarding one's own competencies.

A Self-Efficacy Example

One option for measuring self-efficacy expectations is to record self-efficacy qualitatively as part of progress notes. Guyker (2006) described a 19-year-old Caucasian, heterosexual female who presented at a counseling center with mild depression after a series of academic and personal stressful events. The therapist conceptualized the client as having low self-efficacy for coping with interpersonal problems and a history of low self-esteem; these contributed to the client's ongoing anxiety and depression. The therapist decided to track client statements related to self-efficacy for interpersonal problems (e.g., low assertiveness) and record these in progress notes for ten therapy sessions. Table 8.1 displays examples of the identified self-efficacy themes and associated client statements.

Examination of the content of Table 8.1 suggests that the client frequently expressed a belief that important events in her life were out of her control. In Session 9, for example, she indicates that she has "bad luck" and "a lack of control." In initial sessions, she indicates that she feels unable to do anything in unfavorable situations; she even has difficulty remembering events in which she participated. These descriptions suggest that concepts related to *locus of control* (Rotter, 1966) or a lack of *outcome expectations* (Bandura, 1977) might be better descriptions for this client than self-efficacy per se. Locus of control refers to whether a person believes she or he can influence or affect important events. For persons with an external locus of control (compared to an internal locus), luck and significant others have more influence than the individual. Outcome expectations are beliefs about what behaviors lead to desired outcomes. In this client's case, she appeared to believe that she had little influence with important persons and events in her life, beliefs worthy of further exploration in therapy.

Table 8.1 Qualitative analysis of self-efficacy themes

Session	Themes and Examples
1	Ambivalence toward counseling
	"I know I should do this [counseling], so I'm glad I have to do it."
	Catastrophic thoughts
	"Everything [last semester] was just a mess"
	Difficulty in recalling self-involvement (e.g., *when asked about things that went well for client last semester, client reported, "I don't know. I don't really remember. I remember more about other people than myself."*
2	Perception of inability to do something about an unfavorable situation
	"I just have to wait for him to bring it up."
3	Feelings of happiness when client acquired information by action-taking
	Self-report of feeling based on how people around her are doing
	"I'm really relieved that my problems aren't as bad as [my friend's]… makes me feel like everything I'm going through isn't really that bad."
4	Simply "going with the flow"
	Internal causal attribution
	"I was mean to him over break. That's probably why he didn't come around for a while… I wonder how things would have been different over the past few months if I hadn't said all that."
	Fear of being put in a situation where she feels forced to say yes
	Reported habitual feeling of "not knowing"
5	Expressing happiness/satisfaction over being self-assertive and expressive of own feelings
6	Feeling that counseling has been helpful for her to stop and see what's gone on throughout week and being able to recognize her actions admiration and attraction toward those who do possess self-confidence
	Hope that intoxication will help client express herself
7	Inability to recall how time is spent when client is not in class or at work
	Externalizing
	"I like to avoid drama, but I feel like it just finds me."
8	Helplessness
9	Feeling like she has "bad luck" with situations, feeling like this is unfair and feeling a lack of control
10	Pro-active, identification of areas for improvement, identification of own strengths

Note. Client themes are reported per session, with paraphrases of client quotes in italics

Distress and Remoralization

While alliance and expectations are process factors that influence outcomes, research suggests that for at least initial sessions, a CF related to outcome exists (Meier, 2024). Research supports that clients' *distress* provides motivation for participation in therapy (e.g., Al-Jabari et al., 2019; Anderson et al., 2019). Distress refers to negative affective (NA) states that include feelings such as anxiety, depression, and stress (Campbell-Sills & Barlow, 2007). Initially, clients' subjective experience of distress motivates them to seek therapy (Howard et al., 1996). Once the client contacts a therapist or another representative of the therapy agency (Zilcha-Mano, 2025), the individual begins to establish a working alliance and learn about the behaviors necessary to meet therapeutic goals. Because many clients enter counseling because they are experiencing significant distress, as a result, reduction of distress is a key short-term outcome for many clients. Howard et al. (1996) suggested that therapy participants are initially demoralized: They feel hopeless, unable to cope, and desperate about their personal problems. Modulating client distress to moderate levels appears important to helping clients remain in therapy longer (Meier & Seidel, 2024). Many clients experience substantial decreases in distress after only one or two sessions (Kopta et al., 1994).

Meier et al. (2015) investigated outpatients' self-reports of psychological symptoms and functioning during early sessions of psychotherapy, when the largest amount of change appears (Sperry et al., 1996). Employing a sample of 772 university counseling center clients, they examined clients' relative endorsement of Behavioral Health Questionnare-20 items (BHQ; Kopta & Lowry, 2002) at the start of therapy, as well as which items exhibited the largest change across sessions 1–6. Meier et al. examined effect sizes (ES) for change from Sessions 1–2, Sessions 2–3, and Sessions 3–6. ES was calculated by subtracting item means from the compared sessions and then dividing by the first session's standard deviation. Meier et al. (2015) found that the distress item ("How distressed have you been?") evidenced the largest change from Session 1 to Session 2 (ES = 0.57).

Kopta et al. (1994) found similar results in their study of the SCL-90-R, a widely used symptom checklist. Psychotherapy outpatients' scores on SCL items evidenced three rates of change: (a) acute, that showed a quick response to treatment, (b) chronic, with a moderate response rate, and (c) characterological items, with a slow response rate. The content of acute items included anxiety, depression, and obsessive-compulsive symptoms. Changes in distress early in therapy also fit well with the empirical findings of phase models of psychotherapy: Reducing client distress early in treatment may be crucial to improving clients' sense of hope (i.e., remoralization), satisfaction with therapist and/or treatment, and initial progress (Callahan et al., 2006; Prochaska & Norcross, 2013). Improvements in intermediate and long-term outcomes, however, may not be evident until a more substantial amount of therapy has been completed (Lambert, 2007).

Common factors such as the installation of hope (i.e., remoralization) and the importance of therapeutic relationship also fit with narrative formulations. Narrative therapists believe that when people's lived experiences do not match well with their dominant narratives, this causes distress and provides motivation to seek therapy. In many cases, the client expresses distress initially in therapy by wondering if they are "crazy" or "abnormal." With these clients, competent therapists often start the first session or two by normalizing the client's experiences, typically by providing a therapeutically sound narrative to account for the client's demoralizing events. If accepted by the client, the normalizing narrative, which typically includes a plan and rationale to address the client's presenting problems, is likely to result in a remoralization or installation of hope in the client. The process may become automatic for competent therapists, who routinely produce an alternative narrative for new clients to use to explain their distress.

Client Attendance and Attrition

To employ a medical metaphor, psychotherapy sessions are the primary method by which therapists provide the curative dose of talking therapy (Barkham et al., 2006). Given this premise, factors that influence client attendance and engagement in counseling and psychotherapy are critical to understand why clients begin and remain in therapy (Ong et al., 2018; Wierzbicki & Pekarik, 1993).

One important finding is that many clients who drop out do so quickly (Barrett et al., 2008; Swift & Greenberg, 2012). A relatively large number of clients attend only one session, and a smaller number of clients attend many sessions. In some clinical samples, one-third of clients attend only one session and the median number of sessions attended ranges from three to six (Goldberg et al., 2016; Hansen et al., 2002). Krendl and Lorenzo-Luaces (2022) found that of 264 potential clients who initiated contact at a university mental health training clinic, over half did not schedule an intake and about two-thirds of those placed on a waitlist did not schedule an intake. Only a quarter of the sample completed therapy.

Structural obstacles, such as transportation, cost, and lack of time, hinder attendance for many. These factors can be more important than emotional barriers such as discomfort with talking about problems with a therapist (Bugatti et al., 2023; Mohr et al., 2006). The Mohr et al. (2010) study with a large clinical sample found that cost, time constraints, misfit of therapy to client needs, availability of services, stigma, and emotional concerns were also related to attendance. Although such structural obstacles can occur at any point, they are most likely to be important during early counseling sessions. Other factors related to client characteristics, such as the degree to which male clients identify with traditional male identity, can also influence dropout (Schneeberger et al., 2024).

The number of attended sessions can impact client outcomes. Hatchett (2021, p. 642) observed that "most clients attend only a few sessions and attain only minor improvements in symptomatic distress and psychosocial impairments before ending services." As previously discussed, phase theory proposes that different types of client problems require different amounts of therapy, and more treatment is necessary for intermediate and long-term problems beyond distress reduction (Callahan et al., 2006; Howard et al., 1986). Reducing client distress early in treatment may increase clients' hope, satisfaction with therapist and/or treatment, and initial progress (Callahan et al., 2006; Prochaska & Norcross, 2013).

In a private practice setting, Meier and Seidel (2024) found evidence for a *variable duration effect* on psychotherapy outcomes. Individuals who participate in therapy for a relatively small number of frequently occurring sessions often achieved measurable distress reduction. A combination of moderate distress and an established working alliance helped to form a therapeutic environment that sustained client attendance over longer periods. Lambert's (2007) review found that (a) 50% of patients reached criteria to be classified as recovered at Sessions 11 to 21, and (b) 75% of clients required 25 to 45 sessions to be recovered.

Measurement of Common Factors in Clinical Settings

A major issue with most measurement of CFs is that it occurs exclusively via self-report. The most frequently employed measure for the alliance, for example, is the Working Alliance Inventory (WAI; Horvath & Greenberg, 1989). Interestingly, ceiling effects (CEs) have been frequently documented on the WAI and other alliance measures completed by adult and child clients (Mahon et al., 2024), as well as by supervisees [Authors]. CEs occur when many test scores group near the upper limit of the scale, thereby restricting variability at the high end (Meier & Feeley, 2021). CEs appear even during initial sessions (Babatunde et al., 2017; Paap et al., 2020), and these effects appear consistently across demographic variables (e.g., gender, ethnicity, age), therapeutic modalities, and presenting problems (Meier & Feeley, 2021).

Funder and Gardiner (2025, p. 891) observed that all psychological tests "surely have at least somewhat different properties and implications for different individuals." Self-report data reflect respondents' diverse interpretations of test item content, instructions, and response format. Research indicates that individuals can interpret items on psychological tests differently than test developers intended (Scharz, 2009, influencing the psychometric properties of the test. Dohrenwend (2006) called this problem *intracategory variability*, observing that test-takers respond to item content on self-report measures based on a wide range of personal experiences. The basis on which individuals respond to health-related categories on self-report measures can range "from *the catastrophic* to *the trivial*" (Dohrenwend 2006, p. 479). When reporting on a recent serious illness, for example, test-takers will describe episodes that vary from simple flu to heart attacks.

Rather than rely on self-reports, Meier (2025) employed an advanced AI large language model (LLM; ChatGPT) to analyze client-only speech for linguistic markers of four constructs: client distress, social anxiety, attachment style, and positive transference. Using a transcript of Carl Rogers' first session with Gloria (Shostrum, 1966), ChatGPT was tasked with identifying verbatim client statements corresponding to each construct. The methodology explicitly treated this ChatGPT AI as a psychometric instrument: Outputs were evaluated for construct specificity (whether statements uniquely reflected one construct versus overlapping constructs), temporal stability (replication using a later ChatGPT version), and cross-model validity (comparison with an independent LLM, Claude AI). This design allowed the assessment not only of what the AI identified but also how reliably and consistently it did so across time and models.

Results showed that the AI robustly identified client distress and social anxiety, with many statements demonstrating both replication and cross-validation, suggesting these constructs are linguistically salient and relatively stable in therapeutic discourse. Attachment style and positive transference were detected less consistently, reflecting both their theoretical complexity and the challenges of operationalizing relational constructs through language alone. Importantly, the AI identified overlapping constructs within the same client utterance, highlighting the multidimensional nature of psychotherapy dialogue rather than simple classification error.

Overall, the AI methodology demonstrated its capability for capturing clinically meaningful psychological processes that may increase alliance ratings early in therapy. AI analyses showed promise for identifying emotional and psychological markers related to common factors such as the working alliance and client distress, suggesting that this methodology may be useful for individualized progress monitoring and outcome assessment (PMOA; Janse et al., 2025). While there is a need for human oversight and further validation in larger, real-world clinical samples, linguistic analysis via AI offers a potentially important approach to clinical assessment because it is unobtrusive, avoids reactivity effects, and requires minimal resources from the clinician. In addition, greater consistency, cost-effectiveness, and less bias are also possible with AI analysis of large amounts of text (cf. Tausczik & Pennebaker, 2010).

The Early Therapeutic Environment

The Early Therapeutic Environment (ETE; Meier, 2023) model integrates CF and phase theories. Early sessions constitute a distinct phase in which common factors drive negative affect (NA) reduction, which, in turn, encourages therapeutic engagement, reduces dropout, and prepares clients for later, more intensive therapeutic work. Clinically, this framework suggests prioritizing NA-focused outcome measurement in early sessions; methodologically, it highlights the need for researchers to measure NA explicitly to maximize sensitivity to early therapeutic change.

The ETE model describes the process of transitioning individuals from ordinary interpersonal interactions and conversations to clients who participate in therapeutic discourse and activities. Clients' decision to seek therapy is often motivated by their subjective experience of distress (Howard et al., 1996). Once the client has contacted the therapy organization and therapist, the individual begins to establish a working alliance and learn about the behaviors necessary to meet therapeutic goals. The ETE model proposes that clients who experience difficulties developing the alliance, decreasing distress to moderate levels, or developing expectations relevant to successful therapeutic behaviors are more likely to drop out in initial sessions.

The development of the working alliance may also result from several actions the therapist takes in the beginning of therapy or even before sessions begin. Zilcha-Mano (2025) reported a randomized controlled trial of 100 individuals with major depressive disorder. She found that pre-treatment changes in therapeutic alliance, measured twice *before* patients met their therapists, significantly predicted both alliance development and symptom reduction throughout 16-week treatment. Thus, it appears likely that client participation in intake interactions, administrative procedures, and referral experiences has the potential to influence alliance development (and subsequent client outcomes, particularly distress reduction) as well client outcome expectations relevant to therapy. These findings also align with ceiling effect findings with alliance measures which indicate that clients report and experience the alliance as established as early as the first session.

Providing an explanatory narrative that normalizes the client's current distress may also enhance the development of the alliance. From a narrative perspective, when the client relates a story to a therapist, this act develops the working alliance between client and counselor if the counselor is a skilled listener who conveys empathy. As the counseling process unfolds, the therapist's validation of the client's feelings and thoughts deepens the working alliance, which often improves the subsequent content and quality of the stories the client shares with the therapist. For many clients, developing a working alliance is a prerequisite to telling a deeper story about difficult-to-discuss feelings and issues beyond the initial presenting problem(s).

In the ETE model, discussion of client attrition is based on the client's goals in therapy. With *premature termination*, individuals leave therapy during initial sessions and do not progress beyond their short-term goals, typically focused on distress reduction. A client who terminates prematurely does not engage in specific therapeutic interventions but may experience distress reduction from therapeutic contact. In contrast, *treatment failure* pertains to clients who engage in specific therapeutic interventions but leave therapy before achieving either intermediate goals such as symptom reduction (e.g., decreases in sleep problems or eating difficulties) or longer-term goals such as improved life functioning (e.g., better relationships at work or with family and friends) (Howard et al., 1996; Kopta et al., 1994).

Summary

Common factors (CFs) continue to be an important therapy framework because of their links to client outcomes. Counseling theorists and researchers have proposed descriptions of CFs operating in counseling and psychotherapy, including the working alliance, outcome and efficacy expectations, insight, and corrective experiences. The alliance and client expectations tend to be most important in initial stages of counseling, while insight and corrective experiences more often occur during the intervention phase of psychotherapy and influence intermediate and long-term outcomes. CFs influence client engagement and attendance, and subsequently, progress and outcomes in counseling and psychotherapy. Phase theory indicates that events in counseling take place in a rough sequence involving the initial development of the alliance and client expectations. Distress reduction appears to be a common, early result of counseling, while other interpersonal and behavioral problems require more time in therapy for sustainable improvement to occur. Finally, more research is needed to demonstrate mediation, that is, to show that changes in the common factor(s) precede changes in treatment outcome.

References

Al-Jabari, R., Murrell, A. R., Callahan, J. L., Cox, R. J., & Lester, E. G. (2019). Do distress levels and waitlist impact termination in a training clinic? *Training and Education in Professional Psychology, 13*, 127–137. https://doi.org/10.1037/tep0000223

Anderson, S. R., Tambling, R., Yorgason, J. B., & Rackham, E. (2019). The mediating role of the therapeutic alliance in understanding early discontinuance. *Psychotherapy Research, 29*(7), 882–893. https://doi.org/10.1080/10503307.2018.1506949

Babatunde, F., MacDermid, J., & MacIntyre, N. (2017). Characteristics of therapeutic alliance in musculoskeletal physiotherapy and occupational therapy practice: A scoping review of the literature. *BMC Health Services Research, 17*, 1–23. https://doi.org/10.1186/s12913-017-2311-3

Bailey, R. J., & Ogles, B. M. (2023). *Common factors therapy: A principle-based treatment framework*. American Psychological Association.

Bandura, A. (1977). Self-efficacy: Toward a unifying theory of behavioral change. *Psychological Review, 84*, 191–215. https://doi.org/10.1037/0033-295X.84.2.191

Bandura, A. (1989). Human agency in social cognitive theory. *American Psychologist, 44*(9), 1175–1184. https://doi.org/10.1037/0003-066X.44.9.1175

Bandura, A. (1997). *Self-efficacy: The exercise of control*. W. H. Freeman.

Barkham, M., Connell, J., Stiles, W. B., Miles, J. N. V., Margison, F., Evans, C., & Mellor-Clark, J. (2006). Dose-effect relations and responsive regulation of treatment duration: The good enough level model. *Journal of Consulting and Clinical Psychology, 74*(1), 160–167. https://doi.org/10.1037/0022-006X.74.1.160

Barrett, M. S., Chua, W., Crits-Christoph, P., Gibbons, M., & Thompson, D. (2008). Early withdrawal from mental health treatment: Implications for psychotherapy practice. *Psychotherapy Research: Theory, Research, Practice, Training, 45*, 247–267. https://doi.org/10.1037/0033-3204.45.2.247

Bordin, E. S. (1979). The generalizability of the psychoanalytic concept of the working alliance. *Psychotherapy: Theory, Research & Practice, 16*(3), 252–260. https://doi.org/10.1037/h0085885

Bugatti, M., Richardson, Z., Rasmussen, W., Newton, D., & Owen, J. (2023). Measurement-based care professional practice guideline: Don't forget the therapists! *Psychotherapy, 60*(1), 20–23. https://doi.org/10.1037/pst0000464

Callahan, J. L., Swift, J. K., & Hynan, M. T. (2006). Test of the phase model of psychotherapy in a training clinic. *Psychological Services, 3*(2), 129–136. https://doi.org/10.1037/1541-1559.3.2.129

Campbell-Sills, L., & Barlow, D. H. (2007). Incorporating emotion regulation into conceptualizations and treatments of anxiety and mood disorders. In J. J. Gross (Ed.), Handbook of emotion regulation (pp. 542–559). New York: Guilford.

Constantino, M. J., Vîslă, A., Coyne, A. E., & Boswell, J. F. (2018). A meta-analysis of the association between patients' early treatment outcome expectation and their posttreatment outcomes. *Psychotherapy, 55*(4), 486–495. https://doi.org/10.1037/pst0000168

Cuijpers, P., Reijnders, M., & Huibers, M. J. H. (2019). The role of common factors in psychotherapy outcomes. *Annual Review of Clinical Psychology, 15*, 207–231. https://doi.org/10.1146/annurev-clinpsy-050718-095424

Dohrenwend, B. P. (2006). Inventorying stressful life events as risk factors for psychopathology: Toward resolution of intracategory variability. *Psychological Bulletin, 132*, 477–495. https://doi.org/10.1037/0033-2909.132.3.477

Duncan, B. L., Miller, S. D., Sparks, J. A., Cloud, D. A., et al. (2003). The session rating scale: Preliminary psychometric properties of a "working" alliance measure. *Journal of Brief Therapy, 3*(1), 3–12.

Flückiger, C., Del Re, A. C., Wampold, B. E., & Horvath, A. O. (2018). The alliance in adult psychotherapy: A meta-analytic synthesis. *Psychotherapy, 55*(4), 316–340. https://doi.org/10.1037/pst0000172

Flückiger, C., Del Re, A. C., Wlodasch, D., Horvath, A. O., Solomonov, N., & Wampold, B. E. (2020). Assessing the alliance–outcome association adjusted for patient characteristics and treatment processes: A meta-analytic summary of direct comparisons. *Journal of Counseling Psychology, 67*(6), 706–711. https://doi.org/10.1037/cou0000424

Frank, J. D., Frank, J. B., & Wampold, B. E. (2025). *Persuasion and healing: A comparative study of psychotherapy* (4th ed.). Johns Hopkins University Press.

Funder, D. C., & Gardiner, G. (2025). MIsgivings about measurement invariance. *European Journal of Personality, 38*, 889–8975. https://doi.org/10.1177/08902070241228338

Goldberg, S. B., Babins-Wagner, R., Rousmaniere, T., Berzins, S., Hoyt, W. T., Whipple, J. L., Miller, S. D., & Wampold, B. E. (2016). Creating a climate for therapist improvement: A case study of an agency focused on outcomes and deliberate practice. *Psychotherapy, 53*(3), 367–375. https://doi.org/10.1037/pst0000060

Guyker, W. (2006). *Bridging case conceptualization and assessment*. Unpublished manuscript. University at Buffalo, State University of New York.

Hansen, N. B., Lambert, M. J., & Forman, E. M. (2002). A psychotherapy dose-response study of the effectiveness of brief and long-term therapy. *Psychotherapy Research, 12*(3), 328–343. https://doi.org/10.1093/clipsy.9.3.329

Harris, R., Murphy, M. G., & Rakes, S. (2019). The psychometric properties of the outcome rating scale used in practice: A narrative review. *Journal of Evidence-Based Social Work, 16*, 555–574. https://doi.org/10.1037/0033-295X.102.3.458

Hatchett, G. T. (2021). Implications of clinical significant change research for evidence-based counseling practice. *Journal of Counseling and Development, 99*(4), 462–471. https://doi.org/10.1002/jcad.12398

Horvath, A. O., & Greenberg, L. S. (1989). Development and validation of the working alliance inventory. *Journal of Counseling Psychology, 36*(2), 223–233. https://doi.org/10.1037/0022-0167.36.2.223

Houston, T. K., Allison, J. J., Sussman, M., et al. (2011). Culturally appropriate storytelling to improve blood pressure: A randomized trial. *Annals of Internal Medicine, 154*(2), 77–84. https://doi.org/10.7326/0003-4819-154-2-201101180-00004

Howard, K. I., Kopta, S. M., Krause, M. S., & Orlinsky, D. E. (1986). The dose–effect relationship in psychotherapy. *American Psychologist, 41*(2), 159–164. https://doi.org/10.1037/0003-066X.41.2.159

Janse, P. D., van Sonsbeek, M., Bovendeerd, B., & de Jong, K. (2025). Progress feedback in psychotherapy: Advantages, challenges, and future directions. *Current Opinion in Psychology*.

Kelly, M. A. R., Roberts, J. E., & Ciesla, J. A. (2005). Sudden gains in cognitive behavioral treatment for depression: When do they occur and do they matter? *Behavior Research and Therapy, 43*, 703714. https://doi.org/10.1016/j.brat.2004.06.002

Kopta, S. M., Howard, K. I., Lowry, J. L., & Beutler, L. E. (1994). Patterns of symptomatic recovery in psychotherapy. *Journal of Consulting and Clinical Psychology, 62*, 1009–1016. https://doi.org/10.1037/0022-006X.62.5.1009

Kopta, S. M., & Lowry, J. L. (2002). Psychometric evaluation of the behavioral health questionnaire-20: A brief instrument for assessing global mental health and the three phases of psychotherapy. *Psychotherapy Research, 12*, 413–426. https://doi.org/10.1093/ptr/12.4.413

Krendl, A. C., & Lorenzo-Luaces, L. (2022). Identifying peaks in attrition after clients initiate mental health treatment in a university training clinic. *Psychological Services, 19*(3), 519–526. https://doi.org/10.1037/ser0000469

Lambert, M. J. (2005). Early response in psychotherapy: Further evidence for the importance of common factors rather than "placebo effects." Journal of Clinical Psychology, 61, 855–869. doi:https://doi.org/10.1002/jclp.20130.

Lambert, M. J. (2007). What we have learned from a decade of research aimed at improving psychotherapy outcome in routine care. *Psychotherapy Research, 17*, 1–14. https://doi.org/10.1080/10503300601032506

Longo, L. D., Lent, R. W., & Brown, S. D. (1992). Social cognitive variables in the prediction of client motivation and attrition. *Journal of Counseling Psychology, 39*(4), 447–452. https://doi.org/10.1037/0022-0167.39.4.447

Mahon, D., Minami, T., & Brown, J. (2024). Predicting treatment success and failure using routine outcome data: The role of therapist effects in dynamic predictive modeling. *Counselling and Psychotherapy Research*, e12827. https://doi.org/10.1002/capr.12827

Meier, S. T. (2023). A model of the early therapeutic environment: Predicting client attrition. *Journal of Psychotherapy Integration, 33*, 235–247. https://doi.org/10.1037/int0000293

Meier, S. T. (2024). Initial evaluation of an AI-augmented progress monitoring and outcome assessment. *Counselling & Psychotherapy Research, 25*. https://doi.org/10.1002/capr.12869

Meier, S. T. (2026). An integrative approach to five controversial areas in psychotherapy. *Professional Psychology: Research and Practice, 57*(1), 12–18. https://doi.org/10.1037/pro0000660

Meier, S. T., & Feeley, T. H. (2021). Ceiling effects indicate a possible threshold structure for working alliance. *Journal of Counseling Psychology, 69*(2), 235–245. https://doi.org/10.1037/cou0000564

Meier, S. T., & Seidel, J. (2024). A partial test of the early therapeutic environment model: Association of working alliance and distress with client attendance variables. *Journal of Psychotherapy Integration, 34*, 145–160. https://doi.org/10.1037/int0000323

Meier, S. T., Somova, M., Akin, D., & Altabef, D. (2015). Evidence for rapid decrease in self-reported psychological distress during initial phase of psychotherapy. *Journal of Psychology and Behavioral Science, 3*, 37–43.

Miller, S. D., Duncan, B. L., Sorrell, R., & Brown, G. S. (2005). The partners for change outcome management system. *Journal of Clinical Psychology, 61*(2), 199–208. https://doi.org/10.1002/jclp.20111

Meier, S. T. (2025). Initial evaluation of an AI-augmented progress monitoring and outcome assessment. *Counselling and Psychotherapy Research, 25*. https://doi.org/10.1002/capr.12869

Mohr, D. C., Hart, S. L., Howard, I., Julian, L., Vella, L., Catledge, C., & Feldman, M. D. (2006). Barriers to psychotherapy among depressed and nondepressed primary care patients. *Annals of Behavioral Medicine, 32*(3), 254–258. https://doi.org/10.1207/s15324796abm3203_12

Mohr, D. C., Ho, J., Duffecy, J., Baron, K. G., Lehman, K. A., Jin, L., & Reifler, D. (2010). Perceived barriers to psychological treatments and their relationship to depression. *Journal of Clinical Psychology, 66*(4), 394–409. https://doi.org/10.1002/jclp.20659

Ong, C. W., Lee, E. B., & Twohig, M. P. (2018). A meta-analysis of dropout rates in acceptance and commitment therapy. *Behaviour Research and Therapy, 104*, 14–33. https://doi.org/10.1016/j.brat.2018.02.004

Owen, J., Miller, S. D., Seidel, J., & Chow, D. (2016). The working alliance in treatment of military adolescents. *Journal of Consulting and Clinical Psychology, 84*(3), 200–210. https://doi.org/10.1037/ccp0000035

Paap, D., Schepers, M., & Dijkstra, P. U. (2020). Reducing ceiling effects in the working alliance inventory-rehabilitation Dutch version. *Disability and Rehabilitation, 42*(20), 2944–2950. https://doi.org/10.1080/09638288.2018.1563833

Prochaska, J. O., & Norcross, J. (2013). *Systems of psychotherapy: A transtheoretical analysis* (8th ed.). Wadsworth.

Reese, R. J., Gillaspy, J. A., Jr., Owen, J. J., Flora, K. L., Cunningham, L. C., Archie, D., & Marsden, T. (2013). The influence of demand characteristics and social desirability on clients' ratings of the therapeutic alliance. *Journal of Clinical Psychology, 69*(7), 696–709. https://doi.org/10.1002/jclp.21946

Rotter, J. B. (1966). Generalized expectancies for internal versus external control of reinforcement. Psychological Monographs: *General and Applied, 80*(1), 1–28. https://doi.org/10.1037/h0092976

Schneeberger, M., Ehlert, U., Eggenberger, L., Seidler, Z. E., Wilson, M. J., Fisher, K., & Walther, A. (2024). Men's psychotherapy dropout is associated with conformity to traditional masculinity ideologies. *Journal of Psychotherapy Integration, 34*, 420–433. https://doi.org/10.1037/int0000342

Sharf, J., Primavera, L. H., & Diener, M. J. (2010). Dropout and therapeutic alliance: A meta-analysis of adult individual psychotherapy. *Psychotherapy: Theory, Research, Practice, Training, 47*(4), 637–645. https://doi.org/10.1037/a0021175

Shostrum, E. L. (Producer). (1966). Three approaches to psychotherapy [Film]. Santa Ana, CA: Psychological Films.

Smith, M., & Glass, G. (1977). Meta-analysis of psychotherapy outcome studies. *American Psychologist, 32*, 752–760. https://doi.org/10.1037/0003-066X.32.9.752

Sperry, L., Brill, P. L., Howard, K. I., & Grissom, G. R. (1996). *Treatment outcomes in psychotherapy and psychiatric interventions*. Brunner-Mazel.

Swift, J. K., & Greenberg, R. P. (2012). Premature discontinuation in adult psychotherapy: A meta-analysis. *Journal of Consulting and Clinical Psychology, 80*, 547–559. https://doi.org/10.1037/a0028226

Tausczik, Y. R., & Pennebaker, J. W. (2010). The psychological meaning of words: LIWC and computerized text analysis methods. *Journal of Language and Social Psychology, 29*(1), 24–54. https://doi.org/10.1177/0261927X09351676

Tilden, T., Ulvenes, P., Zahl-Olsen, R., Hoffart, A., Johnson, S. U., Wampold, B. E., & Håland, Å. T. (2021). Predicting change through individual symptoms and relationship distress: A study of within- and between-person processes in couple therapy. *Clinical Psychology & Psychotherapy, 28*(5), 1275–1284. https://doi.org/10.1002/cpp.2575

Tinsley, H. E. A., & Harris, D. J. (1976). Client expectations for counseling. *Journal of Counseling Psychology, 23*, 173–177. https://doi.org/10.1037/0022-0167.23.3.173

Twomey, C., O'Reilly, G., & Goldfried, M. R. (2023). Consensus on the perceived presence of transtheoretical principles of change in routine psychotherapy practice: A survey of clinicians and researchers. *Psychotherapy, 60*(2), 219–224. https://doi.org/10.1037/pst0000489

Wampold, B. (2001). *The great psychotherapy debate: Models, methods, and findings*. Lawrence Erlbaum Associates.

Wierzbicki, M., & Pekarik, G. (1993). A meta-analysis of psychotherapy dropout. *Professional Psychology: Research and Practice, 24*(2), 190–195. https://doi.org/10.1037/0735-7028.24.2.190

Zilcha-Mano, S. (2025). Therapeutic change may begin before the therapist and patient ever meet: Pretreatment alliance changes predict clinical outcomes. *Psychotherapy and Psychosomatics*. https://doi.org/10.1159/000548510

Chapter 9
Narrative and Language

Introduction

Psychotherapy is predominantly a talking therapy. Huler's (2004, p. 91) perspective is "language is technology. It's a tool to accomplish a task." Aspects of client language and narratives are integral to all aspects of the psychotherapy process, including assessment, intervention, and relationship building. Consequently, a narrative model can be conceived as an umbrella theory, connecting concepts that specify what effective therapists do with psychotherapy clients. All therapies, including behavioral, cognitive behavioral, object relations, Gestalt, family therapy, grief, psychodynamic, interpersonal, and client-centered therapies, are narrative therapies in the sense that all use language to assess the client and deliver interventions.

Psychotherapy clients typically communicate through narratives, sharing stories that give shape and meaning to their experiences. Michael White, an Australian social worker and a family therapist, was among the first to articulate this phenomenon in narrative therapy. White (2004, p. 38) emphasized that people are "active, impassioned meaning makers in search of plausible stories." Similarly, Madigan (2011) wrote that a key idea of narrative therapies is "that it is the stories people tell and hold about their lives that determine the meaning they give to their lives" (p. 33). White's collaborative approach, wherein therapists and their clients co-author new, empowering stories, continues to underpin modern narrative practices. In contemporary formulations of narrative therapy, the focus remains on how clients define their lives through language, framing therapists as partners in re-authoring narratives toward hope and possibility. The approach emphasizes concepts and techniques like use of metaphors, deconstruction, and unique outcomes to help clients reshape problem-saturated narratives into healthier stories.

For decades, therapists have relied primarily on clinical intuition and theoretical training to analyze client narratives. They listen for emotional undertones, track recurring themes across sessions, note the metaphors clients use to describe their

R. Hawkins, S. Meier, *Healing Outcomes*,
https://doi.org/10.1007/978-3-032-33611-8_9

experience, and assess whether stories become more coherent over time. This human capacity for nuanced language analysis remains irreplaceable. Yet as our understanding of therapeutic language has deepened, so too has our recognition of the challenges inherent in narrative assessment. Human attention is selective. Memory is fallible, and some bias is inevitable. When therapists speak with dozens of clients each week, consistently tracking subtle language patterns across all cases becomes nearly impossible. Recent advances in natural language processing and large language models, however, have created unprecedented opportunities to augment clinical assessment. Automated text analysis can identify patterns invisible to human perception, track linguistic changes across hundreds of therapy sessions, and provide clinicians with objective data about client progress. These computational tools do not replace the therapist's empathic understanding, but they can offer a complementary lens through which to view the therapeutic process.

This chapter explores how narrative concepts can serve as an integrative framework for psychotherapy assessment, and how emerging AI technologies can operationalize these concepts in clinically useful ways. We begin by examining the theoretical foundations of narrative therapy, including how personal stories are shaped by cultural, familial, and social contexts. We then turn to the question of what therapists should assess in client narratives: Dominant themes, emotional intensity, metaphors, dialectical tensions, and narrative coherence. Finally, we consider how both traditional linguistic analysis methods and cutting-edge AI tools can help therapists systematically evaluate these narrative dimensions to provide timely feedback about client progress and treatment outcomes.

Theories of Narratives

Personal stories are shaped by cultural, familial, and social narratives. The multicultural domain, including race/ethnicity, gender, and culture, is a foundational dimension in narrative therapy. Key questions include: (a) Whose story is considered relevant? (b) Whose story is being heard? and (c) Have cultural power dynamics shaped, distorted, or obscured narratives? Narrative therapists assist clients in examining how their personal narratives are influenced by cultural and sociopolitical contexts, emphasizing what has been omitted or marginalized (Daiute, 2014). Typically, narratives from those with social power are prioritized in broader society. Narrative therapy, in contrast, attends especially to voices historically marginalized—such as women, racial/ethnic minorities, LGBTQ+ individuals, and people from lower socioeconomic backgrounds. Clients are regarded as experts of their experiences; therapists support clients in articulating their stories and claims to identity and agency (White, 2015).

Narrative therapists have drawn upon Michel Foucault's analyses of power, knowledge, and societal normalization. Foucault argued that social power shapes individuals' self-perceptions and behaviors (Guilfoyle, 2025; Lock et al., 2005). For example, cultural norms about female bodies, particularly thinness in Western cultures, are internalized through media, leading many women to self-discipline in ways that can fuel eating disorders (Lock et al., 2005). Brown (2007) underscored how self-regulation becomes normalized: Failure to conform to socially prescribed ideals is often framed as a personal failure rather than as a byproduct of cultural pressure. For men, for example, adherence to narratives that valorize long hours and sacrifice can exact physical and psychological costs, including stress, heart disease, and impaired well-being.

Bruner (1990) noted that people tell themselves stories they hope will be approved by others, which explains why clients encounter difficulty imagining alternative narratives. When normative self-discipline intensifies desire, such as for food or sexual expression, narrative therapy helps clients explore and loosen these controls, facilitating re-authoring toward more self-satisfying and balanced narratives. Polkinghorne (2004) described culture as providing a repertoire of life stories that individuals may adopt. Ideally, narrative therapists help clients identify harmful cultural narratives and create alternative stories aligned with their values. Madigan (2011), for example, documented the formation of an Anti-Anorexia/Bulimia League of activists and therapists who archived lived experiences and used them for public education—an example of narrative therapy's intersection with culture and community activism.

An illustrative case presented by Semmler and Braun (2000) describes Shirley, an African American graduate student who experienced depression, self-doubt, and cultural alienation while studying at a predominantly White institution. Shirley was invited to reexamine experiences of racism (such as a high school counselor's doubts about her academic potential) along with counter-stories of familial affirmation grounded in a strong work ethic. Through this process of re-authoring her personal narrative, she was able to challenge and resist dominant cultural discourses that stereotype Black students as academically inferior. More broadly, narrative therapy aligns with other psychotherapeutic approaches in its commitment to social justice and human rights. However, contemporary mental health services increasingly shaped by for-profit and managed-care models often constrain access to care, shorten treatment duration, and pressure clinicians toward premature termination (Davis & Meier, 2001). In response, narrative therapy practitioners actively contest these systemic limitations by advocating for equitable access to services and resisting practices that undermine client-centered and socially responsive care.

Assessment in Narrative Approaches

Narrative assessment derives from an analysis of client stories. Stories have content, but out of the vast amount of information provided by any client, to what should a therapist primarily attend? To narrative therapists, stories have identifiable characteristics. From a therapeutic perspective, client stories (a) are always partially incomplete or distorted; (b) contain content that evokes strong affect in the storyteller; and (c) represent the storyteller's effort to make sense of life events (Morgan,

2000; White & Epston, 1990). In addition, the dominant themes in a client's personal narratives are central to understanding that person. Most students cannot recall all past exam experiences, for example, but will remember overarching themes. An anxious student may recall past failures despite preparation, while a confident student may remember consistent success tied to effective study strategies. Thus, past behaviors and events are stored in narratives and mobilized for similar future situations (White & Epston, 1990).

The remainder of this chapter describes the *what* and *how* of narrative assessment:

Affect. In the beginning of client storytelling, more emotion is typically present. Strong affect marks key elements of stories that should be assessed in detail. Viney (1993) reported the case of June, a 55-year-old woman who came to a university clinic with difficulties with her marriage and family. Describing her marriage as "30 years of frustration and hell" (Viney, 1993, p. 114), June herself was

> ...ridden with emotions such as frustration, anger, suspicion, as well as depression. Her depressive feelings were linked to feelings of rejection and loneliness and, when her depression welled up to despair, led her to explore a range of ways of committing suicide, none of which she had so far put to the test. The confusion of which she complained appeared to result from the plethora of strong emotions that she was experiencing.

The predominant affect expressed by many clients in the beginning of therapy is some form of psychological distress. As noted, narrative therapists believe people seek therapy when their lived experiences do not match well with their dominant narratives. The resulting demoralization or distress, an upset or persistent negative affect, motivates individuals to seek help despite the social stigma of receiving psychotherapy. Client stories are shaped by their emotional themes (Greenberg & Angus, 2004); emotional reactions to an event increase the likelihood that an event will be remembered and storied for future recall (Payne & Kensinger, 2010). Given that clients' recurrent themes will possess strong emotional components, Linehan (1993) summarized research that noted that "increases in emotional arousal and intensity narrow attention, so that emotion-relevant stimuli become more salient and are more closely attended to" (p. 44).

Recent outcome analyses examined change during psychotherapy at the item level on several outcome measures (Vermeersch et al., 2000, 2004; Weinstock & Meier, 2003). Assessing a broad range of problem domains in a total of 7344 clients who received services at university counseling centers, an outpatient clinic, private practices, and employee assistance programs, these studies found that depression and anxiety-related items evidence larger effect sizes (ES) than items assessing other domains. Krampen (2010) similarly examined change on a brief outcome scale in two studies of psychotherapy outpatients and found that the largest changes appeared on items assessing distress and anxiety. These findings support the importance of focusing on affect that is a key component of narrative approaches.

Meier (2025, 2026) argued that five longstanding psychotherapy controversies (early change, sudden gains, the dose-effect relationship, the effectiveness of brief therapy, and paraprofessional–professional equivalence) can be understood through a single unifying mechanism: Rapid reductions in state negative affect (NA) during the earliest sessions of treatment. Across these diverse phenomena, clients frequently show substantial improvement within the first few sessions, and these early gains tend to persist. Widely employed outcome measures such as the Outcome Rating Scale and Outcome Questionnaire assess distress, which psychometric and emotion-science perspectives identify as state NA. Recognizing NA reduction as the primary short-term outcome across therapies and clients clarifies why early and sudden gains occur, why brief therapies can be effective, and why paraprofessionals often perform comparably to professionals. These early improvements reflect clients' rapid engagement with the therapeutic relationship rather than the operation of modality-specific techniques.

Relatedly, worry and rumination should decrease in improving clients. *Rumination*, or cognitive problem-solving efforts that an individual cannot easily stop, has been linked with the duration and onset of depression and impaired social problem solving (Watkins & Moulds, 2005). Nolen-Hoeksema (1996) maintained that rumination involves a repetition of a theme without movement toward resolution or solution. The continued presence of rumination suggests that those clients are unable to process affect or make meaning of their story events.

Social relationships. Important relationships are another focal point of client stories. Especially in the beginning of therapy, focusing on others can become problematic if it prevents the exploration of the client's feelings and thoughts. Research on writing interventions suggests that self-referential activity (i.e., a focus on the self) early in the process is associated with successful outcomes (Pennebaker et al., 2003). A client who evidences poor interpersonal skills is also likely to experience more difficulty developing a working alliance.

The relationship between client and therapist can also be assessed, particularly as it develops during the beginning of counseling. Telling a story to a therapist helps to develop the working alliance between client and counselor. This is particularly true if the counselor is a skilled listener who conveys empathy as the client tells therapeutically relevant stories. As narratives are shared, validation of the client's feelings and thoughts deepens the working alliance. Anderson (2004) sees social bonds forming when therapist and client co-construct stories; Boothe and Von Wyl (2004) maintain that "listener and narrator are empathic partners in a narrative alliance" (p. 283). Reciprocally, the strength of the working alliance influences the content and quality of the stories the client shares with the therapist. For many clients, developing a working alliance is a prerequisite to telling a deeper story about difficult-to-discuss feelings and issues beyond the initial presenting problem(s). As clients develop a working alliance and gain trust in their therapist, their stories become more elaborate and layered.

Metaphors. Narrative therapists and others interested in language pay attention to several aspects of client stories. First, clients will occasionally employ individual words and phrases that strike the listener as unusual or somehow out of place. The following dialogue is from a well-known training video from the 1960s (Shostrom, 1965) that demonstrated client-centered therapy. Carl Rogers is speaking with Gloria, a recently divorced mother who is expressing her ambivalence about her sexual desires (transcript edited from Wickman, 2000).

Gloria: There's a girl at work who sort of mothers me....I think she thinks I'm all sweet and I sure don't want to show my more *ornery devilish* [italics added] side with her....And it's so disappointing.

Rogers: I get the disappointment, that here, a lot of these things you'd thought you'd worked through and now the guilts and the feeling that, only a part of you is acceptable to anybody else.

Gloria: Regarding for example, my sex life. This is the big thing. If I really fell in love with a man, and I respected him and I adored him, I don't think I'd feel so guilty going to bed with him and I don't think I'd have to make up any excuses to the children because they could see my natural caring for him.

Gloria's description of her desires as a single woman is partially a result of the historical period in which this conversation occurred. "Ornery devilish" is so distinctive a description that it signals a significant conflict between her desire for sex and beliefs about appropriate behavior for a single woman in the 1960s. In another portion of the conversation, Gloria similarly refers to herself as a "demon." Given that distressing relationships were a key reason for Gloria to seek therapy, these salient phrases in her story merit further exploration (which, incidentally, does not happen in the Rogers' interview).

Metaphors illuminate one object by comparing it to another. The object does not have to be a physical object, and with psychotherapeutic conversations, it often refers to a psychological state. A client may describe a feeling of pressure, for example, as a "weight on my chest." This effectively communicates a sense of the client's experience when feeling pressure or stress. Therapists listen for client's use of metaphors to gain a better understanding of the client's subjective experiences. Metaphors also provide therapists with a common language with which to communicate with clients. With the client who describes a feeling of pressure as a weight, the therapist also can refer to that weight when discussing pressure with the client. Equally useful, the therapist can employ the metaphor as an assessment device, asking the client to describe the heaviness of the weight to convey how much pressure the client is experiencing.

Research suggests that people often employ metaphors, as frequently as every 10 to 25 words (Geary, 2011; Wang & Sun, 2024). Thus, metaphors represent one of the most important language tools available to psychotherapists. Describing himself as "a bomb waiting to go off" (Stott et al., 2010, p. 47), a young client had isolated himself from others because of his fear that his anger might harm others. After the therapist began to introduce a more benign metaphor of a pan of water boiling over and then simmering down, therapist and client began to talk about methods for "turning the heat off" to cope with the client's anger. Similarly, Teyber and McClure (2011) used *compacted phrase* to refer to a short phrase or sentence that clients employ repeatedly to communicate their emotional reaction to stressful events. Example phrases include "It's too much for me; I can't stand it" and "I've had it, I'm 'done."

Metaphors can be tracked over time to determine if they reveal differences over time in how a client thinks and feels about a therapy issue. Levitt, Korman and Angus (2000) found that depressed clients who made improvements in therapy, their description of "being burdened" changed to "unloading the burden." No such change occurred in individuals who remained depressed. Metaphors can also be a useful method of ascertaining the client's readiness to terminate. This example is from Viney (1993, p. 118) from a final session with a client who had previously introduced the "ship and crew" metaphor:

Therapist: So I'm wondering whether you feel that you need me to help the process along, or whether you'd like to take off as captain of your own ship?

Client: I would like to try and think as the captain...but I know when I get into rough seas I'm going to need a good navigator.

Therapist: I'm not suggesting that you should see somebody else at this stage or indeed that we should stop having these sessions...but the result of the sessions, that I want to see, is you out there as captain of your own ship.

Client: Well, I think I'm ready for it. When I get into rough seas, I'll feel the need of some support. Will I be able to phone and make an appointment?

Dialectics. George Kelly (1955) maintained that human thought consists of cognitive constructs that contain opposite poles or ends of a continuum. Clients often relate stories in which they are stuck on one end of the continuum when they talk about problem-related constructs. Many therapies have created strategies to deal with this phenomenon; in motivational interviewing, for example, therapists help the client move between the polarities of pros and cons about change. Similarly, Dialectical Behavior Therapy (DBT) emphasizes *dialectics,* the attempt to reconcile opposites in a process of synthesis. Linehan (1993) maintained that borderline and suicidal individuals vacillate between contradictory positions or beliefs ("I am bad" versus "I am good"). Borderlines can become stuck in this *splitting*, in one or the other position when describing themselves or others. In this type of work, DBT therapists combine acceptance and change strategies: Accept clients as who they are *and* look for opportunities to change. Linehan (1993) wrote that "no rigid position is possible, and process and change are inevitable" (p. 201). Narrative therapists might help their clients understand the other end of the continuum as a method of finding missing elements in their clients' stories. But if an individual is unable to resolve the contradictory positions, Linehan described the conflict as a *dialectical failure*.

As with Mergenthaler's (1996) approach (as described in Chapts. 3 and 4), research supports the idea that moving between the client's emotional and cognitive material is important to therapeutic progress (Angus et al., 1999). This shifting is also a focus in narrative approaches. In some narrative approaches, the client's focus shifts between talking about emotional personal narratives and finding meaning in those narratives. The pace of this shifting between affective experiencing and meaning-making is typically unique to a specific therapist-client dyad. With each client, the therapist finds the best method to overcome obstacles to affective experiencing and meaning-making to facilitate client progress. The timing and effectiveness of meaning-making significantly depends on the client's progress in becoming aware of and expressing affect around important events and relationships (Hardtke & Angus, 2004). The therapist also may avoid certain actions, such as advice giving and problem-solving, that have potential to inhibit the client's focus on affective experiencing and meaning-making.

Poorly formed narratives. Client statements can be considered *ill-formed* or *incomplete* at the level of specific words, phrases, sentences, paragraphs, and whole stories. Several approaches to therapy have the concept of maladaptive themes as central to their approach, as in schema therapy (Young et al., 2003) and rational emotive behavior therapy (REBT; Ellis, 1998). Similarly, distorted statements can be characterized in terms of biases such as *generalizations*, ideas about the world or one operates in it that are not literally true, and *deletions*, where individuals selectively focus on certain aspects of their environment and ignore other components. Narrative therapists listen for, explore, and eventually help clients challenge these distortions in a manner like cognitive therapists.

Client stories usually do not encompass all of a person's life experiences, and some of the excluded experiences may be important to a healthy sense of self. Some dysfunction may be evident by the absence of key story elements (Anderson, 2004), while other important life experiences may contradict the dominant story. For example, a therapist in training who sees himself as a natural helper may find it difficult to accept feedback from a supervisor who tells him that he has poor listening skills. Pennebaker et al. (1997) concluded that narratives that became more focused and coherent over writing sessions were associated with health improvements. Verbalizing affective experiences into an organized linguistic form would seem to be a key component (Pennebaker et al., 1997).

Angus and McLeod (2004) proposed a list of potential criteria that suggest that progress in therapy is marked by development of well-formed narratives about the client's problematic situation(s). At the most fundamental level, a good narrative should be internally consistent and make sense to others, meaning that the events should follow a logical progression that feels plausible. A listener should be able to engage with the story without finding it strange or disjointed. Closely related is the need for organization: A well-formed narrative has a clear beginning, middle, and end, with each component carrying meaningful weight. A story that lacks a proper resolution, for instance, leaves the listener without a sense of closure or purpose.

Other strong narratives are distinguished by their richness of themes and the credibility of their elements. A compelling story draws the listener in through vivid descriptions of characters and events; when this depth is absent, attention is difficult to sustain. Credibility is equally important; a narrative loses its power when it contains obvious falsehoods, presents obstacles that feel contrived, or relies on elements so unfamiliar to the audience that they cannot connect with the story. A well-formed story conveys both the motivations and the emotional states of its characters, allowing the listener to empathize with them and understand why they act as they do. When these elements are missing, the narrative can feel flat or emotionally inaccessible.

Finally, two subtler dimensions reflect the narrator's psychological state. The positive/negative balance of a story matters. Individuals experiencing depression, for example, may struggle to acknowledge positive aspects of their experiences, which can skew a narrative toward a uniformly bleak tone. Similarly, the level of generality or specificity offers diagnostic insight; stories that remain overly vague and fail to include concrete details may point to difficulties with working memory. Thus, the quality of a narrative can reveal important information not just about storytelling ability, but also about the narrator's cognitive and emotional functioning.

Dominant themes—and their exceptions. Because clinicians traditionally have kept written records of each therapy session (Sommers-Flanagan & Sommers-Flanagan, 2012), psychotherapy progress notes represent a source of low-cost information that can be applied to narrative assessment. Little consensus exists about the content of such notes; they typically take the form of a general narrative or lists of important material (but compare Wiger's, [1999] structured approach). Progress notes are used for variety of purposes, including documenting service effectiveness, establishing baseline behaviors, and noting progress in relation to the treatment plan (Wiger, 1999).

In a psychotherapy context, qualitative data in progress notes can be a key source of information, including causative process factors that influence client progress and outcomes (Meier, 2003). Themes, stories, issues, and metaphors can provide data about process elements and outcome elements in a case conceptualization. An anxious client, for example, might express that affective state by frequently switching topics within and between sessions. A recording of these topics each session could provide data about when, how often, and why the client switches issues, thereby deepening the case conceptualization and providing more information relevant for subsequent intervention.

As clients make progress in therapy, previously repetitive themes should dissipate and clients should talk less about those topics (Madigan, 2011; Singer & Blagov, 2004). Habermas et al. (2009), for example, conducted research that found that adult narratives of negative events were longer than narratives of positive events. Singer and Blagov (2004) described *repetitive memories* as repeated client reports that contain content related to important personal goals and issues; traumatic memories have been found to be repetitive in the sense that they repeatedly intrude into consciousness (Foa & Riggs, 1993). With effective therapy, what may have been a pressing topic when a client began therapy should lose its sense of urgency. Other topics may replace the presenting problem, but if the presenting problem has been resolved, the client should be less interested in talking about it. In general, a decrease in the presentation and length of discussion of a clinically relevant theme, as well as a decrease in negative affect around that theme, suggest that the client is ready for closure on these topics. If these topics are the primary focus of therapy, the client may also be ready for termination of treatment.

One assessment strategy is tracking the perseverance of client themes over time. Major themes or issues should have *persistent relevance* (Beutler & Hamblin, 1986). That is, clients often repeatedly discuss important topic across sessions. As noted earlier, emotional reactions to an event increase the likelihood that an event

Table 9.1 Persistence table of client themes

Theme	Session:	1	2	3	4	5	Sum
Anxiety and stress		X					**1**
Frustration		X					**1**
Stay here vs. return to Argentina		X			X		**2**
Funding concerns		X	X	X	X		**4**
Lack of motivation		X			X		**2**
Racist comments			X				
Social life			X		X		**2**
Interpersonal conflict			X	X			**2**
Stress over QP (qualifying paper)			X	X		X	**3**
Perfectionism				X			**1**
No balance				X			**1**
Romantic relationship					X		**1**
Lack of academic support				X		X	**2**
School ending						X	**1**
More productive weekend						X	**1**

Note. For this client, *funding concerns* and *stress over qualifying paper* were the two themes discussed most frequently

will be remembered (Payne & Kensinger, 2010); consequently, as problems resolve and negative affect (NA) diminishes, clients should stop discussing the themes that they talked about earlier in therapy. Table 9.1 is an example of what can be termed a *persistence table* showing how themes for a client changed or persisted across five initial sessions. As shown in the Table, a simple sum of the number of times a theme was discussed in session provides a rudimentary indication of the topic's importance for that client.

For this graduate student client, the two themes discussed most often were *funding concerns* and *stress over qualifying paper*, two relatively short-terms stressors for the client. The NA states of anxiety, stress, and frustration were the major topics of Session 1, probably because they were the reasons motivating the client to attend therapy. These NA states were likely present in all subsequent sessions but were less explicitly discussed because the major topics were the causes of the NA. New topics do appear and disappear over these sessions. For this client, short-term issues appear to be primary topics, but longer-term issues such as lack of motivation, where to live post-graduation, and perfectionism are likely to return as topics in future sessions.

Automated methods. Pennebaker and colleagues have described a more structured approach to analysis of word usage. Based on the assumption that psychological information is conveyed through word use independent of semantic context (Pennebaker et al., 2003), computer-based word count systems analyze the content and style of word use to examine grammatical units (e.g., use of personal pronouns) as well as psychological dimensions (e.g., emotional words). *Linguistic Inquiry and Word Count* (LIWC; Pennebaker et al., 2001) is a text analysis software for analyzing large archival datasets of text. LIWC analyzes differences in the extent to which people use different categories of words, including positive and negative emotions, self-references, and causality.

Word use research findings have implications for the identification of language markers for progress and outcome assessment in psychotherapy. First, measures administered during the beginning of therapy should indicate initial increases in or maintenance of higher levels of NA as the client experiences and expresses these states; this should certainly be the case for clients with internalizing disorders such as anxiety and depression. An increase in the use of different pronouns, indicating an understanding of different perspectives on a problematic situation, should also be associated with improvement in psychotherapy. Client statements indicating greater insight into problem causes and an increase in positive emotions should be more evident toward the middle and end of therapy. A reduction in the frequency of the telling of a problematic story or a story's problematic themes should be evident toward the end of successful therapy.

When evaluating a significant amount of text, an automated analysis has the potential for greater consistency, cost-effectiveness, and potentially, less bias than a human rater (cf., Rathje et al., 2024). Linguistic analysis using automated methods is also unobtrusive, avoids reactivity effects, and can be performed without human raters (Meier, 2025). In contrast, human coding of psychotherapy-related language and behavior is labor-intensive and not feasible in many settings (Atzil-Slonim et al., 2021). Automated language analyses can also provide a person-centered idiographic approach (e.g., Allport, 1937, 1968; Beck & Jackson, 2020; Grisso & Springstein, 2025; Stern, 1938) that assesses an individual's unique characteristics over time that may be unrelated to nomothetic traits (e.g., Levenson et al., 2024).

Summary

Clinical assessment in psychotherapy plays a critical role in providing timely feedback about client progress and informing treatment decisions. This function is especially important, given well-documented rates of premature termination, limited improvement, and clinical deterioration in psychotherapy (Kendall et al., 1992; Persons & Mikami, 2002). Narrative therapy concepts offer a particularly useful framework for clarifying *what* clinicians should assess to monitor therapeutic change. These include the persistence and transformation of dominant client themes, shifts in meaning-making, changes in narrative coherence, and most importantly, reductions in negative affect associated with problem-saturated stories.

As Angus and McLeod (2004) observed, narrative therapy has served as a generative catalyst for many clinicians, in part because its principles resonate with therapists' lived experience of clinical work. Seasoned practitioners often apply narrative sensibilities intuitively, drawing upon metaphors, story arcs, and thematic patterns accumulated over years of practice. Importantly, narrative therapy does not stand in opposition to other therapeutic modalities; rather, it overlaps substantially with cognitive-behavioral, psychodynamic, humanistic, systemic, and emotion-focused approaches. In this sense, narrative therapy can function as an integrative meta-framework for understanding core therapeutic processes and outcomes across orientations (Freedman & Combs, 1996).

A narrative-centered approach to assessment also offers a shared conceptual language that complements existing diagnostic and administrative systems without requiring clinicians to abandon their preferred theoretical models. Just as diagnostic categories facilitate communication with medical providers and insurers, narrative constructs can enhance clinicians' ability to track clinically meaningful change within and across sessions. Moreover, advances in automated language analysis and artificial intelligence hold promise for operationalizing narrative concepts in systematic, scalable, and clinically useful ways. When used judiciously, these tools can augment rather than replace the therapist's empathic understanding by identifying patterns of affect, meaning, and thematic persistence that might otherwise go unnoticed.

In sum, attending carefully to client narratives provides clinicians with a powerful lens for monitoring progress and supporting change. By integrating narrative theory with both traditional clinical judgment and emerging computational methods, psychotherapy assessment can become more precise, responsive, and aligned with the lived experience of clients, ultimately enhancing both clinical effectiveness and ethical practice.

References

Allport, G. W. (1937). *Personality: A psychological interpretation*. Holt.

Allport, G. W. (1968). *The person in psychology: Selected essays*. Beacon Press.

Anderson, H. (2004). Collaborative relationships and dialogic conversations: Ideas for a relationally responsive practice. In L. E. Heatherington & G. Friedlander (Eds.), *Family psychology: Science-based interventions* (pp. 399–415). American Psychological Association.

Angus, L., & McLeod, J. (Eds.). (2004). *The handbook of narrative and psychotherapy: Practice, theory and research*. Sage Publications. https://doi.org/10.4135/9781412973496

Angus, L. E., Levitt, H., & Hardtke, K. (1999). The narrative processes coding system: Research applications and implications for psychotherapy practice. *Journal of Clinical Psychology, 55*(10), 1255–1270. https://doi.org/10.1002/(SICI)1097-4679(199910)55:10<1255::AID-JCLP7>3.0.CO;2-F

Atzil-Slonim, D., Bar-Kalifa, E., Fisher, H., Peri, T., Lutz, W., Rubel, J., & Rafaeli, E. (2021). Emotional congruence between clients and therapists and its effect on treatment outcome. *Journal of Consulting and Clinical Psychology, 89*(4), 341–351. https://doi.org/10.1037/ccp0000628

Beck, E. D., & Jackson, J. J. (2020). Personalized prediction of behaviors and experiences: An idiographic approach. *Journal of Personality, 88*(5), 965–978. https://doi.org/10.1111/jopy.12547

Beutler, L. E., & Hamblin, D. L. (1986). Individualized outcome measures of internal change: Methodological considerations. *Journal of Consulting and Clinical Psychology, 54*(1), 48–53. https://doi.org/10.1037/0022-006X.54.1.48

Brown, L. S. (2007). Empathy, genuineness—And the dynamics of power: A feminist responds to Rogers. *Psychotherapy: Theory, Research, Practice, Training, 44*(3), 257–259. https://doi.org/10.1037/0033-3204.44.3.257

Bruner, J. (1990). *Acts of meaning*. Harvard University Press.

Daiute, C. (2014). *Narrative inquiry: A dynamic approach*. Sage Publications. https://doi.org/10.4135/9781544365442

Davis, S. D., & Meier, S. T. (2001). *The elements of managed care: A guide for helping professionals*. Brooks/Cole.

Ellis, A. (1998). *How to control your anxiety before it controls you*. Citadel Press.

Foa, E. B., & Riggs, D. S. (1993). Post-traumatic stress disorder in rape victims. In J. Oldham, M. B. Riba, & A. Tasman (Eds.), *American psychiatric press review of psychiatry* (Vol. 12, pp. 273–303). American Psychiatric Press.

Freedman, J., & Combs, G. (1996). *Narrative therapy: The social construction of preferred realities*. W. W. Norton & Company.

Geary, D. C. (2011). Cognitive predictors of achievement growth in mathematics: A 5-year longitudinal study. *Developmental Psychology, 47*(6), 1539–1552. https://doi.org/10.1037/a0025510

Greenberg, L. S., & Angus, L. (2004). The contributions of emotion processes to narrative change in psychotherapy: A dialectical constructivist approach. In L. E. Angus & J. McLeod (Eds.), *The handbook of narrative and psychotherapy: Practice, theory and research* (pp. 331–349). Sage Publications. https://doi.org/10.4135/9781412973496.d25

Grisso, T., & Springstein, M. I. (2025). Assessment measures for clinical treatment and research. In T. H. Ollendick, S. W. White, & B. A. White (Eds.), *The Oxford handbook of clinical child and adolescent psychology* (2nd ed., pp. 139–160). Oxford University Press.

Guilfoyle, M. (2025). The technologies of power in psychotherapy: A critical Foucauldian analysis. *Clinical Psychology: Science and Practice*.

Habermas, T., Meier, M., & Mukhtar, B. (2009). Are specific emotions narrated differently? *Emotion, 9*, 751–762. https://doi.org/10.1037/a0018002

Hardtke, K., & Angus, L. (2004). The narrative assessment interview: Assessing self-change in psychotherapy. In L. E. Angus & J. McLeod (Eds.), *The handbook of narrative and psychotherapy: Practice, theory and research* (pp. 247–262). Sage Publications. https://doi.org/10.4135/9781412973496.d18

Huler, S. (2004). *Defining the wind: The Beaufort scale, and how a 19th-century admiral turned science into poetry*. Crown Publishers.

Kelly, G. A. (1955). *The psychology of personal constructs* (Vol. 1–2). Norton.

Kendall, P. C., Holmbeck, G., & Verduin, T. (1992). Methodology, design, and evaluation in psychotherapy research. In A. E. Bergin & S. L. Garfield (Eds.), *Handbook of psychotherapy and behavior change* (4th ed., pp. 16–68). Wiley.

Korman, L. M., & Angus, L. (2000). Client emotional productivity: The therapeutic impact of narrative expression of affect. In A. Coles & M. J. Konstam (Eds.), *Empowerment: Approaches to psychotherapy* (pp. 143–159). Guilford Press.

Krampen, G. (2010). Time-series designs in clinical psychology research. In M. Stemmler (Ed.), *Personality and temperament* (pp. 253–280). Hogrefe.

Levenson, J. C., Frank, E., & Friedman, E. S. (2024). Personalized chronotherapeutic approaches in the treatment of mood disorders. *Current Psychiatry Reports, 26*(1), 1–10. https://doi.org/10.1007/s11920-023-01481-5

Linehan, M. M. (1993). *Cognitive-behavioral treatment of borderline personality disorder*. Guilford Press.

Lock, A., Epston, D., Maisel, R., & de Faria, N. (2005). Resisting anorexia/bulimia: Foucauldian perspectives in narrative therapy. *British Journal of Guidance & Counselling, 33*(3), 315–332. https://doi.org/10.1080/03069880500179459

Madigan, S. (2011). *Narrative therapy*. American Psychological Association. https://doi.org/10.1037/12349-000

Meier, S. T. (2003). *Bridging case conceptualization, assessment, and intervention*. Sage Publications.

Meier, S. T. (2025). Initial evaluation of an AI-augmented progress monitoring and outcome assessment. *Counselling and Psychotherapy Research, 25*. https://doi.org/10.1002/capr.12869

Meier, S. T. (2026). An integrative approach to five controversial areas in psychotherapy. Professional Psychology: *Research and Practice, 57*, 12–18. https://doi.org/10.1037/pro0000660

Mergenthaler, E. (1996). Emotion–abstraction patterns in verbatim protocols: A new way of describing psychotherapeutic processes. *Journal of Consulting and Clinical Psychology, 64*(6), 1306–1315. https://doi.org/10.1037/0022-006X.64.6.1306

Morgan, A. (2000). *What is narrative therapy? An easy-to-read introduction*. Dulwich Centre Publications.

Nolen-Hoeksema, S. (1996). Chewing the cud and other ruminations. In R. S. Wyer Jr. (Ed.), *Ruminative thoughts: Advances in social cognition* (Vol. 9, pp. 135–144). Psychology Press.

Payne, J. D., & Kensinger, E. A. (2010). Sleep's role in the consolidation of emotional episodic memories. *Current Directions in Psychological Science, 19*(5), 290–295. https://doi.org/10.1177/0963721410383978

Pennebaker, J. W., Booth, R. J., & Francis, M. E. (2001). *Linguistic inquiry and word count: LIWC*. [Computer software]. LIWC.net.

Pennebaker, J. W., Mayne, T. J., & Francis, M. E. (1997). Linguistic predictors of adaptive bereavement. *Journal of Personality and Social Psychology, 72*(4), 863–871. https://doi.org/10.1037/0022-3514.72.4.863

Pennebaker, J. W., Mehl, M. R., & Niederhoffer, K. G. (2003). Psychological aspects of natural language use: Our words, our selves. *Annual Review of Psychology, 54*, 547–577. https://doi.org/10.1146/annurev.psych.54.101601.145041

Persons, J. B., & Mikami, A. Y. (2002). Strategies for handling treatment failure successfully. *Psychotherapy: Theory, Research, Practice, Training, 39*(2), 139–151. https://doi.org/10.1037/0033-3204.39.2.139

Polkinghorne, D. E. (2004). Narrative therapy and postmodernism. In L. E. Angus & J. McLeod (Eds.), *The handbook of narrative and psychotherapy: Practice, theory and research* (pp. 53–67). Sage Publications. https://doi.org/10.4135/9781412973496.d5

Rathje, S., Roozenbeek, J., Van Bavel, J. J., & van der Linden, S. (2024). Accuracy and social motivations shape judgements of (mis)information. *Nature Human Behaviour, 8*, 731–741. https://doi.org/10.1038/s41562-024-01814-8

Semmler, P. L., & Braun, W. (2000). Culturally-constructed stories of a woman's journey towards self-identity: A narrative analysis. *Journal of Multicultural Counseling and Development, 28*(3), 174–184. https://doi.org/10.1002/j.2161-1912.2000.tb00345.x

Shostrom, E. L. (1965). *Three approaches to psychotherapy*. [Film]. Psychological Films.

Singer, J. A., & Blagov, P. (2004). The integrative function of narrative processing: Autobiographical memory, self-defining memories, and the life story of identity. In D. R. Beike, J. M. Lampinen, & D. A. Behrend (Eds.), *The self and memory* (pp. 117–138). Psychology Press.

Sommers-Flanagan, J., & Sommers-Flanagan, R. (2012). Counseling and psychotherapy theories in context and practice (2nd ed.). New York: Wiley.

Stern, W. (1938). *General psychology from the personalistic standpoint* (H. D. Spoerl, Trans.). Macmillan. (Original work published 1935).

Stott, R., Mansell, W., Salkovskis, P., Lavender, A., & Cartwright-Hatton, S. (2010). *Oxford guide to metaphors in CBT: Building cognitive bridges*. Oxford University Press. https://doi.org/10.1093/med:psych/9780199207053.001.0001

Teyber, E., & McClure, F. H. (2011). *Interpersonal process in therapy: An integrative model* (6th ed.). Brooks/Cole.

Vermeersch, D. A., Lambert, M. J., & Burlingame, G. M. (2000). Outcome Questionnaire: Item sensitivity to change. *Journal of Personality Assessment, 74*, 242–261. https://doi.org/10.1207/S15327752JPA7402_6

Vermeersch, D. A., Whipple, J. L., Lambert, M. J., Hawkins, E. J., Burchfield, C. M., & Okiishi, J. C. (2004). Outcome Questionnaire: Is It Sensitive to Changes in Counseling Center Clients? *Journal of Counseling Psychology, 51*(1), 38–49. https://doi.org/10.1037/0022-0167.51.1.38

Viney, L. L. (1993). *Life stories: Personal construct therapy with the elderly*. John Wiley & Sons.

von Wyl, A. (2004). Narrative processes: Emotion, exchange, and development. In L. E. Angus & J. McLeod (Eds.), *The handbook of narrative and psychotherapy: Practice, theory and research* (pp. 271–286). Sage Publications. https://doi.org/10.4135/9781412973496.d20

Wang, Z., & Sun, Y. (2024). The integration of artificial intelligence in mental health care: Opportunities and challenges. *Journal of Medical Internet Research, 26*(1), e51234. https://doi.org/10.2196/51234

Watkins, E., & Moulds, M. (2005). Distinct modes of ruminative self-focus: Impact of abstract versus concrete rumination on problem solving in depression. *Emotion, 5*(3), 319–328. https://doi.org/10.1037/1528-3542.5.3.319

Weinstock, M., & Meier, S. T. (2003). A comparison of two item selection methodologies for measuring change in university counseling center clients. *Measurement and Evaluation in Counseling & Development, 36*, 66–75. https://doi.org/10.1080/07481756.2003.12069082

White, M. (2004). *Narrative practice and exotic lives: Resurrecting diversity in everyday life*. Dulwich Centre Publications.

White, M. (2015). *Selected papers of Michael White: Adelaide conversations*. Dulwich Centre Publications.

White, M., & Epston, D. (1990). *Narrative means to therapeutic ends*. W. W. Norton & Company.

Wickman, S. A. (2000). Discovering what families want from family therapy: An action research report from trainees in a postmodern family therapy training setting. *Journal of Family Psychotherapy, 11*(1), 19–39. https://doi.org/10.1300/J085v11n01_03

Wiger, D. E. (1999). *The clinical documentation sourcebook* (2nd ed.). John Wiley & Sons.

Young, J. E., Klosko, J. S., & Weishaar, M. E. (2003). *Schema therapy: A practitioner's guide*. Guilford Press.

Chapter 10
Practice–Research Integration: Practice Research Networks for Translating Evidence-Based Interventions into Healthcare Systems

In 2002 Hawkins served as guest editor for a special issue of *The Behavior Therapist* (Hawkins, 2002) that addressed the value of forming practice research networks (PRNs) for graduate training in evidence-based cognitive-behavioral interventions. In that issue, Borkovec (2002) described his "dream" for the development of a set of PRNs at the levels of the training clinic clinical practicum, internship, postdoctoral year, and after professional psychology licensure. The purpose of this chapter is to explore how practice-research integration (also called practice-oriented research; Castonguay et al., 2015) can bridge the gap between real-world clinical practice and clinical science inquiry by leveraging PRNs and translation research, or implementation science systems thinking, to ensure that evidence-based interventions are effectively translated, adopted, and sustained within healthcare systems.

As a professor in research and graduate level teaching, as well as a practicing licensed clinical psychologist, Hawkins developed several archival databases for summarizing and collecting the results of individual and group-based interventions with clients in several settings (see also Hawkins, 2019). Initially, at University of Texas at Austin, in 1976, Hawkins developed and led the Psychological Weight Control Program, a clinic within the student health center, for 4 years and simultaneously gathered assessment and personality measures from a sample of college students for comparison purposes (Hawkins, Fremouw, & Clement, 1984). These efforts were approved by the UT Austin Institutional Review Board.

Subsequently, as a licensed clinical psychologist, he co-developed a group practice called the Austin Stress Clinic. The archived data in that setting were from clients involved in interventions targeting habit control and eating disorders. In 1982, Hawkins became a staff psychologist in an Austin HMO medical group that had a mental health department where he was also able to subcontract conducting extramural research at the Epilepsy Center in San Antonio. There he gathered and archived neuropsychological data from a sample of children who had epilepsy and related conditions, as well as data from their parents (Hawkins et al., 1985). Then, within the Austin medical group, he initiated a series of program evaluation studies

R. Hawkins, S. Meier, *Healing Outcomes*,
https://doi.org/10.1007/978-3-032-33611-8_10

which involved archiving and developing outcome measures for a large sample of mental health clients and a select group of medical patients receiving treatment for hypertension or for substance use disorder. Subsequently, Hawkins directed the UT Austin Clinical Psychology Training Clinic for 3 years and archived data from nearly 30 years of outcomes of evidence-based cognitive behavioral therapy done with clients from the community and UT students (Hawkins, 2019). When he was appointed as a core psychology faculty member at Fielding Graduate University, in 2004, Hawkins created another practice research network archival database at New Life Institute in Austin and, on a larger scale, the Fielding Psychology Practice Research Network, utilizing a standardized outcome measure called the Treatment Outcome Package (Kraus et al., 2005).

An overarching metaphor called "the dam, the garden, and the bond" (Hawkins, 1998, unpublished; Hawkins, 2019) may be useful to illustrate the contrast between the assumptions of hierarchy/power and contextual relations in the SCIM framework. Hawkins lives in a cabin on Lake Buchanan, a flood control lake in the Texas Hill Country that has one of the longest dams in the world. As in managed care that aims to treat specific populations (metaphorically, like fish in a flood control lake), the "dam" model presumes that sufficiently potent specific psychoeducational techniques (e.g., for coping with stress and managing moods) can be developed, manualized, and used effectively to treat clients regardless of their characteristics, the therapists' characteristics, or the nature of the therapeutic relationship. The "garden" model assumes that treatments can be tailored to produce effects for clients with certain characteristics (akin to different species of flora and fauna), including diagnoses, personality types, and cultural features. The competent therapist would thus need to be a kind of field naturalist with an expert knowledge of the clients in the caseload "garden."

Finally, the "bond" model presumes that certain clients with certain characteristics require privileging the therapist-client relationship between specific clients and specific therapists that must be attuned and maintained for maximum therapeutic benefit. This dam–garden–bond metaphor may loosely parallel psychotherapeutic theoretical orientations (from psychoeducation and CBT to humanistic-experiential explorations to psychodynamic attachment-oriented psychotherapy). In addition, the continuum from dam to garden to bond bears resemblance to the agency–communion framework (Bakan, 1966), which has also been applied to end-of life decision making (Hawkins, 2017), cross-cultural psychology (Hawkins, 2016), as well as to addiction and co-dependency (Hawkins & Hawkins, 2014). In the present context, agency connotes an individually controlled, separate focus (i.e., project development by the autonomous clinical researcher) while communion connotes an emphasis upon collaboration or sharing in the development of practice-oriented research (i.e., researchers and clinicians together plan the project and share it with clients in psychotherapy for their input). The dam–garden–bond metaphor also reflects a parallel with the expected duration of psychological interventions (from short-term to long-term duration). One additional implication of this dam–garden–bond metaphor, which is also explicit in the SCIM, is that selection of assessment and outcome measures for use in a PRN should promote psychotherapy integration to accommodate these individual differences in clients' needs and circumstances.

"Best practice" research networks of various kinds can be created as an adjunct to laboratory-based randomized controlled treatments (RCTs) (Borkovec, 2002; Hawkins, 2002, 2019), or simply as a way of doing outcome-informed practice by measuring outcomes to improve one's effectiveness as a psychotherapist. The gap between real-world clinical practice and clinical science must be reduced. Psychotherapy effectiveness can be tested not only using RCTs, which mostly use nomothetic variable-based mono-method outcome measures but also with intensive idiographic person-centered case study analysis using evidence-based interventions that include not only multiple outcome measures but also multiple core process measures (Hawkins, 2019; see also Chap. 5). A core process measure estimates the contribution of the hypothesized treatment active ingredient (as an indicator of a mechanism of action, also called a maintaining factor). The advantage of using case-by-case client-centered interventions and archiving these in a practice research network is that one can examine the changes across sessions in these core process measures as mediators for changes in client functioning before the final end-of-treatment outcome measures are administered.

To illustrate this, consider two related studies of diagnostic subgroups of clients from the UT Austin Clinical Psychology Training Clinic PRN that received evidence-based interventions using exposure-based CBT for social phobia (Hawkins & Grice, 2020) or exposure-based CBT for panic disorder (Hawkins & Grice, 2021). The person-centered Observation-Oriented Modeling approach of Grice (2011) was used for these studies and contrasted with using variable-based outcome measures as well as a measure of a core process mediator administered across sessions. The specific instruments used for the social phobia study included the self-report version of the Liebowitz Social Anxiety Scale (LSAS; Rytwinski et al., 2009) as the outcome measure, and the Appraisal of Social Concerns (ASC; Telch et al., 2004) as the core process measure. As shown in Fig. 10.1, there were systematic decreases in both the outcome measure and the core process measure across sessions. The changes in mean levels of these measures (approaching clinical cutoff thresholds moving from elevated clinical status to normal level) suggest the overall effectiveness of the intervention approach; however, there were numerous differences between clients in the timing of these changes and the contribution of the core process mediation to these changes. To look at these changes in a more person-specific way (Fig. 10.2), we used OOM to see whether changes in the core process mediating measure (i.e., ASC) would occur prior to changes in the outcome measure (LSAS). In approximately two-thirds of these social phobia cases, as hypothesized, the core process measure changed before the outcome measure. The OOM analyses for the panic disorder treated clients also showed statistically significant improvements in both the outcome measure, the Panic Disorder Symptoms Severity Scale (PDSS; Shear et al., 1997), and the core process measures, the Anxiety Sensitivity Index (ASI; Reiss et al., 1986) and the Panic Appraisal Inventory (PAI; Telch et al., 1989). However, the changes in the ASI and PAI core process measures occurred prior to changes in the PDSS outcome measure in only 40% to 48% of the

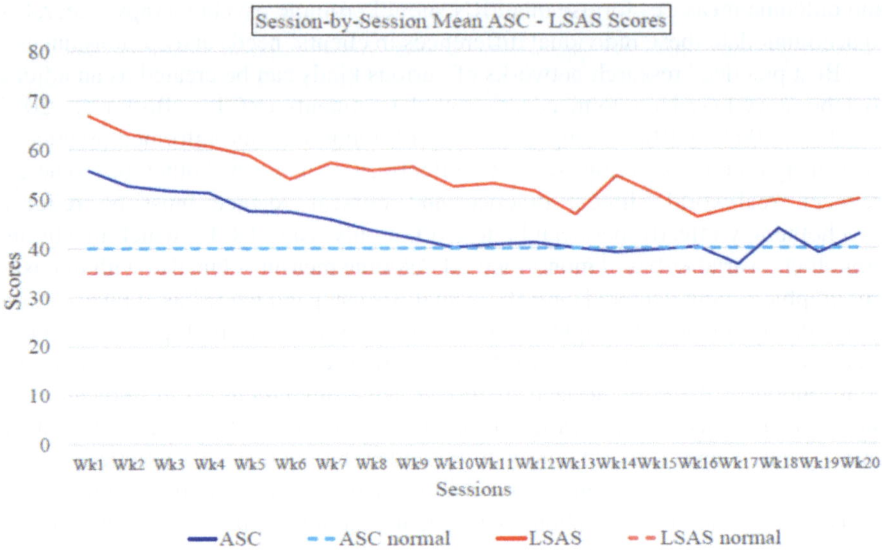

Fig. 10.1 Mean ASC and LSAS across sessions for entire SAD sample (n = 65) (Hawkins & Grice, 2020)

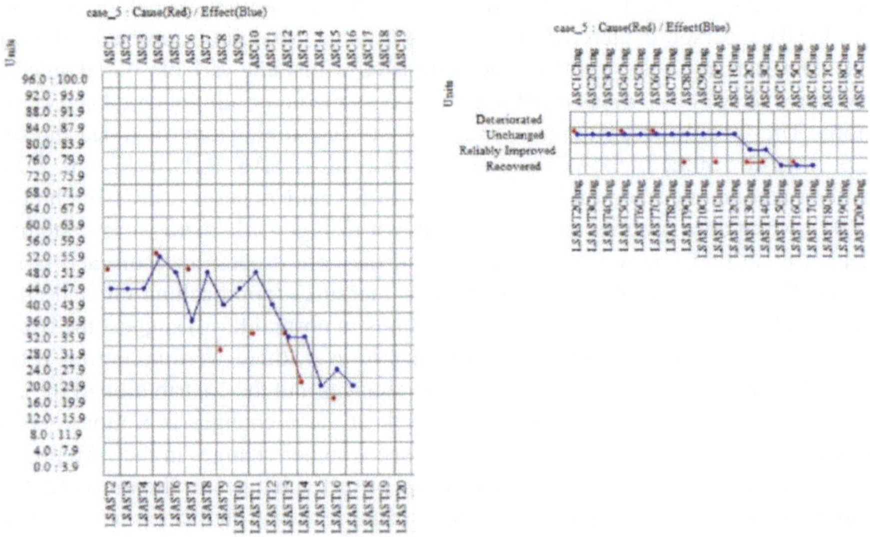

Fig. 10.2 OOM PCC on session-by-session change scores for LSAS lagged one session after ASC (example single case) (Hawkins & Grice, 2020)

cases. The ASI, PAI, and PDSS scores tended to change together in time. Lagging did not improve the results for the raw scores nor for the clinical change categories for panic disorder treatment outcomes (Deteriorated reliably (D), Unimproved (U), Improved reliably (I), or Recovered (R)) (Hawkins & Grice, 2021).

PRN databases can be used to examine treatment outcome effectiveness for other disorders and to analyze general changes in clinical status and overall symptom distress changes using the Treatment Outcome Package (Hawkins et al., 2018). So, what we can see from these examples is that practice research integration (using PRNs) can be studied in such a way that multimethod assessments combined with multiple outcome and core process measures can reveal healing outcomes. These outcomes are not only discernible as mean level group effects but also can be confirmed by the treatment response of individual clients.

Recall the case study presented earlier of a White middle-aged man whose MBTI Type preference was INFP. In Chap. 6, we described the therapist's preferred psychological type as INTJ and pointed out the implications of the degree of mismatch between therapist and client and how this played out in the therapeutic alliance and in the therapeutic process. Looking at this match-mismatch process within the context of the practice research network hypothetically, because actual MBTI measures were not available for all the relationships within meso and macro levels of change, we can observe how the overall temporal ordering of processes can take place on a person-specific basis. In the case of this INFP client, changes in the outcome measure (the Back Depression Inventory) did not occur until the Type mismatch problem in the therapeutic alliance was corrected, and the client's emotional and cognitive processing (i.e., the Healing Cycle) occurred, such that the client was able to discern how his life story was not one of continual victimization, but instead how he could have increased agency in his life doing things that were congruent with his personal values (e.g., reading books on philosophy and religious themes). At that point, depression decreased consistently despite the client's disability status, limited socioeconomic means, and limited social supports. An effort was made at that point to increase social support by including the client in a men's group associated with the client's preferred religious denomination. This, along with encouraging the client to address his social anxiety related avoidance by participating in meetings of a local book club, helped the client to improve his overall mental and physical health. The client was able to remain productively engaged in therapy over several years.

Conclusions

This chapter has provided an overview of practice–research integration, and specifically the value of practice research network archived databases for translating evidence-based interventions within healthcare systems to individual case studies. The Observation Oriented Modeling (OOM) method (Grice, 2011) can be used to show whether, for individual clients, targeted core process maintaining factors change before their respective outcome measures improve.

References

Bakan, D. (1966). *The duality of human existence: Isolation and communion in modern man*. Rand McNally.

Borkovec, T. D. (2002). Training clinic research and the possibility of a national training clinics practice research network. *The Behavior Therapist, 25*(5/6), 98–102.

Castonguay, L. G., Eubanks, C. F., Goldfried, M. R., Muran, J. C., & Lutz, W. (2015). Research on psychotherapy integration: Building on the past, looking to the future. *Psychotherapy Research, 3*, 365–382. https://doi.org/10.1080/10503307.2015.1014010

Grice, J. W. (2011). *Observation-oriented modeling: Analysis of cause in behavioral sciences*. Elsevier.

Hawkins, R. C., II. (2002). Behavior therapy and the training clinic: Can science be integrated with practice and community service? [special issue]. *The Behavior Therapist, 25*(5–6), 97–98.

Hawkins, R. C., II. (2016). Biofeedback and the illusion of control: A functional contextual perspective. *Biofeedback, 44*(4), 225–228. https://doi.org/10.5298/1081-5937-44.4.05

Hawkins, R. C., II. (2017). Agency and communion in end-of-life decision- making. *Illness, Crisis, & Loss, 25*(2), 87–106. https://doi.org/10.1177/1054137315606819

Hawkins, R. C., II. (2019). A conceptual model for practice-oriented research and practice research networks. *Revista Argentina de Clínica Psicológica, 28*(5), 603–609.

Hawkins, R.C. II, & Grice, J. W. (2020, November). *Observation oriented modeling of CBT outcomes for social anxiety disorder*. Poster presented at the annual conference of the Association for Behavioral and Cognitive Therapies, Philadelphia, PA (Virtual).

Hawkins, R.C. II, & Grice, J. W. (2021, November). *Observation oriented modeling of CBT outcomes for panic disorder*. Poster presented at the annual conference of the Association for Behavioral and Cognitive Therapies, New Orleans, LA. (Virtual).

Hawkins, R. C., II, & Hawkins, C. A. (2014). Codependence, contradependence, gender-stereotyped traits, personality dimensions, and problem drinking. *Universal Journal of Psychology, 2*(1), 5–15. https://doi.org/10.13189/ujp.2014.020102

Hawkins, R. C. II, Fremouw, W. J., & Clement, P. F. (Eds.). (1984). *The binge-purge syndrome: Diagnosis, treatment, and research*. New York: Springer.

Hawkins, R. C. II, Hubler, D. W., & Geis, S. (1985). *Neuropsychological assessment as a component of comprehensive treatment planning with seizure disordered children*. Presented at the annual convention of the American Epilepsy Society, New York, NY.

Hawkins, R.C. II, (1998). CBT core process and outcome measures for DSM disorders. (Unpublished chart).

Hawkins, R.C. II, Lopez, M., & Garza, L. (2018, March). *A tale of two practice research networks: Databases for clinical scientist and scholar-practitioner compared*. Poster presented at the Association for Directors of Psychology Training Clinics, Maui, HI.

Kraus, D. R., Seligman, D. A., & Jordan, J. R. (2005). Validation of a behavioral healthcare outcome and assessment tool designed for naturalistic settings: The treatment outcome package. *Journal of Clinical Psychology, 61*(3), 285–314. https://doi.org/10.1002/jclp.20084

Reiss, S., Peterson, R. A., Gursky, D. M., & McNally, R. J. (1986). Anxiety sensitivity, anxiety frequency and the prediction of fearfulness. *Behavior Research and Therapy, 24*(1), 1–8. https://doi.org/10.1016/0005-7967(86)90143-9

Rytwinski, N. K., Fresco, D. M., Heimberg, R. G., Coles, M. E., Liebowitz, M. R., Cissell, S., Stein, M. B., & Hofmann, S. G. (2009). Screening for social anxiety disorder with the self-report version of the Liebowitz social anxiety scale. *Depression and Anxiety, 26*(1), 34–38. https://doi.org/10.1002/da.20503

Shear, M. K., Brown, T. A., Barlow, D. H., Money, R., Sholomskas, D. E., Woods, S. W., Gorman, J. M., & Papp, L. A. (1997). Multicenter collaborative panic disorder severity scale. *American Journal of Psychiatry, 154*(11), 1571–1575. https://doi.org/10.1176/ajp.154.11.1571

Telch, M. J., Brouillard, M., Telch, C. F., Agras, W. S., & Taylor, C. B. (1989). Role of cognitive appraisal in panic-related avoidance. *Behavior Research and Therapy, 27*(4), 373–383. https://doi.org/10.1016/0005-7967(89)90007-7

Telch, M. J., Lucas, R. A., Smits, J. A., Powers, M. B., Heimberg, R., & Hart, T. (2004). Appraisal of social concerns: A cognitive assessment instrument for social phobia. *Depression & Anxiety, 19*(4), 217–224. https://doi.org/10.1002/da.20004

Part III
Summary and Implications

Chapter 11
Toward a Unified Dynamic Model: Summary, Future Directions, and Conclusions

Toward a Unified Dynamic Model

In 1977, George Engel proposed "biopsychosocial" theory as a holistic, integrative model that would supersede the traditional biomedical view, which had characterized medicine and psychiatry for many years. The biopsychosocial model (BPSM) emphasized the importance of considering the psychological and social aspects of the life context as these influence the patient's view of health and illness. In the nearly 50 years since Engel's BPSM has been promulgated, some criticisms have been voiced, and the model has been elaborated. For instance, Lehman et al. (2017) called for situating the BPSM within dynamic systems theory. More significantly, Bolton (2023) emphasized the importance of not merely considering the reciprocal interaction of biology, psychology, and social factors but instead developing the BPSM such that the causal mechanisms can be discerned in this interaction. Also, Card (2023) described the need to consider an overarching view of health and illness as a "complex adaptive system of systems."

Given this discussion of the BPSM, we will now situate the Systems-Contextual Integrative Model (SCIM) proposed in this book. The SCIM is a BPSM variant. This is most clearly seen in its incorporation of Brofenbrenner's (1979) social ecological systems approach looking at the multiple levels of influence, from the "micro" individual level to the "meso" interpersonal level to the "macro" sociocultural level of values. More significantly though, the "engine" of the SCIM has two aspects. The first aspect is that the SCIM driver is based upon dual process complementary system principles: the healthy system principle and the neurotic system principle (Angyal, 1965). These are called the "healing cycle" (HC) and the "trauma cycle" (TC) in the SCIM. Scott Kelso's (2009, 2013; Kelso & Engstrom, 2006) theory of "complementary nature" may also characterize the SCIM in which the contrasting pairs (the Healing Cycle and the Trauma Cycle; Hawkins & Meier, 2015) are synergistically coordinated (Kelso, 2021).

R. Hawkins, S. Meier, *Healing Outcomes*,
https://doi.org/10.1007/978-3-032-33611-8_11

The positive and negative aspects of these complementary pairs are described and contrasted. In the SCIM, qualitative changes (dynamic phase shifts between the HC and the TC) in thoughts, affects, behaviors, and volition are triggered by control parameters within the individual and within the socio-environmental context. Kelso (2021) has described coordination dynamics as integrating contraries into metastable coordinated states. Self-organization (spontaneous) vs. directed (intentional) occurs. In this sense, the SCIM not only is a dynamic system across these multiple levels but also provides testable predictions about how alternations between the HC and TC can be modeled by these opponent dual complementary processes.

Another key aspect of the SCIM is its emphasis upon psychological type theory as a "fractal" lens for viewing dynamic processes within individuals and in their interpersonal transactions. In this sense, then, the SCIM represents a BPSM elaboration which has practical as well as scientific value. The practical value is that the interactions across the levels of the SCIM in conjunction with the shifts back and forth between the HC and TC can be used as a framework for viewing healing processes within and between individuals. Scientifically, the SCIM proposes some testable hypotheses which can be examined in future research. These include elucidating the control parameters for the shifts between the TC and the HC, and examining the individual differences in psychological types and how these type differences influence type dynamics within and between individuals and larger groups.

Summary: The overall thrust of this book has been not only to emphasize how reducing the gap between therapeutic theories and multi-method assessment and outcome measures is an important undertaking, but also to describe new contributions to both theory and measurement in psychotherapy. From both standpoints, it is important to look at the relationship between psychotherapy and the overall framework for organizing and utilizing such measures (e.g., Smith, 2025). In this manuscript, we have updated an earlier paper (Hawkins & Meier, 2015), providing a heuristic Systems-Contextual Integrative Model (SCIM) for levels of change incorporating the interaction of a dual process Trauma Cycle and Healing Cycle. This SCIM framework includes a novel use of a strength-based idiographic person-centered measure (MBTI 16 Types) and a clinician-rated Depression/Anxiety Negative Affect (DANA) scale (Meier, 2012, 2024), and introduces the application of Observation Oriented Modeling (OOM; Grice, 2011), a person-centered non-parametric method for determining the extent to which the results case by case conform to hypothesized models about mechanisms of change in psychotherapy.

We reviewed the important topics of the centrality of healing through emotion, the utilization of emotional processing to reduce avoidance in psychotherapy, and the linking of these processes with measurement tools. We also examined common factors involved in psychotherapy effectiveness, namely the working alliance between therapist and client, and especially client expectations about change and client-determined success along with the utilization of measures not only of client distress but also of strengths and positive values.

This book provides an integrative model (SCIM) for organizing multi-method assessment and outcome measures, and it situates these measures within a dual process dynamic emphasizing Mergenthaler's (1996) therapeutic cycle (here renamed the Healing Cycle), which focuses not only on mono-method decreases in symptoms but also on enhancement of the overall holistic integrative functioning in the client ("healing outcomes"). This therapeutic endeavor involves more than what can be measured using nomothetic variable-based outcome measures. It is very important to use mixed methods, which include narrative language models and artificial intelligence in psychotherapy research.

Chapter 9 described how narratives and language shape therapeutic change, and how artificial intelligence is transforming research and clinical feedback. For example, one RCT pilot study has determined that clients achieved more self-reported symptom change in anxiety and depression following interactions with a Gen-AI–powered chatbot ("Therabot") than did waitlist controls (Heinz et al., 2025). There are some very important ethical challenges that are addressed in this book, or which are pointed out as ethical challenges to be considered future priorities for research and policy. The ethics of including strength-based measures in therapeutic assessment feedback for healing collaboration (e.g., Finn, 2007), and the use of idiographic process measures to account for intra-individual micro level changes are very important. The overall use of the social ecological multilevel SCIM approach provides a reminder to psychotherapy researchers and clinicians that there is a complex interaction across multiple levels affecting individuals within their life contexts. The chief ethical issue that remains to be considered in the future is how to utilize artificial intelligence as an adjunct to the therapeutic alliance in individual psychotherapy, or in group or family therapy, rather than as a replacement for the psychotherapist. In that way machine learning can be both helpful and ethical (e.g., using general language processing models for interpreting session narratives (Meier, 2012, 2024) or narratives of responses given to the Thematic Apperception Test stimulus cards (Hawkins, 2023).

In our book, we have thus revisited the core cycles of healing and trauma, outlined ethical recommendations for the future, and suggested how effective psychotherapy can be offered to all regardless of cultural background. We have described a dynamic client-centered tech-enhanced evaluation framework to be used interactively with individual clients in their life contexts. We have also argued that there is a considerable gap in the linkage between the multitude of therapeutic approaches that exist (Kazdin, 1994; Perez, 1999) and the equally large number of psychological tests potentially relevant to psychotherapy process and outcome. As Faust (1986, p. 423) described this situation:

> There is a universe of potentially available information about patients. One must decide what information is most relevant, how to obtain it, how to integrate what is obtained, and how to relate it to what are often nebulous and ill-defined categories.

However, numerous theoretically derived, reliable, and valid measures have been developed by researchers in the cognitive behavioral, psychoanalytic, interpersonal, and humanistic-experiential traditions to fill this gap. Still, unified theories such as our Systems-Contextual Integrative Model are needed to provide a framework to organize the increasingly large number of theoretically derived measures from these major theoretical orientations that is more coherent, research generating, and useful for practitioners.

Future Directions: We believe that the field should utilize clinical feedback provided by measures specifically designed for progress monitoring and outcome assessment related to psychotherapy theories. The appropriate use of measurement procedures as part of clinical practice offers one approach to reducing the high rates of treatment failure reported in the literature (e.g., between 10% and 50% of all clients, Kraus et al., 2011; Lambert, 2007; Lilienfield, 2007; Persons & Mikami, 2002). Clement (1999, p. 10) observed that for clinicians to employ progress and outcome measures, the usefulness of the information needs to outweigh the additional work. A better integration of psychotherapy theory with measurement is one approach to increasing the apparent and actual usefulness of data produced for the purposes of progress monitoring and outcome assessment (e.g., the findings of Lambert et al., 2005, described earlier). Organizing these measures within a unified framework (e.g., Chap. 3, Table 3.1) may facilitate their use in both clinical research and routine practice.

Regarding everyday practice considerations, clinicians report increased paperwork and required time as major reasons for not employing measurement in treatment (Hatfield & Ogles, 2004). Qualitative studies, surveys, and implementation reviews consistently find that many clinicians report negative or ambivalent attitudes toward outcome data. Common concerns include doubts about the clinical relevance of standardized measures, perceptions that progress monitoring outcome assessment (PMOA) oversimplifies complex cases, and skepticism about whether such data meaningfully improve clinical judgment. Increased workload, time constraints, and poor integration into workflows further reduce PMOA use (Boswell et al., 2015; Hatfield & Ogles, 2004).

Emotional and professional factors also play a role. Some clinicians experience discomfort or threat when confronted with negative feedback, particularly when outcome data are perceived as evaluative rather than supportive. Others worry that formal measurement may harm the therapeutic alliance or shift sessions toward administrative tasks, even though empirical evidence does not strongly support these concerns (Gondek et al., 2016; Kendrick et al., 2016). Taken together, the literature suggests that PMOA with feedback can improve outcomes, yet its impact depends heavily on clinician engagement and responsiveness to the data. Successful implementation appears to require organizational cultures that frame feedback as a tool for learning and client safety, along with systems that minimize burden and provide clear guidance on how to respond when clients are not improving as expected.

Given the usefulness of PMOA and clinical feedback for improving outcomes, it may be helpful to generate other options beyond asking busy clinicians to take on another time-consuming task for which many have received little training. We propose the development of a mental health outcomes specialist whose primary responsibility is the systematic collection, synthesis, and clinical summarization of PMOA data. This specialization would function analogously to assessment-focused roles already established in healthcare (e.g., neuropsychology technicians, radiologists), allowing clinicians to remain focused on treatment delivery while still benefiting from high-quality data. The assessor would (a) oversee measure selection, administration fidelity, and data quality, (b) monitor trajectories of change, (c) identify clients who are failing to improve, and (d) provide concise, clinically interpretable summaries to therapy providers. And, as AI augmentation of clinical assessments develop, the assessor could also supervise AI outputs and resolve differences between AI programs and clinical assessors (Meier, 2024). By translating raw data into actionable insights (e.g., risk flags, alliance concerns, or treatment-response patterns), the assessor's role would directly address one of the most persistent barriers to PMOA use: Clinicians' difficulty integrating data into real-time clinical decision-making.

This specialization may also mitigate other sources of clinician resistance. Separating outcome monitoring from therapist self-evaluation reduces defensiveness and performance anxiety associated with negative feedback, reframing PMOA as a supportive, patient-improvement function rather than a judgment of clinician competence. Moreover, centralized assessment expertise reduces redundancy, increases standardization, and improves organizational learning while maintaining clinician autonomy in treatment decisions. From a systems perspective, a dedicated outcomes assessor enhances quality assurance, supports measurement-based care mandates, and enables more equitable, data-informed treatment planning. Importantly, it allows PMOA to fulfill its intended role as a clinical support technology rather than an administrative burden. In this sense, the creation of a mental health outcomes assessor is not an added layer of bureaucracy, but instead a pragmatic redesign of clinical labor—aligning specialized skills with specialized tasks to improve care quality and patient outcomes. Just as we would not expect a primary care physician or physician assistant to perform X-rays or MRI scans, mental health practice appears to have reached a point where efficient and effective use of PMOA data for clinical feedback requires the creation and use of a new assessment/intervention specialization.

To tackle the early dropout problem, future research should further examine Zilcha-Mano's (2025) findings that challenge the long-standing assumption that the working alliance develops gradually only after therapy begins. Her randomized controlled trial of patients with major depressive disorder demonstrated that changes in alliance measured before patients met their therapists predicted both subsequent alliance development and symptom improvement across treatment. Individuals who showed increases in alliance prior to the first session experienced stronger alliances and greater reductions in depression throughout therapy, even after controlling for expectations, therapist effects, and prior treatment experience. These findings suggest that clinically meaningful therapeutic processes may be active well before formal treatment commences.

Converging evidence from studies of ceiling effects on alliance measures further supports this conclusion (Meier & Feeley, 2021; Sabella & Meier, 2024). Patient-rated alliance scores frequently cluster near the top of available scales as early as the first session, indicating that alliance formation may operate as a rapid, nonlinear threshold phenomenon rather than a slow, incremental process. For many patients, the alliance appears to be either established or not, with little measurable growth thereafter. This pattern also implies that traditional alliance–outcome correlations may underestimate the alliance's true importance once ceiling effects restrict variability.

Together, these findings highlight the importance of pre-therapy and early-session experiences as conceptualized within the Early Therapeutic Environment (ETE). Administrative contacts, referral processes, intake procedures, and early goal clarification may all contribute to alliance formation before the first session. Because many clients terminate treatment within the first few sessions, prioritizing early relational processes may be critical for reducing attrition and improving outcomes. Clinically, these results underscore the need to monitor alliance as early as possible and to view early contact not as peripheral, but as an integral component of effective psychotherapy.

Conclusions

In this book, we have suggested that two separate traditions in psychology, theories of personality and psychotherapy on the one hand, and measurement in psychological assessment and in treatment process/outcome evaluation on the other, can be folded together within one unified model for the mutual advantage of each tradition. The advantages of this integration would be (a) to provide a heuristic conceptual framework that would organize the use of currently available measures and encourage the development of new theoretically derived measures, and (b) to offer an assortment of process and outcome measures for clinicians and trainees to use in practice research networks and evidence-based practices to demonstrate that the therapeutic process described conceptually in our Systems Contextual Integrative Model's Healing Cycle facilitates positive treatment outcomes. Furthermore, as accountability becomes more important with the implementation of healthcare reform in the United States, unified models such as the SCIM may also help to advance policy and dissemination research related to counseling, psychotherapy, and behavioral healthcare (e.g., Chor et al., 2014).

References

Angyal, A. (1965). *Neurosis & treatment: A holistic theory*. Wiley.

Bolton, D. (2023). A revitalized biopsychosocial model: Core theory, research paradigms, and clinical implications. *Psychological Medicine, 53*, 7504–7511. https://doi.org/10.1017/S0033291723002660

Boswell, J. F., Kraus, D. R., Miller, S. D., & Lambert, M. J. (2015). Implementing routine outcome monitoring in clinical practice: Benefits, challenges, and solutions. *Psychotherapy Research, 25*(1), 6–19. https://doi.org/10.1080/10503307.2013.817696

Brofenbrenner, U. (1979). *The ecology of human development: Experiments by nature and design*. Harvard Press. https://doi.org/10.4159/9780674028845

Card, A. J. (2023). The biopsychosociotechnical model: A systems-based framework for human-centered health improvement. *Health Systems, 12*(4), 387–407. https://doi.org/10.1080/20476965.2022.2029584

Chor, K. H. B., Olin, S. S., & Hoagwood, K. E. (2014). Training and education in clinical psychology in the context of the patient protection and affordable care act. *Clinical Psychology: Science and Practice, 21*(2), 91–105. https://doi.org/10.1111/cpsp.12068

Clement, P. W. (1999). *Outcomes and incomes*. Guilford.

Engel, G. L. (1977). The need for a new medical model: A challenge for biomedicine. *Science, 196*(4286), 129–136.

Faust, D. (1986). Research on human judgment and its application to clinical practice. *Professional Psychology: Research and Practice, 17*, 420–430. https://doi.org/10.1037/0735-7028.17.5.420

Finn, S. E. (2007). *In our client's shoes: Theory and techniques of therapeutic assessment*. Taylor & Francis.

Gondek, D., Edbrooke-Childs, J., Fink, E., Deighton, J., & Wolpert, M. (2016). Feedback from outcome measures and treatment effectiveness, treatment efficiency, and collaborative practice: A systematic review. *Administrative Policy and Mental Health, 43*(3), 325–343. https://doi.org/10.1007/s10488-015-0710-5

Grice, J. W. (2011). *Observation-oriented modeling: Analysis of cause in behavioral sciences*. Elsevier.

Hatfield, D. R., & Ogles, B. M. (2004). The use of outcome measures by psychologists in clinical practice. *Professional Psychology: Research and Practice, 35*, 485–491. https://doi.org/10.1037/0735-7028.35.5.485

Hawkins, R.C. II (2023, April). *Integrating LIWC computer text analyses of TAT stories into multimethod personality assessments*. Paper presented at the annual conference of the Society for Personality Assessment, Austin, TX.

Hawkins, R. C., II, & Meier, S. T. (2015). Psychotherapeutic theories of change and measurement: An integrative model. *Journal of Unified Psychotherapy and Clinical Science, 3*(1), 80–119.

Heinz, M. L., et al. (2025). Randomized trial of a generative AI Chatbot for mental health treatment. *NEJM AI, 2*(4), 1–14. https://doi.org/10.1056/AIoa2400802

Kazdin, A. E. (1994). Psychotherapy for children and adolescents. In A. E. Bergin & S. L. Garfield (Eds.), *Handbook of psychotherapy and behavior change* (4th ed., pp. 543–594). Wiley. https://doi.org/10.1097/00004583-199405000-00013

Kelso, J. A. S. (2009). Synergies: Atoms of brain and behavior. *Advances in Experimental Medicine and Biology, 629*, 83–91. https://doi.org/10.1007/978-0-387-77064-2_5

Kelso, J. A. S. (2013). Coordination dynamics. In R. A. Meyers (Ed.), *Encyclopedia of complexity and system science* (pp. 1537–1564). Springer. https://doi.org/10.1007/978-0-387-30440-3_101

Kelso, J. A. S. (2021). The Haken–Kelso–Bunz (HKB) model: From matter to movement to mind. *Biological Cybernetics, 115*(4), 305–322. https://doi.org/10.1007/s00422-021-00890-w

Kelso, J. A. S., & Engstrom, D. A. (2006). *The complementary nature*. The MIT Press. https://doi.org/10.7551/mitpress/1988.001.0001

Kendrick, T., El-Gohary, M., et al. (2016). Routine use of patient reported outcome measures (PROMs) for improving treatment of common mental health disorders in adults. *Cochrane Database Systematic Review, 7*(7), CD011119. https://doi.org/10.1002/14651858.CD011119.pub2

Kraus, D. R., Castonguay, L., Boswell, J. F., Nordberg, S. S., & Hayes, J. A. (2011). Therapist effectiveness: Implications for accountability and patient care. *Psychotherapy Research, 21*(3), 267–276. https://doi.org/10.1080/10503307.2011.563249

Lambert, M. J. (2007). What we have learned from a decade of research aimed at improving psychotherapy outcome in routine care. *Psychotherapy Research, 17*, 1–14. https://doi.org/10.1080/10503300601032506

Lambert, M. J., Harmon, C., Slade, K., Whipple, J. L., & Hawkins, E. J. (2005). Providing feedback to psychotherapists on their patients' progress: Clinical results and practice suggestions. *Journal of Clinical Psychology, 61*, 165–174. https://doi.org/10.1002/jclp.20113

Lehman, B. J., David, D. M., & Gruber, J. A. (2017). Rethinking the biopsychosocial model of health: Understanding health as a dynamic system. *Social and Personality Psychology Compass, 11*, e12328. https://doi.org/10.1111/spc3.12328

Lilienfield, S. O. (2007). Psychological treatments that cause harm. *Perspectives on Psychological Science, 2*, 53–70. https://doi.org/10.1111/j.1745-6916.2007.00029.x

Meier, S. T. (2012). Nomothetic outcome assessment in counseling and psychotherapy: Development and preliminary psychometric analyses of the depression/anxiety negative affect scale. *Psychological Test and Assessment Modeling, 54*, 343–362. https://doi.org/10.1037/t25540-000

Meier, S. T. (2024). Initial evaluation of an AI-augmented progress monitoring and outcome assessment. *Counselling and Psychotherapy Research, 25*(1), e12869. https://doi.org/10.1002/capr.12869

Meier, S. T., & Feeley, T. H. (2021). Ceiling effects indicate a possible threshold structure for working alliance. *Journal of Counseling Psychology, 69*(2), 235–245. https://doi.org/10.1037/cou0000564

Mergenthaler, E. (1996). Emotion-abstraction patterns in verbatim protocols: A new way of describing psychotherapeutic processes. *Journal of Consulting and Clinical Psychology, 64*, 1306–1315. https://doi.org/10.1037/0022-006X.64.6.1306

Perez, J. E. (1999). Clients deserve empirically supported treatments, not romanticism. *American Psychologist, 54*, 205–206. https://doi.org/10.1037/0003-066X.54.3.205

Persons, J. B., & Mikami, A. Y. (2002). Strategies for handling treatment failure successfully. *Psychotherapy: Theory/Research/Practice/Training, 39*, 139–151. https://doi.org/10.1037/0033-3204.39.2.139

Sabella, S. A., & Meier, S. T. (2024). Pervasive ceiling effect in supervisory working Alliance measurement: An exploratory meta-analysis. *The Clinical Supervisor, 43*(2), 248–268. https://doi.org/10.1080/07325223.2024.2393299

Smith, J. (2025). Psychotherapy integration from the bottom up: A unifying, science-based view of psychotherapy's infrastructure. *Journal of Psychotherapy Integration, 35*(4), 256–271. https://doi.org/10.1037/int0000371

Zilcha-Mano, S. (2025). Therapeutic change may begin before the therapist and patient ever meet: Pretreatment alliance changes predict clinical outcomes. *Psychotherapy and Psychosomatics*. https://doi.org/10.1159/000548510

Index

R. Hawkins, S. Meier, *Healing Outcomes*,
https://doi.org/10.1007/978-3-032-33611-8